Job Creation
Prospects & Strategies

The Black Worker in the 21ST Century

Volume 1

DISCARD

Job Creation
Prospects & Strategies

Edited by

Wilhelmina A. Leigh
& Margaret C. Simms

Joint Center for Political and Economic Studies
Washington, DC

The Joint Center for Political and Economic Studies informs and illuminates the nation's major public policy debates through research, analysis, and information dissemination in order to: Improve the socioeconomic status of black Americans; Expand their effective participation in the political and public policy arenas; and promote communications and relationships across racial and ethnic lines to strengthen the nation's pluralistic society.

Opinions expressed in Joint Center publications are those of the authors and do not necessarily reflect the views of the staff, officers, or governors of the Joint Center or of the organizations supporting the Center and its research.

The Joint Center gratefully acknowledges the support of the Rockefeller Foundation in making this publication possible.

University Press of America,® Inc.
4720 Boston Way
Lanham, MD 20706

12 Hid's Copse Rd.
Cumnor Hill, Oxford OX2 9JJ

Library of Congress Cataloging-in-Publication Data
Job creation prospects and strategies / editors, Wilhelmina A. Leigh,
Margaret C. Simms.
p.   cm. —(Black worker in the 21st century)
Includes bibliographical references.
1. Afro-Americans—Employment. 2. Afro-Americans—Economic conditions. 3. Job creation—Government policy—United States. 4. Full employment policies—United States. 5. Labor market—United States. 6. Discrimination in employment—United States. I. Leigh, Wilhelmina.   II. Simms, Margaret C.   III. Series.
HD8081.A65.J63   331.6'396073—dc21   99-I0620 CIP

ISBN 0-7618-1349-7 (cloth: alk. ppr.)
ISBN 0-7618-1350-0 (pbk: alk. ppr.)

⊖™ The paper used in this publication meets the minimum requirements of American National Standard for Information Sciences—Permanence of Paper for Printed Library Materials, ANSI Z39.48—1984

T he Joint Center for Political and Economic Studies has conducted research on economic policy issues for well over a decade, even before we added "Economic" to our name. However, it was not until three years ago, at the urging of the Rockefeller Foundation, that we added a specific focus on the issue of job creation. This book is one product of that new thrust.

Job Creation Prospects and Strategies is the first in a series of three volumes that will address policy issues associated with the role and prospects for the black worker in the 21st century. It focuses on the demand for African American labor—what it has been in the past two decades; how black workers are viewed by employers; and what stategies policymakers can implement to increase the demand for black workers in the future. Later volumes will address education and training (the supply side) and the compensation workers receive. All three volumes are designed to offer clear, thorough analyses of the position of black workers in the labor market and promising policy solutions that can reduce racial disparities and improve the economic status of these workers and their families.

The Black Worker in the 21st Century publication series was originally designed by Dr. Edward Montgomery, a senior research associate at the Joint Center just prior to his 24-month tour of duty as chief economist at the U.S. Department of Labor. We remain grateful to him for providing the framework and to Dr. Milton Morris, former vice president for research, who challenged Dr. Montgomery to develop an effective vehicle for actively engaging public officials in identifying and implementing programs that support the economic advancement of the African American population.

The creation of this volume began with the commissioning of papers on selected topics related to job creation. Drafts of those papers served as catalysts for a very lively conference in which the scholars' analyses were reviewed and critiqued by policymakers and practitioners in the field. Before they became the final chapters in this book they were made stronger by this infusion of the "real world" view. We are particularly grateful to Congressman William Jefferson, Diane Bell, Edward Blakely, Gerald Jaynes, Franklin Raines, William Spriggs, and Margery Austin Turner for their participation in the conference discussion.

The support of the Rockefeller Foundation was essential to our efforts, but we owe a special thank-you to Julia Lopez, director of the Equal Opportunity Program, for making us stretch ourselves to do this. The hard work of the two volume editors, Dr. Wilhelmina Leigh and Dr. Margaret Simms, is to be commended. We also wish to thank Denise Dugas, vice president for communications and marketing, and her staff for overseeing the editing, design, and production of this book.

We hope that the publication of this volume will help policymakers move forward with effective policies, whether they be "tried and true" or bold and innovative.

Eddie N. Williams
President
Joint Center for Political
and Economic Studies

Contents

List of Tables

EMPLOYMENT PATTERNS AND LIKELY OPPORTUNITIES

Appendix Tables

Introduction

Margaret C. Simms

Since the Joint Center launched its job creation initiative in 1996, unemployment has fallen, the proportion of the United States workforce with jobs has increased, and the poverty rate for the African American population has fallen to historic lows. It could be assumed that with successful manipulation of the macroeconomy, targeted job creation strategies are not necessary. Yet, as the first section of this volume demonstrates, African American workers still enter the labor force with less education and training than their white counterparts, and even when they have the same level of education, blacks seem to have fewer job opportunities than whites. Moreover, they are geographically isolated, with many living in communities with little job growth.

The future for young black workers is not likely to be bright given the projected contours of the workplace. As Wilhelmina Leigh notes in the conclusion of her chapter, policy intervention is desirable "if we decide that the social costs [of] . . . idle minds and hands . . . are more than we are willing to continue to pay." This volume reviews the nature of black workers' labor-market difficulties and examines several policies that are part of the public sector's economic development and job creation arsenals, including the recently added Empowerment Zone initiative. In the first part of the book, the current and likely future demand for African American workers is assessed. In the second part, the authors analyze whether the programs identified are effective means of increasing blacks' employment opportunities.

The Labor Market Situation of Black Workers

The disadvantage that African Americans face in the labor market is not new, and the persistence of racial (and gender) differences is documented in Wilhelmina Leigh's chapter. Blacks are less likely to be employed than whites and, when employed, are more likely to work part-time. While blacks have made progress since 1980 in terms of the types of jobs they hold, they are still more concentrated in the less prestigious, lower-paying jobs. For labor force participation, employment rates, and occupation, these racial differences are greater for men than for women.

Since 1995, the last year of the trend analysis in Leigh's chapter, nearly 4 million members of the U.S. population entered the labor market (U.S. Department of Labor 1998, 9). The number of workers who actually got jobs increased by even more, over 4.6 million. As a result, the proportion of the civilian population with jobs increased by nearly one percentage point to 63.8 percent, and the annual unemployment rate moved below 5 percent for the first time since 1970. In other words, nearly two of every three individuals over the age of 15 had a job in 1997, and very few of those who wanted work failed to find employment. Black workers shared in the job expansion, with nearly a half million more African Americans employed at the end of 1997 than at the end of the prior year. Black unemployment continued to be below 10 percent, quite low by recent standards. Yet the black-white unemployment ratio had changed little by the end of 1997 and into 1998. Blacks were almost 2.5 times as likely to be unemployed as whites, a ratio that remained fairly constant throughout the 1980s and 1990s.

The outlook for the new millennium is not much better. Even though the black labor force is not projected to grow as much as the Hispanic and Asian labor forces, and therefore should be more easily absorbed in the labor market, a number of obstacles block further improvement in the labor market position of black workers. First, African Americans are likely to continue to be the most geographically isolated of all racial groups (Council of Economic Advisers 1998[1]). More important, the occupations in which African Americans currently work are less likely to grow, except for low-paying service jobs, especially those in the health care industry. Without major intervention, Leigh suggests, the racial gaps in employment are likely to grow.

To some extent, African Americans will suffer because of differences in their level of educational attainment and their access to training. It is well documented that African Americans have lower levels of formal education and seem to have somewhat less access to other types of training. But some differences may be due to employers' perceptions of black workers rather than to actual differences in their preparation. This is one of several issues explored in the second chapter by Harry Holzer. Among the barriers to employment by African Americans, Holzer cites employers' requirements for a wide range of credentials and social skills, even for jobs that do not require a college education. The jobs that require these skills and credentials are less likely to be occupied by blacks.

While this may be the result of differences in qualifications, it is also possible that employers merely assume that blacks have fewer of these skills and thus do not hire them.

Aspects of the recruitment and referral process also seem to disadvantage black jobseekers. The new jobs that are being created in the economy are disproportionately located in suburban areas. Particularly disadvantaged as a result of this relocation of jobs are those black workers who live in inner-city neighborhoods. They have less access to the jobs in the suburbs and are less likely to be hired when they do apply for these jobs. Moreover, they seem less likely to be aware of job opportunities because they are not in the informal networks where that type of information is shared among friends and family. Black men are most affected by the combination of obstacles, a situation that will exacerbate existing differences between them and white men.

Holzer ends his chapter with a discussion of the policy options available to improve job access for African American workers. Some of these options rely on job search strategies and mentoring of new job entrants, others on reducing barriers caused by geographic isolation through such means as transportation assistance and improved access to information. Attention is given to wage subsidies and to strengthening community institutions. His review sets the stage for the succeeding chapters that address the effectiveness of several policy options he mentions.

Seeking Solutions

Clearly, any serious attempt to bring us closer to parity in employment between blacks and whites will require a multifaceted policy agenda. Essential items in that agenda are the maintenance of antidiscrimination measures and improvements in the quality and level of education available to blacks. But this volume focuses on a specific set of strategies, namely, those that increase the number of jobs available to the existing workforce. That means creating jobs which those currently in the workforce either are already prepared for or can be easily trained to take. These jobs must also be in locations accessible to African American workers. The balance of this book presents the evidence on several approaches that have been suggested.

The chapter by William Rodgers examines the likely job-creation effectiveness of Empowerment Zones. The Empowerment Zone/Enterprise Community initiative was the only geographically targeted job development program proposed by the Clinton administration and passed by the U.S. Congress. It is designed to foster public-private collaborations to bring economic development into distressed neighborhoods and to provide jobs for local residents. Empowerment Zones, the focus of Rodgers' analysis, combine large block grants that can be used to support an array of economic and social initiatives along with tax incentives and subsidies for businesses that choose to locate in the zones. Rodgers examines the incentive side only, estimating the impact of the current labor and capital subsidies on zone employment for both black and white residents in the nine zones named in the 1994 selection process. He then recommends adjustments in those subsidies to increase the positive impact on employment and wages for zone residents. In particular, he raises the possibility of adjusting the current subsidies so that labor is more attractive relative to new capital investment. This would boost the job creation aspects of the Empowerment Zone, as would incentives that are attractive to industries with the greatest potential for expanded production. These recommendations should prove helpful to the new zones selected for round two of the program.

Empowerment Zones are geographically targeted strategies that could increase minority employment, but at least in theory, they are neutral with regard to the race of the business owner. The last two chapters in the volume address the role of minority business in job creation and strategies that might be particularly helpful to the growth of these firms. The rationale behind this approach is the well-documented fact that minority firms disproportionately hire minority workers, regardless of the location of their businesses. While the subject is the same, the two chapters take slightly different approaches to public policy and minority business development.

In his chapter on improved access to markets for minority-owned businesses, Timothy Bates identifies a subsector of minority firms that he thinks should be the focus of public policy initiatives. The chapter documents the growth of firms with the greatest potential for employing minority workers and identifies the markets that they serve. These firms, located in emerging industries, do not market to the minority community, as was the case in the past, but sell to a broader clientele and to other businesses and government entities. To generate greater employment within these firms, Bates asserts, it is necessary to reduce even further the market barriers that confront them.

While they have made great strides by moving into new markets, minority firms still have less government and private-sector business than nonminority firms with similar capacity. Therefore, programs designed to provide market access are still needed. Bates addresses the economic issues raised in court cases that seek to eliminate minority business programs. In particular, he refutes the contention that minority firms have less government business because they lack the capability to perform on government contracts. In fact, even when the firms have similar capacity, minority firms have less government business than their nonminority counterparts. Even larger disparities exist in private-sector contracting. Bates points out that opportunities in the private sector far exceed those in the public sector in terms of potential volume. He further shows that minority firms that have gained business contracts have been quite successful. Yet the research shows that minority firms are less likely than nonminority firms of similar size and experience to have private-sector business clients. Bates argues that minority business programs should remove the remaining barriers that disproportionately handicap minority firms, providing them equal access to all groups of clients so that they can generate the jobs so desperately needed in minority communities.

The final chapter, by Randall Eberts and Edward Montgomery, takes a different approach to minority business growth. It focuses on a more general set of economic development incentives by examining the responses of both minority and nonminority firms to changes in the economic environment. In some ways, the arsenal of policies that they analyze are similar to those used by Empowerment Zones—tax breaks, publicly subsidized training programs, loans, and such. While the Rodgers chapter focuses on the jobs created by these incentives, Eberts and Montgomery analyze the impact on firms. They try to answer two questions: (1) Can a place-based strategy assist black-owned firms? and (2) Are black-owned firms more sensitive than other firms to the incentives used?

Their analysis suggests that black-owned businesses are more positively affected by incentives that lower business costs than are businesses in general. This means that local government policies to provide more favorable economic conditions for all firms could have a disproportionate impact on the growth of black firms and the size of their workforce. However, there are several caveats to this conclusion in terms of employment growth. First, black firms are not disproportionately concentrated in areas of high economic distress (which is consistent with Bates' analysis), so economic incentive programs that target only those areas may not be of special assistance to black-owned firms. Thus, broader economic development incentives, beyond Empowerment Zones, are necessary if the focus is on promoting the growth of firms that are known to hire black workers regardless of location. Second, the types of firms that seem to benefit most from general economic assistance programs are in industries, such as manufacturing, in which blacks continue to be underrepresented as owners. This suggests that when economic development programs are combined with policies that open up markets for black-owned firms in emerging industries, as recommended by Bates, the impact on employment opportunities for African American workers could be substantial.

Conclusion

The need for positive and forceful action to improve the labor market status of black workers has not been eliminated by the overall economic expansion the United States has witnessed in the past five years. While blacks have achieved gains in employment, significant racial differences remain, with some African American communities altogether outside the expansion. However, even for members of these isolated communities, there are effective strategies to create jobs that can be used by public policymakers working in conjunction with the private sector. The analysis in this volume is by no means exhaustive, but it does offer both place- and business-specific policies that can be implemented or enhanced to make jobs more accessible to African Americans as we cross the divide into the new millennium.

1. This report documents the greater isolation of blacks in central cities (page 9) and their tendency to be in racially homogenous neighborhoods (page 67).

Council of Economic Advisers. 1998. *Changing America: Indicators of Social and Economic Well-being by Race and Hispanic Origin*, a report for the President's Initiative on Race, September.

U.S. Department of Labor. 1998. *Employment and Earnings*: January 1998. Washington, D.C.: Government Printing Office.

Into the Millennium (1994–2005): Employment Patterns and Likely Opportunities for Blacks and Whites

Wilhelmina A. Leigh

L abor market differences by race and sex, as reflected in measures such as labor force participation and unemployment, have existed throughout the post–World War II era.[1] Since 1980, however, changes in the U.S. economic system have altered the employment options and opportunities for members of all racial and gender groups. Goods-producing industries no longer power the U.S. economy; service-producing industries instead fill that role. Further, the emergence of a global economic system means that nations can substitute lower-cost foreign labor for more expensive domestic labor. As a result, job loss or displacement has become a major cause of unemployment for all U.S. workers, black and white, male and female.

In this chapter, we first examine current trends in employment and unemployment by race and sex. In light of these current labor market patterns, we then look at job growth by industry and occupation during the 1994–2005 period and assess the likely implications of projections for the employment of blacks in the early years of the 21st century. Finally, we discuss what roles the private and public sectors should play in matching available jobs to workers with appropriate skills.

CURRENT EMPLOYMENT PATTERNS

Labor Force Participation

- Between 1980 and 1995, labor force participation rates continued to follow previously established trends, with white men more likely to be in the labor force than black men, and black women more likely to be employed than white women. However, by 1995, the participation rates for black and white women had nearly converged.

The basis for most measures of employment, the civilian labor force, has grown for both blacks and whites, and for men and women, since 1980. Defined as members of the civilian noninstitutionalized population (i.e., those not in the military and not in institutions such as prisons and nursing homes), ages 16 and older, who are either working or seeking work, the white labor force grew from 92.2 million members in 1980 to 107.2 million members in 1990.[2] Over the period, white women increased their share of these totals from 42 percent to 45 percent. In 1995, there were nearly 112 million whites in the labor force, and men were still in the majority at 55 percent (61.1 million); women still constituted 45 percent (50.8 million). (See table 1.1.) For the decade from 1980 to 1990, the black labor force grew from 12.5 million to 13.5 million, with the share of women rising from 48 percent to 50 percent over the period. By 1995, the black labor force had grown to 14.8 million persons, and women outnumbered men— 7.6 million (52 percent) to 7.2 million (48 percent).

Generally, in this country, labor force participation rates for white men have exceeded those for black men, while the reverse has been true for women, with labor force participation rates higher for black women than for white women. In other words, white men are more likely to be in the labor force than are their black counterparts. Black women, however, are generally more likely to be in the labor force than are their white counterparts.

Data for the 1980–1995 period show these patterns continuing, although labor force participation rates for black and white women have nearly converged during this time. White men in the labor force constituted between 76 and 77 percent of the white male population in 1990, 1994, and 1995. (See table 1.1.) These figures have varied only slightly since 1980, when the percentage of white men in the labor force was 77 percent. Over the same period, nearly 71 percent of black men were in the labor force in 1980, declining only slightly to 70 percent in 1990 and to 69 percent in both 1994 and 1995. (See table 1.1.) Among women, the labor force as a percentage of the population increased for both blacks and whites between 1980 and 1995. The percentage of white women in the labor force grew from 50 percent of the total population of white women in 1980 to nearly 58 percent in 1990 and to 59 percent in both 1994 and 1995. The percentage of black women who were in the labor force grew from 53 percent in 1980 to nearly 58 percent in 1990, 59 percent in 1994, and 60 percent in 1995. (See table 1.1.)

Employment-to-Population Ratios

- Although black women are more likely than white women to be in the labor force (that is, either working or seeking work), white women are more likely to actually be employed.

While labor force participation rates include both those persons who are employed and those seeking employment, employment-to-population ratios exclude those seeking work who have not found jobs and compare only employed persons to the total population. These ratios reveal greater employment among white women than among black women. As with labor force participation rates, the employment-to-population ratios for white men between 1980 and 1995 remain greater than the ratios for black men. In 1980, the employment-to-population ratio for white men was nearly 74 percent; the corresponding ratio for black men was 61 percent. By 1990, the ratio for white men had fallen slightly to 73 percent, and it had declined further to 72 percent in 1994 and 1995. The employment-to-population ratios for black men in 1990 and 1995 had increased slightly above the 1980 level of 61 percent to 62 percent in 1990 and 1995, although the 1994 rate had dipped slightly to 61 percent. (See table 1.2.)

The employment-to-population ratios for white and black women in 1980 were 48 percent and 46 percent, respectively. By 1990, the ratios for both groups of women had risen, to nearly 55 percent for white women and to nearly 52 percent for black women. (See table 1.2.) In 1994 and 1995, employment-to-population ratios for white women rose above the 1990 level to 56 percent; ratios for black women in these years (1994 and 1995) were around 52 percent and 53 percent, also slightly higher than their 1990 level.

Among those who reported being employed, the extent of full-time employment differs by race. White men and women were more likely than black men and women of the same ages to report that they were employed full-time. Specifically, between 1990 and 1995, 94 percent to 95 percent of whites reported full-time employment. (See table 1.3.) In 1995, about 90 percent of employed blacks reported working full-time. In 1990 and other subsequent years, the percentage of black workers who were full-time ranged between a low of 85 percent for black men in 1992 and a high of 89 percent for black women in both 1990 and 1994.

Occupational Distribution

- The largest share of white men have managerial and professional occupations, while black men are concentrated in lower-paying service occupations.

Both white and black female workers are most likely to be in technical, sales, and administrative support positions.

The data show vast differences in occupation by both race and gender. While sizable shares of whites have managerial and professional occupations, comparably large shares of blacks have service occupations. Among white men, the largest occupational category in 1982 (the earliest year in the 1980s for which data are available) was managerial and professional. (See table 1.4.) In that year, over a fourth of all employed white men held managerial and professional jobs. Nearly 14 percent of white men held positions in the executive, administrative, and managerial occupational subcategory and 12 percent held jobs in the professional specialty occupational subcategory, the largest percentages employed in any of the subcategories among all the occupational groups. A fifth of all employed white men had occupations in three categories—technical, sales, and administrative support; precision production, craft, and repair; and operators, fabricators, or laborers. The only other occupational subcategory in which a sizable share of white men were employed was sales, accounting for nearly 12 percent.

By the 1990s (i.e., 1990, 1994, and 1995), the shares of white men in various occupations had changed only slightly. The percentage of white men with occupations in the managerial and professional category had increased slightly from 26 percent in 1982 to 27 percent and 28 percent in 1990, 1994, and 1995. The shares in the executive, administrative, and managerial occupational subcategory had increased from 14 percent to around 15 percent, and the shares in the professional specialty occupational subcategory had grown to between 12 percent and 13 percent. In the 1990s, about a fifth of all jobs held by employed white men continued to be in the categories of technical, sales, and administrative support; precision production, craft, and repair; and operators, fabricators, and laborers. Sales continued to account for 12 percent of jobs held by white men, with all other occupational subcategories accounting for much smaller shares.

The major occupational category among black men in 1983 (the first year in which data are available) was operators, fabricators, and laborers, accounting for a third of all jobs held. (See table 1.4.) Each of the three occupational subcategories under operators, fabricators, and laborers—machine operators, assemblers, and inspectors; transportation and material moving; and handlers, equipment cleaners, helpers, and laborers—accounted for around 11 percent of all jobs held by black men. The second most common occupation for black men was service jobs (nearly 19 percent), and the dominant subcategory was "service except private household/protective," including business service and health service occupations. The occupational categories of precision production, craft, and repair occupations and technical, sales, and administrative support accounted for about 16 percent and 15 percent, respectively, of the jobs held by black men in 1983.

By 1994 and 1995, the share of black men with occupations as operators, fabricators, and laborers had declined to between 30 percent and 31 percent. The next largest shares of jobs held by black men were in the categories of service (19 percent in 1994 and 18 percent in 1995); technical, sales, and administrative support (18 percent in 1994 and 1995); and managerial and professional (16 percent and 18 percent in 1994 and 1995, respectively). As in 1983, the dominant subcategory of service occupations was "service, except private household/protective" (14 percent and 13 percent in 1994 and 1995, respectively). The share of professional specialty occupations, a subcategory of managerial and professional occupations, held by black men was close to 8 percent in 1994 and 9 percent in 1995, as was the share in the executive, administrative, and managerial subcategory. Under the technical, sales, and administrative support occupational category, over 8 percent of black men in both 1994 and 1995 were employed in administrative support occupations, including clerical. Sales occupations employed 7 percent in those years.

The largest shares of employed black women and white women both in 1982 and in the early 1990s were in technical, sales, and administrative support occupations. (See table 1.5.) However, the second largest occupational category for black women was service occupations, while managerial and professional was the second largest occupational category for white women.

Nearly half of all employed white women in 1982 (47 percent) held technical, sales, and administrative support jobs. The "administrative support (including clerical)" subcategory accounted for the largest share of these jobs (31 percent). (See table 1.5.) Managerial and professional occupations provided jobs for nearly a fourth (23 percent) of all white women that year, with the professional specialty subcategory accounting for most of these (14 percent). Service occupations employed 18 percent of white women in 1982, and occupations in "service, except private household/protective" accounted for most of these.

By the 1990s, the percentage of white women employed in the following occupations had declined from their 1982 levels: technical, sales, and administrative support; service; and operators, fabricators, and laborers. By 1990, the share of white women in technical, sales and administrative support occupations had declined to 45 percent from 47 percent in 1982. In 1994 and 1995, the share was even lower at 43 percent. Service occupations employed fewer white women (between 16 percent and 17 percent) by the 1990s than in 1982, while the share of white women working as operators, fabricators, and laborers fell from 10 percent in 1982 to about 7 percent in 1994 and 1995. The only occupation in which white women increased their employment share between 1982 and the 1990s was managerial and professional. The percentage of white women employed in managerial and professional occupations increased from nearly 23 percent in 1982 to nearly 31 percent in 1995. The split of managerial and professional occupations among white women was 17 percent in professional specialties and 13 percent in executive, administrative, and managerial occupations. (See table 1.5.)

In 1982, over a third of black women (36 percent) held technical, sales, and administrative support occupations, while nearly a third (31 percent) had service occupations. (See table 1.5.) Black women with technical, sales, and administrative support occupations mainly were in the administrative support/clerical subcategory (27 percent), while the majority in service occupations worked in "service, except private household/protective" (24 percent). Nearly equal shares— 16 percent and 15 percent, respectively—were in the managerial and professional occupational category and the operators, fabricators, and laborers occupational category. The majority of the black women with managerial and professional occupations were in the professional specialties subcategory (11 percent).

By the 1990s, the shares of black women in the categories of managerial and professional occupations and in technical, sales, and administrative support occupations had increased; the shares accounted for by service occupations and by occupations as operators, fabricators, and laborers had decreased. About a fifth of employed black women in the 1990s held managerial and professional occupations, and nearly two-fifths held technical, sales, and administrative support occupations. Professional specialties and administrative support/clerical remained the largest subcategories within their respective occupational categories. By the 1990s, service occupations had declined from nearly a third to around a fourth of the occupations held by black women. The share of black women in private household service occupations, in particular, was reduced by two-thirds between 1982 (6 percent) and 1994 and 1995 (2 percent in both years). Over this same period, black women doubled their share in protective service occupations (from 0.7 percent in 1982 to 1.4 percent and 1.5 percent in 1994 and 1995, respectively). Their share in service occupations "except private household/protective" declined slightly (from 24 percent in 1982 to 22 percent in both 1994 and 1995). The percentage of black women with occupations as operators, fabricators, and laborers decreased from nearly 15 percent in 1982 to between 11 percent and 12 percent in the 1990s.

Occupations by Industries

- Looking at occupations by the type of industry shows the same basic distribution by race—that is, whites are more likely to hold the higher paying managerial and professional jobs, and blacks are more likely to be in the lower-rung service and laborer jobs.

Within many of the different industries, blacks and whites generally are distributed among occupations as noted above, with whites more likely to hold managerial and professional occupations and blacks more likely to have service occupations and occupations as operators, fabricators, and laborers. The distribution of the occupations by race in the services industry in 1985 illustrates these racial differences. Over two-fifths (43 percent) of whites had managerial and professional occupations; nearly a fourth (24 percent) had technical, sales, and administrative support occupations; and about a fifth (22 percent) were in service occupations. For blacks in the services industry, the occupational distribution was starkly different, however, with 44 percent in service occupations, almost a fourth

(24 percent) in managerial and professional occupations, and a fifth (21 percent) in technical, sales, and administrative support occupations. (See table 1.6.) Within managerial and professional occupations, nearly a third (32 percent) of whites were in professional specialty occupations and 11 percent were in executive, administrative, and managerial occupations. Most blacks with managerial and professional occupations were in the professional specialty subcategory (18 percent). Most whites in the services industry with technical, sales, and administrative support occupations worked in administrative support (17 percent), rather than as technicians (5 percent), or in sales (2 percent). Like whites, most blacks with technical, sales, and administrative support occupations provided administrative support (15 percent). (See appendix tables A.1 and A.5 at the end of this volume.)

As another example, in the retail trade industry in 1985, the dominant occupation for both whites and blacks was technical, sales, and administrative support (51 percent for whites and 43 percent for blacks). (See table 1.6.) The largest shares of the technical, sales, and administrative support occupations held by both blacks and whites were in sales—42 percent of whites and 35 percent of blacks. (See appendix tables A.1 and A.5.) The second most common occupation in the retail trade sector for both racial groups was service occupations, but nearly a third of blacks (31 percent) held service occupations while only a fifth (22 percent) of whites did so.

Employment in the construction and manufacturing industries in 1985 also reflected the similarities and differences between the occupational distributions of blacks and whites noted previously. The majority of both racial groups (58 percent of whites and 52 percent of blacks) in the construction industry held precision production, craft, and repair occupations. Although the second most common occupation in the construction industry for both racial groups was operators, fabricators, and laborers, the percentage of blacks (37 percent) in this line of work was nearly double that of whites (19 percent). (See table 1.6.) The widest gap in the construction industry was in the area of managerial and professional occupations. Fourteen percent of whites in the construction industry held these positions compared with only 5 percent of blacks. The vast majority of both blacks and whites with managerial and professional occupations in the construction industry had positions in the executive, administrative, and managerial occupational subcategory—12 percent of whites and 4.7 percent of blacks (See appendix tables A.1 and A.5.)

In 1985, the manufacturing sector reported the largest shares of blacks and whites in the same occupation—operators, fabricators, and laborers. However, the shares differed considerably. (See table 1.6.) Over three-fifths of blacks (62 percent) but less than two-fifths of whites (38 percent) were employed as operators, fabricators, and laborers in the manufacturing industry. The next most prevalent occupation categories among blacks in this sector were occupations in precision production, craft, and repair (15 percent of blacks) and in technical, sales, and administrative support (12 percent of blacks). Nearly three-quarters of blacks in this industry with technical, sales, and administrative support positions were in administrative support occupations. (See appendix tables A.1 and A.5.)

Of the whites not employed as operators, fabricators, and laborers in the manufacturing industry, about a fifth held jobs in each of the following categories—managerial and professional; technical, sales, and administrative support; and precision production, craft, and repair. (See table 1.6.) About three-fifths of the whites in the managerial and professional category (12 percent) had executive, administrative, and managerial positions. Slightly more than three-fifths of the whites with technical, sales, and administrative support occupations (13 percent) in the manufacturing industry held administrative support positions. (See appendix table A.1.)

By the 1990s, the occupational distributions within all these industries—services, retail trade, construction, and manufacturing—had changed very little for either blacks or whites. In the 1990s, the largest percentage of white workers in the services industry had managerial and professional occupations—46 percent in 1994 and 47 percent in 1995, up from 43 percent in 1985. (See tables 1.6, 1.8, and 1.9.) Around a fourth of white employees in this sector had technical, sales, and administrative support occupations and a fifth had service occupations. Professional specialty occupations was the dominant subcategory under managerial and professional occupations—between 31 percent and 33 percent of all employment in the years 1985, 1990, 1994, and 1995. Administrative support was the dominant subcategory under the category of technical, sales, and administrative support occupations, between 15 percent and 17 percent in these same years. (See appendix tables A.1–A.4 and A.6.)

The occupational distribution in the services industry continued to differ by race in the same way it did in 1985, although the percentage of black workers in the industry who held service occupations declined to 38 percent and 37 percent, respectively, in 1994 and 1995, down from 44 percent in 1985. Likewise, the percentage of blacks in managerial and professional occupations grew to 29 percent in 1994 and 30 percent by 1995, up from 24 percent in 1985. (See tables 1.6, 1.8, and 1.9.) Twenty-one percent of the blacks employed in the services industry in both 1994 and 1995 held professional specialty occupations, up from 18 percent in 1985, and this was still the biggest share of blacks in the managerial and professional occupational category. (See appendix tables A.3 and A.4.) Technical, sales, and administrative support occupations among blacks increased from about a fifth (1985) to nearly a fourth (23 percent) in 1994 and 1995, with most in these occupations providing administrative support (16 percent in both years). (See appendix tables A.1, A.3, and A.4.)

In the retail trade industry, in the 1990s, slightly over half of whites had technical, sales, and administrative support occupations, followed by about a fifth in service occupations. (See tables 1.7, 1.8, and 1.9.) More than 42 percent of the white retail trade industry employees in these years had sales occupations, amounting to more than 80 percent of all whites with technical, sales, and administrative support jobs. (See appendix tables A.2, A.3, and A.4.) The percentage of blacks in the retail trade industry who held technical, sales, and administrative support occupations increased from 43 percent in 1985 to nearly half by 1995. These employees were mostly concentrated in sales jobs—38 percent in 1990, 40 percent in 1994, and 43 percent in 1995. (See appendix tables A.6–A.8.) Over the same period, the share of blacks with service occupations fell from nearly a third in 1985 to a fourth in 1995. (See tables 1.6 and 1.9.)

Occupational patterns for blacks and whites in the construction industry remained the same as in 1985. The major occupation for blacks and whites continued to be precision production, craft, and repair, with the shares of the two groups remaining nearly constant between 1985 and 1995—around 52 percent for blacks and around 58 percent for whites. (See tables 1.6 and 1.9.) Operators, fabricators, and laborers remained the second most common occupation for both groups, although the share for blacks decreased from 37 percent in 1985 to about 32 percent in 1995. The share of whites who were operators, fabricators, and laborers remained between 18 percent and 19 percent over the same period. The percentage of whites in managerial and professional occupations grew from 14 percent in 1985 to 17 percent in 1994 and 1995. Executive, administrative, and managerial occupations, a subcategory of managerial and professional occupations, constituted 15 percent of the jobs held by whites in the construction industry in 1994 and 1995, an increase from their 12 percent share in 1985. (See appendix tables A.3 and A.4.) The percentage of blacks in the construction industry who held managerial and professional occupations nearly doubled from 5 percent in 1985 to 9 percent in 1995. Most managerial and professional occupations held by blacks in the construction industry—7.5 percent in 1994 and nearly 7 percent in 1995—were executive, administrative, and managerial positions. (See appendix tables A.1, A.3, and A4.)

In the manufacturing industry, the occupational patterns for blacks and whites were carried forward into the 1990s largely unchanged from 1985. The dominant occupation for both blacks and whites was still operators, fabricators, and laborers; nearly three-fifths of blacks and nearly two-fifths of whites had this occupation. The percentage of whites in managerial and professional jobs, however, increased from a fifth in 1985 to nearly a fourth in 1994 and 1995. By the mid-1990s, the shares of whites in the other two occupations—technical, sales, and administrative support and precision production, craft, and repair—had fallen slightly below the one-fifth level of 1985. (See tables 1.6, 1.7, 1.8, 1.9 and appendix tables A.5, A.7, and A.8.) In 1994 and 1995, 14 to 15 percent of the jobs held by whites in the manufacturing industry were executive, administrative, and managerial, an increase over the 12 percent share in 1985. (See appendix tables A.1, A.3, and A.4.) The percentage of blacks in precision production, craft, and repair occupations rose slightly, from 15 percent in 1985 to 17 percent in 1995, while the share in technical, sales, and administrative support occupations in the manufacturing industry remained stable, between 12 percent and 13 percent. (See tables 1.6 and 1.9.) As in the 1980s, administrative support remained the major technical, sales, and administrative support occupational subcategory for blacks—8 percent in 1994 and 9 percent in 1995. (See appendix tables A.1, A.3, and A.4.)

Education and Employment

- For both blacks and whites, the percentage employed increased with higher educational achievement; however, employment rates for blacks at all educational levels were still considerably lower than for their white counterparts.

As might be expected, for both black and white populations, the percentage employed increases with educational attainment. However, in all the years 1990 through 1995 and at almost every level of educational attainment, the percentage of whites between ages 16 and 24 not in school who were employed exceeded the corresponding percentage for blacks. The only exception occurred in 1994, when black and white college graduates had approximately equal employment rates.

In 1990, 83 percent of 16-to-24-year-old whites with less than a high school diploma were employed, compared to 92 percent of white high school graduates without any college education and 95 percent of whites with a college degree. (See table 1.10.) The 1995 figures were about the same: 82 percent of whites with less than a high school diploma were employed, 90 percent of white high school graduates without any college were employed, and 95 percent of white college graduates were employed.

Although the corresponding employment rates for blacks in 1990 and 1995 were considerably less than the rates among whites, they also increased with educational achievement. Among blacks with less than a high school education, 59 percent were employed in 1990, and 57 percent were employed in 1995. Among black high school graduates without any college education, 78 percent and 77 percent reported employment in 1990 and 1995, respectively. Among black college graduates, 91 percent in 1990 and 93 percent in 1995 were employed.

Income and Earnings

- In terms of both annual family income and median weekly income for workers, whites continued to earn considerably more than their black counterparts.

Although median annual income (in current dollars) for both black and white families nearly doubled between 1980 and 1994, the sizable gap between them remained. (See table 1.11.) In 1980, current dollar median annual income for white families was $21,949; by 1994 that number had increased to $40,884. Between 1980 and 1994, median annual income in current dollars for black families increased from $12,662 to $24,698. Among married-couple families in which only the husband worked full-time in 1987 (earliest year for which data are available), the median annual income for white families was $36,072, about 1.5 times the median annual income for black families of $24,776. The income gap between white and black married-couple families in which both the husband and wife worked full-time was considerably less in 1987, with white families earning $49,307 and corresponding black families earning $43,702. By 1994, the income gap between white and black married-couple families in which both the husband and wife worked had increased; white families earned $63,184, black families only $55,883. However, in families in which only the husband worked full-time, the gap between white and black families was smaller than in 1987. The $43,065 white median annual family income was about 1.3 times the corresponding annual black median family income of $32,365. For both racial groups, families maintained by women had the lowest annual median incomes. The gap between the incomes of white and black families maintained by women was sizable in 1980 and remained so in 1994.

Median weekly earnings of full-time workers by race and sex in 1995 exhibited patterns consistent with those found in median annual family incomes. White men had the largest median weekly earnings ($566), followed by white women ($415), and black men ($411). Black women had the lowest median weekly earnings, $355. This rank ordering of median weekly earnings has held over the years 1992, 1993, 1994, and 1995. In 1990, median weekly earnings of black men slightly exceeded those of white women; in 1991, median weekly earnings of these two groups were equal. (See table 1.12.)

Although median weekly earnings for white women in the aggregate were greater than for both black men and black women in most of the years from 1990 to 1995, the only occupation in which white women had higher median weekly earnings than both black women and black men was technicians. (See table 1.13.) In this occupation, white men earned the most, with median weekly earnings of $644, followed by white women with median earnings of $479, then black women at $462, and black men at $421. In most of the remaining occupations, the greatest earnings were reported for white men, then black men, then white women, and finally black women.

Unemployment

- For most of the period 1980 to 1995 and for most age groups, unemployment among black men and women was at least double that among the white population. Although the reasons for unemploy-ment for both blacks and whites were either job loss or reentering the labor force, periods of unemployment were likely to last longer for blacks than for whites.

Black men and women in the labor force are more likely to report being unemployed than are white men and women. In most years between 1980 and 1995 and for most age groups, unemployment rates for black men and black women were at least double those for white men and white women. (See table 1.14.) Occasional exceptions to this pattern were found most often among women and among the older age groups (55 to 64 years of age and 65 years of age and older). In 1995, for persons of all ages, 5 percent of white men were unemployed, compared to 11 percent of black men, 5 percent of white women, and 10 percent of black women.

Job loss and reentering the labor force are the dominant reasons for unemployment among blacks and whites. The main reason for unemployment among whites—reported by half of the 5.5 million unemployed whites in 1995—was losing a job, with market reentry the second most frequently reported reason (32 percent). (See table 1.15.) This pattern was reversed among blacks, with 43 percent of the unemployed indicating that they were market reentrants and 38 percent reporting they had lost jobs in 1995. For the entire 1980–1995 period, the relative shares of whites who reported job loss and market reentry as reasons for their unemployment were unchanged. For blacks, the dominance of job loss as a reason for unemployment held only for the decade 1980 to 1990. This differing pattern could suggest that the U.S. labor market in the early 1990s was perceived by blacks as having improved to such an extent that persons who previously had dropped out decided to reenter in large enough numbers to outweigh those seeking jobs because of recent losses.

Spells of unemployment lasted slightly longer among blacks than among whites. Although the duration of unemployment increased for both blacks and whites throughout the 1990 to 1995 period, in 1995, the largest percentage of unemployed black men and black women reported unemployment lasting between 5 and 14 weeks, while the largest percentage of unemployed white men and white women reported unemployment lasting less than 5 weeks. (See table 1.16.) In 1990, 39 percent of unemployed black men reported unemployment of less than 5 weeks, and 35 percent reported unemployment of between 5 and 14 weeks. By 1995, 29 percent reported unemployment of less than 5 weeks and 31 percent reported unemployment lasting between 5 and 14 weeks. Fifteen percent of black men reported 27 weeks or more of unemployment in 1990, while 23 percent reported such lengthy unemployment in 1995. Forty-four percent of white men reported unemployment of less than 5 weeks, and 32 percent reported being unemployed for between 5 and 14 weeks in 1990; in 1995, the largest share (37 percent) continued to report unemployment of less than five weeks, with 32 percent reporting unemployment of between 5 and 14 weeks' duration.

Similar trends were noted among black and white women. In 1990, over half (52 percent) of white women reported less than five weeks of unemployment, and 31 percent reported between five and 14 weeks of unemployment. By 1995, the share reporting unemployment of less than five weeks had fallen to 41 percent, while the share reporting being unemployed between five and 14 weeks had risen slightly to 32 percent. Among black women, the percentage reporting unemployment lasting less than five weeks fell from 48 percent in 1990 to 31 percent by 1995. Over the same period, the percentage of black women reporting unemployment for 27 weeks or more increased markedly, from 9 percent to 21 percent.

Unemployed black and white male jobseekers used similar job search techniques in 1995. (See table 1.17.) Roughly two-thirds of both groups of unemployed men reported contacting employers directly to seek jobs. Over two-fifths (43 percent of white men and 45 percent of black men) reported sending resumes or filing applications to seek employment. About a fifth reported using a public employment agency for this purpose. Unemployed black and white female jobseekers in 1995 also reported similar job search methods, with 64 percent of both black and white women indicating that they contacted employers directly to seek work. Nearly half (49 percent) of unemployed white women and 46 percent of unemployed black women indicated that they sent a resume or filed an application to seek employment. A larger share of white women (20 percent) than black women (14 percent) indicated using their friends or relatives to search for jobs; comparable shares of black women (20 percent) and white women (17 percent) reported using a public employment agency to help them find a job. The general consistency by race and sex in the distribution of job search methods suggests a consensus on the most effective strategies to find a job.

PROJECTED EMPLOYMENT PATTERNS

Regardless of the assumptions used to make projections from 1994 to the year 2005, both the total adult population and the total labor force are expected to grow. Using moderate growth assumptions, the total population is projected to grow from nearly 197 million to 219 million, an overall increase of 11 percent, with an annual growth rate of 1 percent (Fullerton 1995). Projections for the size of the labor force in the year 2005 range between 144 million and 153 million. Using moderate growth assumptions, the labor force should grow by 12 percent, from 131 million in 1994 to 147 million in the year 2005, also reflecting annual growth at a 1 percent rate. (See table 1.18.)

Labor Force: Size and Participation Rate Projections

- Although whites will continue to dominate the labor force, Hispanics and Asians will double their labor force participation rates. Black participation rates will only rise modestly.

Using moderate growth assumptions, in the year 2005, the white labor force is projected to contain nearly 123 million persons. Black workers, numbering nearly 17 million, and Hispanic workers, numbering slightly over 16 million, are projected to be the next largest components of the U.S. labor force, followed by Asian (and other) workers, totaling nearly 8 million. (See table 1.18.) Although whites will continue to dominate the total U.S. labor force in the year 2005, constituting 84 percent of its members, blacks and Hispanics each are projected to be about 11 percent, and Asians and others are anticipated to make up 5 percent.

These labor force shares represent nearly a doubling of the Hispanic presence and more than a doubling of the presence of Asians and others in the U.S. labor force between 1982 and the year 2005. Over this same period, only a modest increase from 10 percent to 11 percent is projected for the share of blacks in the labor force (Fullerton 1995). Between 1994 and 2005, the Hispanic labor force is projected to increase by over a third (36 percent), while growth of nearly two-fifths (39 percent) is anticipated for the Asian-and-others component of the labor force. (See table 1.18.) The projected growth rate for blacks in the labor force over the period (15 percent) exceeds that for whites (11 percent) but is less than the rates predicted for either Hispanics or for Asians and others.

The relationship between the labor force participation rates of white men and black men observed through the mid-1990s is projected to hold in the year 2005, that is, the white rate is expected to be greater than the black rate. White men reported a labor force participation rate of 76 percent in 1994, which is anticipated to fall by two percentage points to 74 percent in 2005. The 1994 rate for black men was 69 percent, also projected to decline by 2005 to 66 percent. Although the labor force participation rates for black and white women were the same in 1994 (both 59 percent), by the year 2005, the labor force partic-ipation rate for white women is expected to have surpassed that for black women. In the year 2005, the rate for white women is projected to be nearly 63 percent, while the rate for black women is projected to remain at the 1994 level of 59 percent. (See table 1.19.)

Occupational Distribution

- Blacks are concentrated in occupations that are expected to experience below-average growth in the near future. Of the occupations held by large percentages of blacks, only those in the low-paying service sector are expected to grow rapidly in the early 21st century.

Looking at the current occupational distributions by race and using moderate growth assumptions for future projections, employment opportunities for whites are likely to be greater than for blacks. Between 1994 and 2005, the occupation projected to grow the most (29 percent) is professional specialty occupations, which is expected to add more than five million jobs. In the year 2005, as in 1994, professional specialty occupations are projected to be the third largest occupational group. In 1994, this occupational category accounted for 13 percent of the jobs held by employed white men, but only 8 percent of the jobs held by employed black men. (See tables 1.4 and 1.20.) A larger share of white women (17 percent) than black women (13 percent) also had professional specialty occupations in 1994. (See table 1.5.) If current occupational distributions indi-cate likely future access to positions, then the groups most likely to benefit by growth in professional specialty occupations can be anticipated to be those cur-rently employed in this occupation. This can be expected to remain true unless targeted and effective retraining and job placement initiatives are implemented for other members of the labor force.

Occupations as operators, fabricators, and laborers, which were held by 31 percent of employed black men in 1994, are expected to increase by only 4 percent between 1994 and 2005, an addition of 757,000 jobs. This suggests an employment disadvantage for blacks if current occupational patterns hold in the future. However, by this same reasoning, the projected 23 percent growth rate (and nearly 4.6 million new jobs) in service occupations over the 1994–2005 period may benefit black men more than white men since, in 1994, 19 percent of black men but only 9 percent of white men had these occupations. Fourteen percent of black men and 7 percent of white men in 1994—the majority of both groups of men with service occupations—had occupations in the subcategory "services except private household/protective." (See tables 1.4 and 1.20.) This is the subcategory of service occupations projected to exhibit the greatest growth between 1994 and 2005 (Silvestri 1995). The projected increase in service occupations paired with the projected decrease in occupations as operators, fabricators, and laborers, however, may leave black men on balance worse off financially than they are today. Wages for occupations as operators, fabricators, and laborers generally exceed wages for the service occupations projected to become more numerous in the early years of the 21st century.

Growth in service occupations is expected to be fueled by the continuing graying of the population and by changes within the system for delivering health care to this group. The greatest projected percentage increase in occupations is in personal and home care aides, a 119 percent increase from 179,000 to 391,000 jobs between 1994 and 2005. (See table 1.21.) The second largest projected percentage increase is in home health aides—102 percent, growing from 420,000 jobs to 848,000 jobs. Both of these are service occupations. (See table 1.21.) Half of the 10 fastest growing occupations are health-related, and these 10 occupations will account for more than one-fourth of total projected employment growth. (U.S. Department of Labor 1995a.)

Both black women and white women may be hurt because projected occupational growth over the 1994 to 2005 period does not favor the occupations in which they are most often employed. In 1994, technical, sales, and administrative support occupations employed 43 percent of white women and 38 percent of black women. Within this broad occupational category, both black women and white women are most likely to hold administrative support (including clerical) occupations, which are projected to grow by only 4 percent between 1994 and 2005. In 1994, 26 percent of white women and 25 percent of black women held these occupations. The other two subcategories under "technical, sales, and administrative support" occupations—technicians and related support occupations, and marketing and sales occupations—are projected to grow by nearly 20 percent (876,000 jobs) and 18 percent (2.5 million jobs), respectively, over the 1994–2005 period. (See tables 1.5 and 1.20.) Black women and white women will need to redistribute themselves among these three occupational subcategories to take advantage of this projected job growth. In 1994, only 4 percent of white women and 3 percent of black women had technician and related support occupations, while 13 percent of white women and 10 percent of black women had sales occupations. (See table 1.5.)

Executive, administrative, and managerial occupations also are expected to grow substantially between 1994 and 2005. The category should expand by nearly 17 percent or 2.2 million jobs. Based on the shares holding these occupations in 1994, white men (15 percent) and white women (13 percent) are likely to have an advantage over black men (8 percent) and black women (9 percent) in moving into these additional positions. (See tables 1.4, 1.5, and 1.20.)

Limited projected future growth—6 percent and 833,000 jobs—in precision production, craft, and repair occupations is likely to affect men more than women since 19 percent of white men and 14 percent of black men reported these occupations in 1994. (See tables 1.4 and 1.20.) These occupations are expected to experience below-average growth over the 1994–2005 period because of continuing advances in technology, changes in production methods, and the overall decline in manufacturing employment (Silvestri 1995). Since only 2 percent of white women and nearly 3 percent of black women held jobs in this category, projected low growth for these occupations is not likely to influence the employment prospects of very many women. (See table 1.5.)

Occupations by Industries

- Between 1994 and 2005, service-producing industries are expected to continue to account for most of the growth in employment, with growth expected in each of these industries. Among goods-producing industries, only construction is expected to grow during the period.

As they did between 1983 and 1994, the service-producing industries are projected to account for most of the growth in employment between 1994 and 2005. (See table 1.22.) Using moderate growth assumptions, goods-producing industries are expected to lose 985,000 jobs over the 1994–2005 period, while service-producing industries are projected to add nearly 18 million jobs. Growth is anticipated in each of the service-producing industries—transportation, communications, utilities; wholesale and retail trade; finance, insurance, and real estate; services; and government. Over 12 million of the 17.8 million jobs, or 7 of 10 jobs, expected to be added in service-producing industries are projected to be in the services industry itself, primarily in the areas of health services, business services, and social services. Of the goods-producing industries (mining, construction, and manufacturing), only construction is expected to add jobs (490,000) over the 1994–2005 period. (See table 1.22.)

Based on their current industry of employment, both blacks and whites are working in industries expected to grow. Among all industries, the services industry employed the largest shares of both whites (34 percent) and blacks (40 percent) in 1994. (See table 1.7.) Substantial shares of whites (23 percent) and blacks (27 percent) worked in the professional services industry. Wholesale and retail trade industries employed large shares of whites (21 percent) and blacks (17 percent) as well, with most in retail, rather than wholesale, trade. The only goods-producing industry that employed a sizable proportion of whites (16 percent) and blacks (16 percent) in 1994 was manufacturing, which is projected to lose 1.3 million jobs over the 1994–2005 period. (See table 1.22.) The construction industry, the only goods-producing industry whose employment is expected to grow in the 12-year period, employed small shares of both whites (6 percent) and blacks (4 percent) in 1994.

The distribution of professional and managerial occupations and of technical, sales, and administrative support occupations is basically the same in the industries for which high growth is projected as in those for which little job growth is anticipated. The distribution within occupational subcategories varies among industries, however. For example, in both 1994 and 1995, in all industries except the services industry, more employees in the managerial and professional occupational category have executive, administrative, and managerial occupations than professional specialty occupations. In the services industry, especially in "other service industries" (which include professional services), more jobs are in professional specialties than in the other managerial and professional occupations. (See appendix.) A similar pattern is evident across industries for technical, sales, and administrative support occupations. In all industries except wholesale and retail trade in both 1994 and 1995, the dominant sub-occupational category is "administrative support," ahead of both sales occupations and occupations as technicians and related support personnel. In the wholesale and retail trade industries, the largest shares of occupations are in sales. (See appendix tables A.3 and A.4.)

Education and Employment

- The jobs created in the early 21st century are projected to require even more education and training, further widening the already consider-able gap in employment opportunities between those with a college degree and those without a high school diploma.

The correlation between level of educational attainment and employment noted for recent entrants into the labor market in the first half of the 1990s may become more pronounced during the 1994–2005 period. For both blacks and whites in 1994, the likelihood of being employed increased as the level of educational attainment increased. For example, 95 percent of both black and white college graduates were employed in 1994, while only 56 percent of blacks and 80 percent of whites with less than a high school diploma were employed. (See table 1.10.)

In the near future, the distribution of employment by education/training category is projected to shift away from jobs requiring less education, toward jobs requiring more education or training. Projected growth rates for jobs, based on their educational requirements, range from 5 percent for occupations requiring moderate on-the-job training, to 28 percent for occupations requiring a master's degree. Occupations requiring an associate's degree or more are projected to grow at 24 percent, faster than the 14 percent average growth rate for all occupations (U.S. Department of Labor 1995b). Occupations requiring a bachelor's degree or more will account for job growth of nearly 6 million, representing 34 percent of the total growth among occupations over the 1994–2005 period. This 34 percent share of total growth is greater than the 21 percent share that these jobs represented of all employment in 1994 and portends increases in the educational requirements for future employment. On the other hand, jobs requiring less than a year of on-the-job training are projected to account for 7.4 million new jobs, representing 42 percent of total job growth over the 1994–2005 period. When compared to the share that jobs at this level of training represented in 1994 (52 percent), this growth rate suggests a future decline in jobs requiring relatively little training and education.

Data on employment by education level in the early 1990s suggest that the job outlook for blacks should improve as both the number and growth rate of jobs requiring a bachelor's degree or higher increase. However, as growth rates decline for jobs requiring less education or training, the unemployment gap between less-educated blacks and less-educated whites may increase since blacks with less education or training have lower employment rates than whites with comparable levels of education. This gap may widen at the same time that the employment gap between less-educated blacks and more-educated blacks also widens.

Role of the Public and Private Sectors

- Without specifically tailored public and private initiatives, the confluence of a number of trends, including continued racial discrimination, is likely to lead to an even wider racial gap in employment and even greater costs to society.

Projected job growth between 1994 and 2005 is related to the increasingly global nature of the U.S. economy and to the aging of the population. As the 21st century approaches, the country will have to contend with a labor market that not only reflects chronic disparities in employment outcomes between blacks and whites but also projects a pattern of growth in job opportunities that could worsen the existing gap. Age-adjusted unemployment rates for blacks remain multiples of two or more times comparable rates for whites, while earnings differentials and labor market "testing" suggest continued discrimination against blacks (Turner

1991; Fix 1993). Although educational attainment is improving for blacks, racial gaps in employment remain at all levels of education.

Blacks and members of other racial and ethnic minority groups will become a larger portion of the U.S. labor force between 1994 and the year 2005, at the same time that occupations such as operators, fabricators, and laborers, which large shares of blacks (especially men) hold, are projected to experience slower than average growth. Professional specialty occupations, which employ smaller percentages of black men and women than do occupations as operators, fabricators, and laborers, are projected to grow rapidly, as are service occupations, which employ larger percentages of blacks. Because service occupations employ many blacks, depending on the growth rates in particular service occupational subcategories, black workers in future decades could perhaps find avenues for advancement in the various growth sectors, such as health care. Three of the five occupations projected to grow fastest between 1994 and 2005 (e.g., personal and home care aides, home health aides, and physical and corrective therapy assistants and aides) are in the health care sector.

Decisions related to bridging the chronic racial employment gap pivot around the nature of society's goals with respect to employment. If we as a nation can be content with the traditional economist's definition of full employment as unemployment of 5 percent or less, then we as a nation could decide that federal government intervention in the labor market to create jobs for members of the labor force who are underemployed, unemployed, or are viewed as unemployable, is neither necessary nor a priority. However, if we note that a 5 percent national unemployment rate masks unemployment rates for young black men as high as 40 percent or 50 percent in many urban areas, and if we decide that the social costs associated with these high rates—idle minds and hands resulting in high-risk behaviors such as drug trafficking and other criminal activity—are more than we are willing to continue to pay, we as a nation might decide to expend the necessary energy, effort, and funds to create a labor market that reduces aggregate unemployment well below 5 percent.

Making and acting upon the decision to reduce unemployment rates among all subpopulations will require resources and input from both the public and private sectors. The federal and state governments can provide tax incentives to private businesses to encourage employment for the underemployed, unemployed, and unemployable as one way to close the employment gap. Federal job creation programs like those that existed during the Depression are another, along with Enterprise Communities, Empowerment Zones, minority business set-asides, Workfare, and a host of other more recent initiatives. Such public initiatives will be most successful if complemented by job training and outreach programs among private employers that can establish rungs further up the employment ladder than those government programs can achieve.

Our nation has a history of attempts to target job training and employment support to the unemployed and underemployed. The 1994–2005 period is not the time to scrap these efforts and start again from scratch. It is instead the time to build on those initiatives that have proven their worth and to discard those that have not, in a concentrated effort to bring both public and private voices and resources together to address the chronic U.S. racial unemployment gap.

1.   For details, see Leigh (1996).

2.   Throughout this chapter, unless otherwise specified, all references to the labor force, population, or population subgroups apply to civilian, noninstitutionalized persons, 16 years of age and older.

3.   For more complete data on occupational distribution by industry and race, see appendix at the back of the book.

Fix, Michael. 1993. *Clear and Convincing Evidence: The Measurement of Discrimination in America.* Washington, D.C.: The Urban Institute Press.

Franklin, James C. 1995. "Industry Output and Employment Projections to 2005." *Monthly Labor Review* 118 (11, November):45–59.

Fullerton, Howard N. Jr. 1995. "The 2005 Labor Force: Growing, but Slowly." *Monthly Labor Review* 118 (11, November): 29–44.

Leigh, Wilhelmina A. 1996. *Employment Trends 1980–1992: A Black-White Comparison.* Washington, D.C.: Joint Center for Political and Economic Studies.

Silvestri, George T. 1995. "Occupational Employment to 2005." *Monthly Labor Review* 118 (11, November): 60–84.

Turner, Margery Austin. 1991. *Opportunities Denied, Opportunities Diminished: Racial Discrimination in Hiring.* Washington, D.C.: The Urban Institute Press.

U.S. Department of Labor. 1995a. "BLS Releases New 1994–2005 Employment Projections." *News Release.* (December). Washington, D.C.: Bureau of Labor Statistics.

U.S. Department of Labor. 1995b. *Employment Outlook: 1994–2005—Job Quality and Other Aspects of Projected Employment Growth.* Bulletin 2472. (December). Washington, D.C.: Bureau of Labor Statistics.

U.S. Department of Labor. *Employment and Earnings.* Selected issues. Washington, D.C.: Bureau of Labor Statistics.

Table 1.1

Employment Status of the Civilian Noninstitutional Population, 16 Years of Age and Older, by Race and Gender, Selected Years, 1980–1995

(Numbers in Thousands)

	Men					Women				
	1980[a]	1985	1990	1994	1995	1980[a]	1985	1990	1994	1995
Blacks										
Civilian Noninstitutional Population	9,204	8,790	9,567	10,258	10,411	11,282	10,873	11,733	12,621	12,835
Civilian Labor Force	6,518	6,220	6,708	7,089	7,183	6,029	6,144	6,785	7,413	7,634
% of Population	70.8	70.8	70.1	69.1	69.0	53.4	56.5	57.8	58.7	59.5
Employed	5,651	5,270	5,915	6,241	6,422	5,239	5,231	6,051	6,595	6,857
Unemployed	868	951	793	848	762	790	913	734	818	777
Unemployment Rate (%)	13.3	15.3	11.8	12.0	10.6	13.1	14.9	10.8	11.0	10.2
Not in Labor Force	2,686	2,570	2,859	3,169	3,228	5,253	4,729	4,948	5,208	5,201
Whites										
Civilian Noninstitutional Population	69,634	73,373	77,082	80,059	80,733	76,489	80,306	83,332	85,496	86,181
Civilian Labor Force	53,627	56,472	59,298	60,727	61,146	38,544	43,455	47,879	50,356	50,804
% of Population	77.0	77.0	76.9	75.9	75.7	50.4	54.1	57.5	58.9	59.0
Employed	50,337	53,046	56,432	57,452	58,146	36,043	40,690	45,654	47,738	48,344
Unemployed	3,289	3,426	2,866	3,275	2,999	2,501	2,765	2,225	2,617	2,460
Unemployment Rate (%)	6.1	6.1	4.8	5.4	4.9	6.5	6.4	4.6	5.2	4.8
Not in Labor Force	14,868	16,901	17,785	19,332	19,587	36,618	36,852	35,453	35,141	35,377

Source: *Employment and Earnings,* January issues, 1981, 1986, 1991, 1995, 1996.
[a] Blacks are defined as "Blacks and Others" in 1980.

Table 1.2

Employment-to-Population Ratios by Race, Age, and Gender, Selected Years, 1980–1995
(In Percents)

	Men					Women				
	1980[a]	1985	1990	1994	1995	1980[a]	1985	1990	1994	1995
Blacks										
16 Years and Older	61.4	60.0	61.8	60.8	61.7	46.4	48.1	51.6	52.3	53.4
16 to 19 Years	28.2	26.3	27.6	25.4	25.2	22.7	23.1	25.7	24.4	26.1
20 to 24 Years	61.3	60.4	61.2	59.5	61.5	46.9	46.5	50.1	51.8	52.4
25 to 54 Years	80.0	77.6	79.1	76.8	77.5	60.7	63.4	67.3	67.0	68.6
55 to 64 Years	59.7	54.2	54.8	51.2	51.9	42.9	42.6	41.6	43.0	45.5
65 Years and Older	16.0	12.6	12.4	11.7	13.7	9.3	8.9	9.3	8.8	7.3
Whites										
16 Years and Older	73.5	72.3	73.2	71.8	72.0	48.0	50.7	54.8	55.8	56.1
16 to 19 Years	53.5	49.9	51.0	48.3	49.4	48.0	47.1	48.4	47.5	48.1
20 to 24 Years	77.5	78.0	79.5	78.0	78.4	64.6	67.5	68.7	68.0	67.0
25 to 54 Years	90.7	90.2	90.7	88.9	89.1	60.0	65.7	71.5	72.6	73.3
55 to 64 Years	71.0	66.1	66.2	63.7	64.8	39.8	39.9	44.4	47.5	47.8
65 Years and Older	18.8	15.5	16.3	16.6	16.3	4.6	6.8	8.3	8.8	8.7

Source: *Employment and Earnings*, January issues, 1981, 1986, 1991, 1995, 1996.
[a] Blacks are defined as "Blacks and Others" in 1980.

EMPLOYMENT PATTERNS AND LIKELY OPPORTUNITIES

Table 1.3

Percentage of Employed Persons 16 Years of Age and Older Who Work Full-Time, by Race and Gender, 1990–1995

	1990	1991	1992	1993	1994	1995
Blacks	88.8	87.6	85.8	87.2	88.4	89.7
Males	88.3	87.0	84.7	86.2	88.1	89.6
Females	89.4	88.3	86.9	88.1	88.6	89.7
Whites	95.4	94.0	93.5	94.1	94.7	95.3
Males	95.4	93.8	93.3	93.9	94.8	95.3
Females	95.5	94.4	93.9	94.3	94.6	95.1

Source: *Employment and Earnings*, January issues, 1991–1995.

Table 1.4

Distribution of Employed Black and White Civilian Men, by Occupation, Selected Years, 1980–1995
(N in Thousands)

	1980	1982	1983	1990	1994	1995
Blacks		N= 4,637 (%)	N= 4,753 (%)	N= 5,915 (%)	N= 6,241 (%)	N= 6,422 (%)
Managerial/Professional	n.a.	n.a.	12.2	13.3	16.0	17.7
Executive, Administrative, and Managerial	n.a.	n.a.	(5.8)	(6.8)	(8.4)	(9.2)
Professional Specialty	n.a.	n.a.	(6.4)	(6.5)	(7.6)	(8.6)
Technical, Sales, and Administrative Support	n.a.	n.a.	14.9	17.1	17.7	17.7
Technicians and Related Support	n.a.	n.a.	(2.0)	(2.2)	(2.4)	(2.3)
Sales	n.a.	n.a.	(4.7)	(5.8)	(6.8)	(7.0)
Administrative Support, Including Clerical	n.a.	n.a.	(8.2)	(9.1)	(8.5)	(8.4)
Service	n.a.	n.a.	18.5	18.2	19.1	17.8
Private Household	n.a.	n.a.	(0.2)	(0.1)	(a)	(0.1)
Protective Service	n.a.	n.a.	(4.1)	(4.4)	(5.1)	(4.7)
Service, Except Private Household/Protective	n.a.	n.a.	(14.3)	(13.7)	(14.0)	(12.9)
Precision Production, Craft, and Repair	n.a.	n.a.	15.7	15.6	13.9	14.3
Operators, Fabricators, Laborers	n.a.	n.a.	33.5	32.7	30.6	30.3
Machine Operators, Assemblers, and Inspectors	n.a.	n.a.	(11.6)	(10.3)	(10.1)	(10.4)
Transportation and Material Moving	n.a.	n.a.	(10.7)	(11.6)	(10.7)	(10.5)
Handlers, Equipment Cleaners, Helpers, and Laborers	n.a.	n.a.	(11.3)	(10.8)	(9.8)	(9.4)
Farming, Forestry, and Fishing	n.a.	n.a.	5.2	3.2	2.6	2.2

a Less than 0.05 percent.

Continued...

Table 1.4 (Continued)

Whites	1980	1982	1983	1990	1994	1995
		N= 50,287 (%)	N= 50,621 (%)	N= 56,432 (%)	N= 57,452 (%)	N= 58,146 (%)
Managerial/Professional	n.a.	25.6	25.6	26.9	27.5	28.4
Executive, Administrative, and Managerial	n.a.	(13.6)	(13.5)	(14.6)	(14.7)	(15.4)
Professional Specialty	n.a.	(12.0)	(12.1)	(12.3)	(12.8)	(13.0)
Technical, Sales, and Administrative Support	n.a.	19.9	19.9	20.3	20.3	20.0
Technicians and Related Support	n.a.	(2.9)	(2.8)	(3.1)	(2.8)	(2.9)
Sales	n.a.	(11.5)	(11.5)	(11.8)	(11.9)	(11.9)
Administrative Support, Including Clerical	n.a.	(5.5)	(5.6)	(5.5)	(5.5)	(5.2)
Service	n.a.	8.5	8.8	8.7	9.2	9.0
Private Household	n.a.	(a)	(0.1)	(a)	(a)	(a)
Protective Service	n.a.	(2.4)	(2.4)	(2.5)	(2.6)	(2.6)
Service Except Private Household/Protective	n.a.	(6.0)	(6.3)	(6.2)	(6.5)	(6.3)
Precision Production, Craft, and Repair	n.a.	19.9	20.5	20.0	19.1	18.9
Operators, Fabricators, Laborers	n.a.	20.4	19.7	19.4	19.3	19.2
Machine Operators, Assemblers, and Inspectors	n.a.	(7.8)	(7.6)	(7.2)	(6.9)	(6.9)
Transportation and Material Moving	n.a.	(6.6)	(6.5)	(6.4)	(6.7)	(6.6)
Handlers, Equipment Cleaners, Helpers, and Laborers	n.a.	(5.9)	(5.6)	(5.8)	(5.8)	(5.6)
Farming, Forestry, and Fishing	n.a.	5.7	5.5	4.6	4.6	4.6

Source: *Employment and Earnings*, January issues, 1984, 1991, 1995, 1996.
Notes: For blacks and whites, N is expressed in thousands and equals all employed civilians of that group. *n.a.* indicates not available. Percents may not sum because of rounding. Numbers in parentheses show the breakdown by subcategory within categories.
a Less than 0.05 percent.

Table 1.5

Distribution of Employed Black and White Civilian Women, by Occupation, Selected Years, 1980–1995
(N in Thousands)

	1980	1982	1983	1990	1994	1995
Blacks		N=4,552	N=4,622	N=6,051	N=6,595	N=6,857
		(%)	(%)	(%)	(%)	(%)
Managerial/Professional	n.a.	15.6	16.1	18.6	21.3	22.1
Executive, Administrative, and Managerial	n.a.	(4.4)	(4.9)	(7.5)	(8.7)	(9.4)
Professional Specialty	n.a.	(11.2)	(11.2)	(11.2)	(12.6)	(12.7)
Technical, Sales, and Administrative Support	n.a.	36.3	36.2	39.1	38.4	39.0
Technicians and Related Support	n.a.	(3.1)	(3.4)	(3.6)	(3.4)	(3.4)
Sales	n.a.	(6.7)	(7.3)	(9.4)	(9.6)	(10.7)
Administrative Support, Including Clerical	n.a.	(26.5)	(25.6)	(26.1)	(25.3)	(25.0)
Service	n.a.	31.0	30.6	27.3	25.7	25.4
Private Household	n.a.	(6.3)	(5.7)	(3.1)	(2.0)	(1.9)
Protective Service	n.a.	(0.7)	(0.7)	(1.2)	(1.4)	(1.5)
Service Except Private Household/Protective	n.a.	(24.0)	(24.2)	(23.0)	(22.3)	(22.0)
Precision Production, Craft, and Repair	n.a.	1.7	2.1	2.3	2.6	2.3
Operators, Fabricators, Laborers	n.a.	14.8	14.3	12.2	11.6	11.1
Machine Operators, Assemblers, and Inspectors	n.a.	(11.1)	(11.5)	(9.1)	(8.2)	(8.0)
Transportation and Material Moving	n.a.	(0.9)	(0.9)	(1.0)	(1.2)	(1.2)
Handlers, Equipment Cleaners, Helpers, and Laborers	n.a.	(2.8)	(1.9)	(2.1)	(2.3)	(1.9)
Farming, Forestry, and Fishing	n.a.	0.6	0.6	0.3	0.3	0.2

Continued...

Table 1.5 (Continued)

Whites	1980	1982 N=37,615 (%)	1983 N=38,272 (%)	1990 N=45,654 (%)	1994 N=47,738 (%)	1995 N=48,344 (%)
Managerial/Professional	n.a.	22.5	22.6	27.2	29.8	30.6
Executive, Administrative, and Managerial	n.a.	(8.3)	(8.3)	(11.6)	(12.9)	(13.3)
Professional Specialty	n.a.	(14.2)	(14.3)	(15.6)	(16.9)	(17.3)
Technical, Sales, and Administrative Support	n.a.	47.1	47.2	45.3	43.1	42.5
Technicians and Related Support	n.a.	(3.2)	(3.3)	(3.5)	(3.6)	(3.5)
Sales	n.a.	(12.6)	(13.5)	(13.6)	(13.4)	(13.4)
Administrative Support, Including Clerical	n.a.	(31.3)	(30.5)	(28.2)	(26.2)	(25.7)
Service	n.a.	17.5	17.5	16.4	16.6	16.5
Private Household	n.a.	(1.9)	(1.7)	(1.2)	(1.3)	(1.3)
Protective Service	n.a.	(0.4)	(0.5)	(0.5)	(0.6)	(0.5)
Service, Except Private Household/Protective	n.a.	(15.2)	(15.3)	(14.7)	(14.8)	(14.7)
Precision Production, Craft, and Repair	n.a.	1.9	2.2	2.1	2.1	2.0
Operators, Fabricators, Laborers	n.a.	9.6	9.0	7.8	7.0	6.9
Machine Operators, Assemblers, and Inspectors	n.a.	(7.0)	(6.8)	(5.5)	(4.7)	(4.5)
Transportation and Material Moving	n.a.	(0.7)	(0.7)	(0.8)	(0.8)	(0.8)
Handlers, Equipment Cleaners, Helpers, and Laborers	n.a.	(1.9)	(1.5)	(1.5)	(1.5)	(1.6)
Farming, Forestry, and Fishing	n.a.	1.4	1.4	1.1	1.4	1.4

Source: *Employment and Earnings*, January issues, 1984, 1991, 1995, 1996.
Notes: For blacks and whites, N is expressed in thousands and equals all employed civilians of that group. *n.a.* indicates not available. Percents may not sum because of rounding. Numbers in parentheses show the breakdown by subcategory within categories.

Table 1.6

Black and White Civilians Employed in the Construction, Manufacturing, Retail Trade, and Services Industries, by Occupation, 1985

	Total Number Employed (000s)	Managerial & Professional (%)	Tech., Sales & Admin. Support (%)	Service (%)	Precision Production, Craft & Repair (%)	Operators, Fabricators, & Laborers (%)	Farming, Forestry, & Fishing (%)
Blacks							
Construction	473	5.1	4.2	1.5	51.6	37.2	0.2
Manufacturing	2,085	5.6	12.2	3.9	15.3	62.2	0.8
Retail Trade	1,422	6.2	42.6	30.8	4.4	16.0	0.1
Services	3,879	24.1	20.7	44.3	3.3	6.2	1.3
Private Household	350	0.6	1.1	90.3	0.3	1.4	6.3
Other Services Industries	3,529	26.4	22.6	39.8	3.6	6.7	0.8
Whites							
Construction	6,409	14.4	8.4	0.4	57.9	18.6	0.2
Manufacturing	18,216	20.2	20.0	1.7	19.7	38.1	0.4
Retail Trade	15,948	9.7	51.0	22.2	6.7	10.3	0.1
Services	28,483	43.1	24.1	21.5	5.8	4.3	1.2
Private Household	873	1.0	1.6	85.3	0.8	3.2	8.0
Other Services Industries	27,610	44.4	24.8	19.5	6.0	4.3	0.9

Source: *Employment and Earnings*, January issue, 1986.
Note: Percents across each row may not sum to 100% due to rounding.

EMPLOYMENT PATTERNS AND LIKELY OPPORTUNITIES

Table 1.7

Black and White Civilians Employed in the Construction, Manufacturing, Retail Trade, and Services Industries, by Occupation, 1990

	Total Number Employed (000s)	Managerial & Professional (%)	Tech., Sales & Admin. Support (%)	Service (%)	Precision Production, Craft & Repair (%)	Operators, Fabricators, & Laborers (%)	Farming, Forestry, & Fishing (%)
Blacks							
Construction	498	7.2	4.6	0.8	53.0	33.5	0.6
Manufacturing	2,141	6.6	12.6	3.0	15.6	61.4	0.7
Retail Trade	1,716	6.6	45.7	27.8	4.0	15.9	0.1
Services	4,459	25.2	22.4	41.1	3.8	6.5	1.1
Private Household	241	1.7	0.4	90.9	0.8	2.1	4.6
Other Services Industries	4,218	26.5	23.6	38.3	3.9	6.7	0.9
Whites							
Construction	7,047	14.3	7.5	0.4	57.6	18.5	0.3
Manufacturing	18,338	22.0	19.0	1.6	19.0	37.8	0.5
Retail Trade	17,166	10.1	51.3	21.7	6.2	10.6	0.1
Services	33,237	44.6	24.9	20.3	5.0	4.2	1.0
Private Household	749	1.7	1.7	84.0	1.9	2.9	7.7
Other Services Industries	32,488	45.6	25.4	18.8	5.0	4.3	0.9

Source: *Employment and Earnings*, January issue, 1991.
Note: Percents across each row may not sum to 100% due to rounding.

Table 1.8

Black and White Civilians Employed in the Construction, Manufacturing, Retail Trade, and Services Industries, by Occupation, 1994

	Total Number Employed (000s)	Managerial & Professional (%)	Tech., Sales & Admin. Support (%)	Service (%)	Precision Production, Craft & Repair (%)	Operators, Fabricators, & Laborers (%)	Farming, Forestry, & Fishing (%)
Blacks							
Construction	482	8.3	4.4	1.7	54.1	30.9	0.2
Manufacturing	2,032	7.5	12.4	2.1	16.3	61.2	0.5
Retail Trade	1,869	6.9	46.0	28.0	3.3	15.8	0.0
Services	5,095	28.8	23.0	37.7	3.2	6.6	0.7
Private Household	171	1.2	0.6	94.2	0.6	0.0	0.0
Other Services Industries	4,924	29.7	23.7	35.8	3.3	6.8	0.7
Whites							
Construction	6,810	16.5	7.5	0.3	57.3	18.0	0.3
Manufacturing	17,230	23.7	17.8	1.4	19.2	37.6	0.4
Retail Trade	18,144	10.2	50.6	22.7	5.7	10.6	0.1
Services	36,095	46.4	23.8	19.7	5.0	4.1	1.0
Private Household	761	1.2	1.2	89.9	0.8	2.0	5.0
Other Services Industries	35,333	47.3	24.3	18.1	5.1	4.1	0.9

Source: *Employment and Earnings*, January issue, 1995.
Note: Percents across each row may not sum to 100% due to rounding.

EMPLOYMENT PATTERNS AND LIKELY OPPORTUNITIES

Table 1.9

Black and White Civilians Employed in the Construction, Manufacturing, Retail Trade, and Services Industries, by Occupation, 1995

	Total Number Employed (000s)	Managerial & Professional (%)	Tech, Sales & Admin. Support (%)	Service (%)	Precision Production, Craft & Repair (%)	Operators, Fabricators, & Laborers (%)	Farming, Forestry, & Fishing (%)
Blacks							
Construction	509	9.2	4.3	0.6	53.4	32.2	0.4
Manufacturing	2,131	7.8	12.7	2.7	17.0	59.3	5.2
Retail Trade	1,924	7.5	49.9	25.3	3.3	13.9	0.1
Services	5,265	30.4	23.1	37.0	2.9	6.0	0.6
Private Household	178	1.7	1.1	92.1	0.6	2.8	1.1
Other Services Industries	5,088	31.4	23.8	35.0	3.0	6.1	0.6
Whites							
Construction	6,945	17.1	7.3	0.4	57.1	17.9	0.2
Manufacturing	17,401	24.4	17.7	1.3	18.9	37.1	0.6
Retail Trade	18,178	10.5	50.6	22.4	5.5	10.8	0.2
Services	36,877	47.3	23.4	19.5	4.8	4.0	1.0
Private Household	739	1.4	1.4	91.5	0.7	1.5	3.7
Other Services Industries	36,138	48.2	23.9	18.0	4.9	4.1	0.9

Source: *Employment and Earnings*, January issue, 1996.
Note: Percents across each row may not sum to 100% due to rounding.

Table 1.10

Percentage of Black and White Persons 16–24 Years of Age, Not Currently Enrolled in School, Who Are Employed, by Educational Attainment, 1990–1995

	1990	1991	1992	1993	1994	1995
Blacks	75.8	74.3	71.3	73.3	75.5	76.0
Less Than HS Diploma	59.4	59.1	55.7	56.4	55.8	56.7
HS Graduate, No College	78.0	76.0	73.3	74.5	77.1	77.2
Less Than Bachelor's Degree	85.6	83.5	79.4	82.2	83.8	86.6
College Graduates	90.6	88.4	91.4	88.6	95.0	92.8
Whites	90.7	88.3	88.1	89.0	89.4	89.9
Less Than HS Diploma	83.0	79.4	78.5	80.4	80.2	82.1
HS Graduate, No College	91.6	89.3	88.5	89.3	90.1	89.8
Less Than Bachelor's Degree	94.6	92.4	92.6	92.9	93.5	94.4
College Graduates	95.2	93.5	93.6	94.3	94.7	94.6

Source: *Employment and Earnings*, January issues, 1991–1995.

EMPLOYMENT PATTERNS AND LIKELY OPPORTUNITIES

Table 1.11

Median Income of Black and White Families, by Type of Family, Selected Years, 1980–1994
(In Current Dollars)

	1980	1985	1987	1990	1994
Black Families					
All Families	12,662	16,665	18,406	21,423	24,698
Married-Couple Families	18,593	24,570	27,311	33,784	40,432
Husband Working Full-Time Only[a]	n.a.	n.a.	24,776	30,065	32,365
Husband & Wife Working Full-Time[a]	n.a.	n.a.	43,702	49,265	55,883
Families Maintained by Women	7,425	9,305	9,844	12,125	13,943
Families Maintained by Men	12,557	16,416	18,050	21,848	20,977
White Families					
All Families	21,949	29,253	32,385	36,915	40,884
Married-Couple Families	23,501	31,602	35,434	40,331	45,474
Husband Working Full-Time Only[a]	n.a.	n.a.	36,072	39,903	43,065
Husband & Wife Working Full-Time[a]	n.a.	n.a.	49,307	55,668	63,184
Families Maintained by Women	11,908	15,825	17,013	19,528	20,795
Families Maintained by Men	18,731	24,190	26,513	30,570	29,460

Source: *Current Population Reports*, Series P-60.
Note: *n.a.* indicates not available.
[a] Includes only families in which the employed person(s) work(s) full time.

Table 1.12

Median Weekly Earnings of Black and White Full-Time Salary Workers, by Gender, 1990–1995
(In Current Dollars)

	1990	1991	1992	1993	1994	1995
Blacks						
Males	329	348	357	370	371	383
Females	360	374	380	392	400	411
	308	323	336	349	346	355
Whites						
Males	427	446	462	478	484	494
Females	497	509	518	531	547	566
	355	374	388	403	408	415

Source: *Employment and Earnings,* January issues, 1991-1996.

Table 1.13

Median Weekly Earnings of Full-Time Salary Workers, by Occupation, Gender, and Race, 1995
(In Current Dollars)

	Men		Women	
	White	Black	White	Black
Total	566	411	415	355
Executive	854	607	570	563
Professional Specialty	835	678	637	568
Technicians	644	421	479	462
Sales Occupations	594	378	347	260
Administrative Support	503	410	384	383
Service Occupations	377	307	264	263
Service Occupations Except Private Household	306	270	264	258
Precision Production, Crafts, and Repair	546	483	384	340
Operators, Fabricators, Laborers	425	368	302	288
Farming, Forestry, and Fishing	298	268	247	278
Non-Farm Total	577	414	416	355

Source: Unpublished data from the Bureau of Labor Statistics, 1995.

Table 1.14

Unemployment Rates, by Race, Age, and Gender, Selected Years, 1980–1995
(In Percents)

	Men					Women				
	1980[a]	1985	1990	1994	1995	1980[a]	1985	1990	1994	1995
Blacks										
16 Years and Older	13.3	15.3	11.8	12.0	10.6	13.1	14.9	10.8	11.0	10.2
16 to 19 Years	34.9	41.0	32.1	37.6	37.1	36.9	39.2	30.0	32.6	34.3
20 to 24 Years	22.3	23.5	20.2	19.4	17.6	21.8	25.6	19.7	19.6	17.8
25 to 54 Years	9.6	11.6	9.4	9.1	7.8	9.5	11.5	8.7	8.7	7.7
55 to 64 Years	6.0	7.9	5.5	6.0	4.4	4.7	6.0	3.7	4.9	3.6
65 Years and Older	8.8	8.9	4.6	8.2	7.6	4.7	5.2	5.8	4.4	5.6
Whites										
16 Years and Older	6.1	6.1	4.8	5.4	4.9	6.5	6.4	4.6	5.2	4.8
16 to 19 Years	16.2	16.5	14.2	16.3	15.6	14.8	14.8	12.6	13.8	13.4
20 to 24 Years	11.1	9.7	7.6	8.8	7.9	8.5	8.5	6.8	7.4	7.4
25 to 54 Years	4.5	4.9	3.9	4.3	3.9	5.3	5.4	3.9	4.4	4.0
55 to 64 Years	3.1	4.0	3.6	4.1	3.4	3.1	4.1	2.7	3.7	3.5
65 Years and Older	2.5	2.7	2.8	3.7	4.0	2.9	3.1	2.8	3.9	3.5

Source: *Employment and Earnings,* January issues, 1981, 1986, 1991, 1995, 1996.
[a] Blacks are defined as "Blacks and Others" in 1980.

EMPLOYMENT PATTERNS AND LIKELY OPPORTUNITIES

Table 1.15

Black and White Unemployed Persons (Percentage Distribution), by Reason for Unemployment, Selected Years, 1980–1995
(N in thousands)

	1980[a]	1985	1990	1994	1995
Blacks	N=1,658	N=1,864	N=1,527	N=1,666	N=1,538
Job Losers	48.5	47.8	44.4	39.0	38.0
On Layoff	(14.3)	(8.1)	(9.5)	(8.1)	(7.6)
Other Job Losers	(34.2)	(39.6)	(34.9)	(31.0)	(30.4)
Job Leavers	8.8	5.9	12.2	6.9	8.0
Reentrants	27.3	29.3	30.2	43.8	42.7
New Entrants	15.4	17.0	13.2	10.3	11.3
Whites	N=5,790	N=6,191	N=5,091	N=5,892	N=5,459
Job Losers	52.8	50.8	49.8	50.4	49.6
On Layoff	(21.3)	(15.9)	(16.6)	(13.6)	(15.7)
Other Job Losers	(31.5)	(34.9)	(33.2)	(36.9)	(34.0)
Job Leavers	12.4	11.7	15.5	10.8	12.1
Reentrants	24.5	26.4	26.4	32.2	31.7
New Entrants	10.3	11.0	8.3	6.5	6.6

Source: *Employment and Earnings,* January issues, 1981, 1986, 1991, 1995, 1996.
Notes: Percents may not sum to 100% due to rounding. N equals the number of unemployed persons by race, expressed in thousands.
[a] Blacks are defined as "Blacks and Others" in 1980.

Table 1.16

Duration of Unemployment for Unemployed Persons, Age 16 and Older, by Race and Gender, 1990 and 1995
(N in Thousands)

	Blacks		Whites	
	1990	1995	1990	1995
Men	N=793	N=762	N=2,866	N=2,999
	(%)	(%)	(%)	(%)
Less Than 5 Weeks	38.5	28.7	43.5	36.6
5 to 14 Weeks	34.6	31.2	31.9	31.5
15 to 26 Weeks	12.2	17.5	12.9	14.1
27 Weeks or More	14.6	22.6	11.7	17.7
Women	N=734	N=777	N=2,225	N=2,460
	(%)	(%)	(%)	(%)
Less Than 5 Weeks	47.5	30.8	51.8	41.0
5 to 14 Weeks	32.4	32.6	31.1	31.8
15 to 26 Weeks	10.8	16.1	10.4	13.7
27 Weeks or More	9.3	20.6	6.7	13.5

Source: *Employment and Earnings*, January issues, 1991, 1996.

Notes: Percents may not add to 100% due to rounding. N equals number of unemployed persons, expressed in thousands.

Table 1.17

Unemployed Jobseekers, Age 16 and Older, by Race, Gender, and Job Search Methods Used, Selected Years, 1980–1995
(Numbers in Thousands)

	Men					Women				
	1980[a]	1985	1990	1994	1995	1980[a]	1985	1990	1994	1995
Blacks										
Total Unemployed	868	951	793	848	762	790	913	734	818	777
Total Jobseekers	711	852	691	766	694	699	848	681	766	727
% of Unemployed Seeking Jobs	81.9	89.6	87.1	90.3	91.1	88.5	92.9	92.8	93.6	93.6
Job Search Methods[b]										
Public Employment Agency	35.7	28.9	26.2	24.3	21.1	31.2	26.3	24.3	23.7	19.8
Private Employment Agency	5.8	5.5	8.3	7.2	6.4	6.2	5.9	8.5	7.1	7.0
Contacted Employer Directly	70.7	78.5	74.6	69.5	65.3	70.2	74.3	69.8	67.7	63.9
Placed or Answered Ads	23.2	27.7	32.1	18.8	14.7	26.3	31.0	35.2	19.7	16.1
Sent Resume/Filed Application	n.a.	n.a.	n.a.	33.9	44.5	n.a.	n.a.	n.a.	38.2	45.6
Friends or Relatives	16.0	19.5	21.5	17.1	16.3	10.6	14.2	15.1	13.2	14.1
Other	7.0	4.1	3.3	5.9	6.4	5.2	3.7	3.4	5.2	5.1

Continued....

Note: *n.a.* indicates data not available.
[a] Blacks are defined as "Blacks and Others" for 1980.
[b] Percentage of jobseekers using method.

Table 1.17 (Continued)

	Men					Women				
	1980	1985	1990	1994	1995	1980	1985	1990	1994	1995
Whites										
Total Unemployed	3,289	3,426	2,866	3,275	2,999	2,501	2,765	2,225	2,617	2,460
Total Jobseekers	2,389	2,693	2,242	2,765	2,454	2,055	2,366	1,903	2,328	2,150
% of Unemployed Seeking Jobs	72.6	78.6	78.2	84.4	81.8	82.2	85.6	85.5	89.0	87.4
Job Search Methods[b]										
Public Employment Agency	28.6	25.2	23.9	21.3	20.0	22.7	20.8	19.6	17.8	16.8
Private Employment Agency	6.2	5.8	8.9	6.6	6.6	6.2	6.1	8.9	6.4	6.4
Contacted Employer Directly	75.2	77.5	72.5	70.0	67.3	72.7	74.9	71.0	67.7	63.8
Placed or Answered Ads	30.4	33.3	40.0	22.7	19.0	35.5	39.1	43.4	23.2	19.9
Sent Resume/Filed Application	n.a.	n.a.	n.a.	38.2	42.7	n.a.	n.a.	n.a.	43.5	48.7
Friends or Relatives	16.4	20.0	23.1	16.7	14.8	11.0	14.9	17.3	22.2	20.0
Other	7.2	6.0	6.3	10.3	9.5	3.9	3.5	4.1	7.8	7.3

Source: *Employment and Earnings*, January issues, 1981, 1986, 1991, 1995, 1996.
Note: *n.a.* indicates data not available.
[b] Percentage of jobseekers using method.

Table 1.18

Civilian Labor Force (Age 16 and Older), by Race and Hispanic Origin, 1994, With Moderate Growth Projection to 2005
(Numbers in Thousands)

| | 1994 | | 2005 | | 1994-2005 Change | | Annual Growth |
	No.	(%)	No.	(%)	No.	(%)	Rate
Total	131,056	100.0	147,106	100.0	16,050	12.2	1.1
White	111,082	84.8	122,867	83.5	11,785	10.6	0.9
Black	14,502	11.1	16,619	11.3	2,116	14.6	1.2
Hispanic	11,975	9.1	16,330	11.1	4,355	36.4	2.9
Asian and Other	5,474	4.2	7,632	5.2	2,158	39.4	3.1

Source: Fullerton, 1995.
Note: Percents will not sum to 100% because the category *Hispanic* includes persons of all races, thus leading to persons being counted in more than one category.

Table 1.19

Civilian Labor Force Participation Rates for Population Age 16 and Older, by Race and Gender, 1982, 1993, and 1994, With Moderate Projection to 2005
(In Percents)

	1982	1993	1994	2005
Blacks				
Males	61.0	62.4	63.4	61.9
Females	70.1	68.6	69.1	65.8
	53.7	57.4	58.7	58.8
Whites				
Males	64.3	66.7	67.1	67.7
Females	77.4	76.1	75.9	73.9
	52.4	58.0	58.9	62.6

Source: Fullerton, 1995.

EMPLOYMENT PATTERNS AND LIKELY OPPORTUNITIES

Table 1.20

Employment by Major Occupational Group, 1994 and 2005, Moderate Alternative Projection
(Numbers in Thousands)

	1994		2005		Employment Change 1994-2005	
	No.	(%)	No.	(%)	No.	(%)
Total	127,014	100.0	144,708	100.0	17,694	13.9
Executive, Administrative, and Managerial	12,903	10.2	15,071	10.4	2,168	16.8
Professional Specialty	17,314	13.6	22,387	15.5	5,073	29.3
Technicians and Related Support	4,439	3.5	5,316	3.7	876	19.7
Marketing and Sales	13,990	11.0	16,502	11.4	2,512	18.0
Administrative Support, Including Clerical	23,178	18.2	24,172	16.7	994	4.3
Service	20,239	15.9	24,832	17.2	4,593	22.7
Agriculture, Forestry, Fishing, and Related	3,762	3.0	3,650	2.5	-112	-3.0
Precision Production, Craft, and Repair	14,047	11.1	14,880	10.3	833	5.9
Operators, Fabricators, and Laborers	17,142	13.5	17,898	12.4	757	4.4

Source: Silvestri, 1995.

Table 1.21

Employment in Fastest Growing Occupations, 1994–2005, Moderate Alternative Projection
(Numbers in Thousands)

	Employment		Numerical Change	Percent Change
	1994	2005		
Personal and Home Care Aides	179	391	212	119
Home Health Aides	420	848	428	102
Systems Analysts	483	928	445	92
Computer Engineers	195	372	177	90
Physical and Corrective Therapy Assistants and Aides	78	142	64	83
Electronic Pagination Systems Workers	18	33	15	83
Occupational Therapy Assistants and Aides	16	29	13	82
Physical Therapists	102	183	81	80
Residential Counselors	165	290	126	76
Human Services Workers	168	293	125	75

Source: Silvestri, 1995.

Table 1.22

Employment in Nonfarm Wage and Salary Industries, by Major Industry Division, 1983, 1994, and 2005, Moderate Alternative Projection

(Numbers in Thousands)

	Employment Level			Change	
	1983	1994	2005	1983–1994	1994–2005
All Nonfarm Wage and Salary Industries	89,734	113,340	130,185	23,605	16,846
Goods-Producing	23,328	23,914	22,930	587	-985
Mining	952	601	439	-351	-162
Construction	3,946	5,010	5,500	1,064	490
Manufacturing	18,430	18,304	16,991	-126	-1,313
Durable	10,707	10,431	9,290	-275	-1,141
Nondurable	7,723	7,873	7,700	149	-172
Service-Producing	66,407	89,425	107,256	23,019	17,830
Transportation, Communications, Utilities	4,958	6,006	6,431	1,048	425
Wholesale Trade	5,283	6,140	6,559	857	419
Retail Trade	15,587	20,438	23,094	4,850	2,657
Finance, Insurance, and Real Estate	5,466	6,933	7,373	1,468	439
Services	19,242	30,792	42,810	11,550	12,018
Government	15,870	19,117	20,990	3,247	1,873

Source: Franklin, 1995.

Barriers to Higher Employment Rates Among African Americans

Harry J. Holzer

The problem is well known: employment rates among African Americans lag well behind those of white Americans (Freeman and Holzer 1986; Badgett 1994). In 1996, the unemployment rate averaged roughly 4.8 percent for whites and 10.5 percent among blacks. The gaps among the young are even greater: for teens in 1996, unemployment rates were roughly 14 percent for whites and 33 percent for blacks.

Racial differences in employment rates have increased in each of the last several decades. Earnings gaps between the two groups, which had narrowed in earlier decades and especially in the aftermath of the Civil Rights legislation of the 1960s, have also widened in recent years (Bound and Freeman 1992; Bound and Holzer 1996).

What accounts for the labor market difficulties of African Americans, and why have these problems worsened during the past few decades? Do blacks face particular barriers in the labor market to higher employment and earnings, and if so, what are these barriers? Can these barriers be weakened or removed by public policies, and is there some special role for private-sector organizations or institutions to play?

This chapter addresses those concerns with a focus on barriers to improved employment that blacks in general, and less-educated blacks in particular, face on the demand side of the labor market, that is, barriers posed by the characteristics of jobs and the attitudes or behavior of those who make decisions about hiring and pay. Clearly, in recent years, workers of all races have been affected by enormous changes in labor markets, generated mostly by changes on the demand side of the market. If these demand-side changes have occurred so rapidly that adjustments among blacks on the supply side of the market have not kept pace, then various mismatches might exist that exacerbate the problems of blacks (Holzer 1994; Moss and Tilly 1992).

The next section reviews the major hypotheses advanced by social scientists in recent years to explain the relative deterioration in labor market performance among blacks. The third section reviews recent evidence on these hypotheses, including some work from my own survey of employers in major metropolitan areas. The final section discusses the policy implications of these findings.

A DISCUSSION OF DEMAND-SIDE HYPOTHESES

The declines that have occurred in recent years in both relative earnings and employment rates among blacks suggest that labor demand has shifted away from them.[1] The questions of why these shifts have occurred and what barriers to better employment and earnings blacks currently face in the market have recently been addressed by a variety of labor market economists, as well as by sociologists such as William J. Wilson and John Kasarda, among others. While no certain consensus on the answers to these questions has emerged, there is some agreement on the relevant hypotheses.

Rising Demand for Skills

In the past two decades, the gaps in earnings between workers with varying amounts of education and experience have grown quite dramatically (Levy and Murnane 1992). Returns to other measures of cognitive ability, such as scores on standardized tests, have risen as well, and at least partially account for the growing gaps between high school and college graduates (Murnane et al. 1995).

The fact that both employment and earnings have deteriorated among the less-educated relative to the more-educated suggests that labor demand has shifted away from the former towards the latter. The primary hypothesis for this shift involves "skill-biased technological change" in the workplace, that is, changes in workplace technology and organization, perhaps related to the growing use of personal computers, that lead to relatively less demand for unskilled workers (Berman et al. 1994). Growing international trade, including the outsourcing of assembly from domestic to foreign plants, appears to play some role as well, though likely a smaller one (Freeman 1995). Rising immigration, particularly of large numbers of less-educated immigrants from Asia and Latin America in recent years, also has likely reduced the demand for less-educated native-born workers, especially high school dropouts (Friedberg and Hunt 1994; Borjas et al. 1997). While these factors, and perhaps others, appear to be responsible for major demand shifts, other institutional factors, such as the declining power of unions and declining real value of the minimum wage, have likely contributed as well to the growing earnings gaps between more- and less-skilled workers.

The declining demand for the labor of less-educated workers probably hurts black workers especially, as they are disproportionately represented among these workers. Even among whites and blacks with comparable levels of education, blacks lag behind in other measures of skills, such as test scores. While the racial gaps in education levels and test scores have closed somewhat in recent years, this may not have occurred quickly enough to offset the recent rising returns to skill (Hauser and Phang 1993; Grissmer et al. 1994; Kane 1994; Bound and Holzer 1996). Furthermore, blacks were somewhat more concentrated and had experienced even greater benefits relative to whites in the manufacturing and unionized jobs that have declined especially rapidly in recent years (Freeman and Medoff 1984; Bound and Holzer 1993).

Geographic Imbalances

For several decades now, jobs have generally been relocating from central cities to suburbs and "exurbs." Indeed, employment growth has been particularly strong in suburbs located in outlying areas not close to the central cities (Hughes and Sternberg 1992; Kasarda 1995). Of course, both white and black residential populations also have been relocating in similar fashion. But to the extent that blacks remain relatively more concentrated in the central cities, suburbanization has probably diminished their access to these jobs, creating a spatial mismatch between jobs and workers.

Urban economists generally postulate that people choose their optimal residential locations, often involving some trade-off between the amenities of suburban life, such as lower housing prices, better schools, and safer neighborhoods, and the longer commute times to jobs. But the ability of blacks to choose their residences is constrained by residential segregation and housing market discrimination. Zoning practices also limit the availability of low-income housing in suburban areas. Where such housing exists, it is more frequently obtained by lower-income whites than by blacks (Yinger 1995).

Even if blacks are not fully free to choose residences near employment, why would they not have access to jobs anywhere in the metropolitan area? Why can't they simply search for jobs regardless of location and then commute to any jobs they find and accept?

For one thing, transportation costs may be particularly high, especially for those low-income residents who lack access to automobiles. Public transit to many suburban neighborhoods may either not exist or be so time-consuming as to be impractical. If the time and money costs of commuting are deducted from gross wages earned, particularly for low-wage jobs, the net earnings in these positions might well fall below the "reservation wages" of black workers, that is, the lowest wages considered acceptable. Alternatively, if they refuse to commute and seek work only close to home, their crowding into very local labor markets might also depress wages, and therefore employment, in a similar fashion. Furthermore, many inner-city residents may lack the information necessary to obtain suburban employment. They may be unfamiliar with the local geography itself, with the employers and jobs located in suburban areas, or with the residents from whom information and contacts with such employers can be obtained. Even if they have both the transportation and information, the perception of racial hostility in these environments, whether accurate or not, may inhibit inner-city blacks from seeking jobs in suburban areas.

Information and Employment Networks

The preceding discussion raises an important point about the nature of the job search in the United States: much of it occurs informally, through friends and relatives of the jobseeker. Employer search patterns reinforce this tendency. Many employers seek workers by soliciting referrals from their current employees and from other acquaintances.

While this may suggest the importance of nepotism in labor markets, employer reliance on informal referrals may actually generate quite efficient outcomes. The information obtained regarding the potential work performance of job candidates may be more accurate than what they would otherwise receive (Rees 1996; Granovetter 1974). Incumbent employees have an incentive to only forward candidates whom they think would be good employees and to be honest in their evaluations of these candidates; otherwise, their own position with the employer could be compromised. Indeed, some evidence indicates that employees who have obtained their jobs through informal referrals have lower quit rates and higher performance than those hired through other means, suggesting that these are better, more-informed matches between employers and employees (Holzer 1987a).

However, while the use of informal search mechanisms might be relatively efficient for the overall labor market, it also creates disadvantages for those who lack access to large networks of employed people. This is particularly true for blacks who live in poor neighborhoods where few adults are employed. Furthermore, even blacks who have access to employment networks may find themselves limited to jobs with relatively lower pay or status than those to which whites have access. Indeed, gains in efficiency that result from the spreading of information through labor market networks also will be limited if a large segment of potentially productive employees do not have access to these networks.

Finally, the social isolation of low-income blacks, caused by the interaction of racial and class segregation, may not only inhibit their ability to obtain information about potential job openings, but may also generate neighborhood effects that lower educational attainment or lead to nonmainstream behavior such as crime and drug abuse, especially among the young (Wilson 1987; Massey and Denton 1992; Harrell and Peterson 1992).

Discrimination

The passage of Civil Rights legislation in the 1960s and early 1970s, along with the implementation of affirmative action procedures for federal contractors, seems to have greatly lessened labor market discrimination facing blacks and resulted in major improvements in their relative market outcomes (Freeman 1973; Heckman and Payner 1989; Leonard 1990). But discrimination continues to exist in some areas of the labor market, especially where Equal Employment Opportunity (EEO) laws are weakly enforced or do not apply.

This may especially be true of small establishments since the laws do not apply to firms with fewer than 15 employees, and the federal monitoring of racial employment patterns is generally limited to even larger establishments.[2] Furthermore, enforcement of EEO laws seems limited in areas where few blacks live or apply for jobs. Indeed, discriminatory employers may deliberately choose to locate in those areas to avoid black job applicants (Bloch 1994). The perceived preferences of white customers or employees in these areas may induce employers to avoid hiring blacks, even if they themselves have no discriminatory preferences (Becker 1971).

Furthermore, some employers may choose not to employ blacks because they believe they will face more complaints and legal action from blacks who are hired (over such issues as pay and promotion) than from those who are rejected. To the extent that most discrimination litigation in recent years has been from incumbent employees rather than from rejected job applicants, this behavior by discriminatory employers might be particularly sensible (Donohue and Siegelman 1991). In this case, wage discrimination may simply be replaced by employment discrimination (Shulman 1987).

Despite the widespread decline of labor market discrimination 20 to 30 years ago, there may have been some recent upsurge in such behavior. One possible reason could be a decline of federal enforcement of existing EEO and affirmative action statutes (Leonard 1990). Sectoral shifts in the labor market might also generate greater employment discrimination against blacks for a variety of reasons. For instance, employment shifts away from central-city areas toward suburbs or from manufacturing to service jobs with more customer contact could result in greater discrimination from coworkers or customers. Rapid sectoral shifts could also lead to a temporary rise in statistical discrimination against blacks. Because of these employment shifts, employers would have less actual experience or information on which to base judgments about the relative abilities of black and white applicants, so they might treat race as a signal of weaker average ability. Statistical discrimination against individuals should lessen with rising job tenure, as employers gain more information about specific employees (Oettinger 1996), but if employment relationships are generally becoming less stable, the result could be a longer-term rise in such discrimination as well.

Finally, employer fears of young, less-educated black males may have risen in conjunction with public perceptions of increased crime and drug involvement among this group. Thus, the rising crime rates of young blacks and their diminishing opportunities for regular employment may reinforce each other (Freeman 1992).

THE EMPIRICAL EVIDENCE

The hypotheses mentioned above have received considerable attention from academics as well as the news media and policymakers. But are they, in fact, supported by empirical evidence? The first part of this section reviews the recent empirical literature on these issues. The second part presents data from a new survey of employers that documents some of the particular barriers that blacks face today as they seek employment, especially at wages above the lowest levels.

A Review of the Literature

To what extent have the economywide changes in labor demand and the rising returns to skills in the labor market been responsible for the recent deterioration in relative earnings and employment among blacks? A number of sources note the relatively strong effects on blacks of shifts in the occupational and industrial distributions away from less-educated workers, particularly in the industrial Midwest (Bound and Freeman 1992; Bound and Holzer 1993, 1996; Bluestone et al. 1992; and Johnson and Oliver 1992). Juhn et al. (1993) also note that trends in relative wages for blacks appear to move very closely with those of other less-skilled workers, though this point is disputed somewhat by Card and Lemieux (1994).

More direct evidence of the importance of skills to black-white differences in earnings can be found in a series of recent papers (O'Neill 1990; Ferguson 1993; Neal and Johnson 1996). Using the National Longitudinal Survey of Youth (NLSY), the authors find that controls for education as well as Armed Forces Qualifying Test (AFQT) scores account for most of the current black-white difference in hourly wages. But the effects on annual earnings differences, which reflect employment as well as wage differences, are not explained completely by these differences. Although Rivera-Batiz (1992) finds some effect of test scores on the probabilities of employment, a larger racial difference remains in employment than in hourly wages after controlling for differences in test scores. This suggests that blacks may now face greater discrimination in obtaining jobs in the first place than in obtaining comparable returns to skills once they are hired.

Furthermore, some questions about these findings have recently been raised by Rodgers and Spriggs (1996) and Cawley et al. (1996). These authors show that returns to different parts of the AFQT differ between blacks and whites. Thus, the same skills are rewarded in somewhat different relative proportions in the labor market between the two groups, perhaps suggesting some continued employer discrimination in evaluations of black skills. The former paper, in particular, shows that math scores are more highly rewarded among whites while verbal scores are more highly rewarded among blacks.

The importance of verbal skills among blacks is also underscored in recent work by Moss and Tilly (1995), who focus on employer demand for and perceptions of "soft" skills, such as communication skills and general work attitudes. In open-ended interviews with a sample of employers in Detroit and Los Angeles, they found that employers perceived major gaps between blacks and whites in these skills, and those employers who put relatively greater weight on these skills in their hiring decisions were less likely to employ blacks. Of course, the extent to which these perceptions are accurate or discriminatory remains unclear in this work. Interestingly, the psychometric literature on test score differences between blacks and whites generally finds racial differences in basic reading and math abilities but not in general attitudes or personality attributes (Hunt 1995).

Finally, young blacks seem to have particular difficulty with the school-to-work transition and with the costs of lost work experience. While the evidence about these effects has never been totally clear, it is likely that these contribute to lower wages of blacks throughout their working lives (Ellwood 1982; Meyer and Wise 1982; Ballen and Freeman 1986; Hotz and Tienda 1994).

Regarding the extent to which black employment is reduced by spatial mismatch, a body of research has long existed that relates black employment rates by geographical areas to measures of job access within and across metropolitan areas

(Jencks and Mayer 1990a; Holzer 1991; Kain 1992). While a wide range of results has been found, most recent research suggests some link between the two. The evidence for this link is strengthened in recent work by Raphael (1996), who finds a strong relationship between the employment rates of blacks and nearby rates of job growth, which are generally highest in outlying suburban areas. Given their greater residential proximity to central business districts, blacks continue on average to be located closer than whites to established jobs, but further away from new jobs and much of current hiring.

Furthermore, recent micro-level research lends more support for this view. Studies of single large firms that have relocated from central city to suburban locations find that black employees are more likely than white employees to quit after the relocation (Fernandez 1994; Zax and Kain 1996). Zax and Kain particularly link this tendency to increasing commute times and distances for individuals. Similarly, Ross (1996) finds that blacks are less likely than whites to move their residences because of a job change, especially when they live in metropolitan areas where jobs are highly suburbanized. These findings suggest that constraints on residential locations limit the abilities of blacks to adjust to various shocks that affect the demand for their labor.

Regarding the limited abilities of blacks to commute or search for work over the entire metropolitan area, Holzer et al. (1994) find that the time spent per mile of travel to work is significantly higher for blacks than for whites, at least partly due to racial differences in the use of automobiles for commuting. These differences in search and travel mode are at least partly related to differences in wages and employment rates between whites and blacks. The study also finds that young, central-city blacks do not offset the growing suburbanization of employment by longer search and commute distances. Holzer (1997) also finds that the tendency of blacks to search for work in the suburbs primarily when there is a residential presence of blacks in these areas, along with general perceptions of friendliness toward blacks, suggests the importance of social contacts and networks as well as perceptions of hostility. Ihlanfeldt (1997) also finds that spatial information about job availability in the local labor market varies somewhat by race and education level of the worker. Thus, transportation, information/networks, and racial perceptions all seem to play some role in the persistence of spatial imbalances in local labor markets.

A few other points are worth mentioning here. For one thing, imbalances can exist between as well as within local labor markets. Differences in labor demand across states or metropolitan areas are generally offset by migration flows across these areas within a period of 5 to 10 years (Blanchard and Katz 1992; Bartik 1992). But Bound and Holzer (1996) find that blacks and less-educated workers are somewhat less able to make this adjustment to shifting demand through migration than are whites and the more-educated; they are thus more likely to be concentrated in declining local areas.

Furthermore, residential segregation per se has been linked to poor employment outcomes among blacks in a variety of recent studies, even when travel

---

times and other measures of job access are controlled for (Massey and Denton 1992; Cutler and Glaeser 1997; O'Regan and Quigley 1996a, 1996b). These studies suggest that independent of its effect on access to jobs, the social isolation that accompanies residential segregation may limit human capital accumulation and lead to non-mainstream behavior such as crime.[3]

Finally, it is important to stress the difficulty of sorting out studies and surveys emphasizing space from those stressing race or skills. Racial differences in outcome that are correlated with geographic location might really reflect other underlying conditions. For example, more highly skilled blacks may be more likely to live in mixed neighborhoods or commute to the suburbs to find work, and employers with discriminatory preferences may be more likely to locate in suburban areas far away from black populations. The difficulty of distinguishing between these different interpretations varies with individual studies.[4]

Evidence of difficulties with informal search and job networks, independent of geographic location, has also appeared in several studies. Holzer (1987b) finds that young blacks are much less likely than young whites to gain employment using informal search methods, with the biggest racial gap in hiring occurring among persons who walk in from the street and apply for jobs without referrals. Browne and Hewitt (1996) found that when blacks did obtain jobs informally, their wages were likely to be lower than those of comparable whites using these methods. This suggests that networks that are strong enough to generate employment for blacks may not be strong enough to generate relatively high wages.

Regarding employer discrimination, it has always been difficult to infer labor market discrimination from statistical differences in observed outcomes between blacks and whites since these differences could just as easily reflect factors such as unobserved differences in ability or preferences between blacks and whites that could not be controlled for with available data. But recent results from audit studies in which matched pairs of black and white applicants with identical credentials in terms of education and experience were sent out to apply for jobs generate the strongest evidence yet of labor market discrimination against blacks (Fix and Struyk 1994).[5] However, it remains unclear whether this reflects pure discrimination (employer preferences for different racial groups) or statistical discrimination, which results from imperfect employer information about worker abilities by race. Further, the relationship of this hiring behavior to actual marketwide differences in other abilities is not accounted for in these studies.[6]

The tendency for employers to view blacks negatively, suggested by the audit studies, is clearly portrayed in recent ethnographic work with employers in Chicago by Kirschenman and Neckerman (1991). They found that employers perceive blacks quite negatively in terms of basic skills and attitudes toward work. Employer views of black males were especially harsh and reflected somewhat greater fear of black males than of black females or whites (Kirschenman 1991). Of course, it is difficult to tell from this work the extent to which these perceptions are accurate. Interestingly, black employers in their sample were as likely as white employers to make negative comments, thus casting some doubt on an interpretation of these findings that stresses racial discrimination only.

Overall, we can say that a fairly large body of evidence suggests that skills, locational imbalances, lack of effective informal networks, and discrimination all play some role in generating barriers to greater employment opportunities for blacks. But, as stressed above, distinguishing among the individual hypotheses has often been difficult. Furthermore, despite the central importance of barriers on the demand side of the labor market in virtually all of this work, the lack of direct data from this side of the labor market in most of these studies leaves unanswered a number of important questions, such as:

- Which jobs really are accessible to blacks, and what makes them so?
- Exactly which cognitive skills do employers think are in such short supply among blacks?
- What characteristics of employers are associated with discriminatory preferences?
- Are there identifiable mechanisms, such as availability of public transit, through which the geographic locations of firms affect black employment rates?

In the next section, we explore these questions with data directly from the demand side of the labor market.

EVIDENCE FROM A NEW EMPLOYER SURVEY

The evidence presented below is from a telephone survey between 1992 and 1994 of employers in four large metropolitan areas—Atlanta, Boston, Detroit, and Los Angeles.[7] The survey focused on the characteristics of each establishment and its workforce as well as the most recently filled job and most recently hired worker. Thus, considerable information was generated about the firm's location, customers, job applicants, skill requirements, recruiting and screening activities, and demographics of those hired, including their race. Overall response rates, conditional on a successful screening, were 67 percent; a variety of data characteristics suggest that selection biases are not severe.[8] Since the sample of firms drawn was already weighted by establishment size, we can consider the last job filled for each firm and thus have a relatively representative sample of the kinds of jobs that current jobseekers are likely to find in the labor market. What do these data tell us about the barriers that blacks currently face in obtaining new jobs? Below we present some summary data on each of the barriers discussed above.[9]

Skill Needs and Credentials

Employers were asked a series of questions about the skills needed to perform the most recently filled job in their establishment and how frequently these skills are used. The skills reflect basic cognitive and social skills, such as direct contact with customers (in person or over the phone), reading or writing paragraph-length material, arithmetic computations, and using a computer. A variety of questions also dealt with required applicant credentials that might indicate important skills. These credentials include high school diploma, general work experience, specific job-related work experience, and previous vocational training or certification.

Table 2.1 presents data on the extent to which these tasks and credentials are required on newly filled jobs. The results are means of responses to questions about whether each task is performed daily, and whether each credential is required, either "absolutely" or "strongly preferred." To account for differences in occupational categories or educational requirements, jobs are listed separately according to whether they require a college diploma. Those that do not require college degrees are further broken down into white-collar and blue-collar/service jobs.

The results show that these credentials and tasks are required quite extensively on new jobs. Almost three-fourths of all new jobs involve some direct customer contact, over two-thirds require significant reading/writing, a similar fraction require arithmetic calculations, and well over half now involve some use of a computer. In terms of credentials, over three-quarters of these new jobs require a high school diploma, though GEDs are widely acceptable as a substitute.[10] About 70 percent require some general work experience, and almost two-thirds require experience specifically related to the particular kind of work. Over 40 percent require some previous training or certification. Indeed, very few new jobs are available that require none of the tasks or credentials listed above. These findings are at least broadly consistent with those of Howell and Wolff (1991), who find growth over time in the cognitive skill requirements of jobs, and particularly a shift from low-skill jobs in the manufacturing sector, which paid relatively well, to medium-skill jobs in the services sector, which pay less well.

As one would expect, the incidence of these skill requirements varies somewhat by the educational requirements or occupational category of the job. Those requiring college degrees involve more tasks and require more credentials, while white-collar jobs that do not require college degrees involve more tasks and require more credentials than do blue-collar/service jobs. But even in the latter category, where the jobs are generally considered quite unskilled, over half of the new jobs require several credentials or performance of certain tasks, such as customer contact, reading/writing, arithmetic calculation, and specific work experience. Few jobs require none of these.

To what extent do these skill requirements represent barriers to the hiring of blacks? Table 2.2 presents the percentage of new jobs filled by blacks, according to what tasks are used daily and what credentials are required. Again data is presented for all jobs and according to educational or occupational category. The sample is limited to jobs filled by blacks or whites, in order to sharpen the focus on differences in hiring between these two groups. This is important since Hispanics are even more likely than blacks to hold jobs that require few skills (Holzer 1996).

Table 2.2 clearly indicates that blacks are more likely to be hired into jobs that do not require these tasks or credentials than into those jobs that do. Jobs that do not require any of the listed tasks or credentials are also filled more often by blacks than are jobs that require at least some of them. This is particularly true for jobs that do not require college, whether white-collar or blue-collar, even after controlling for the worker's educational attainment (Holzer 1998a).

In data presented in Holzer (1998a), the skill requirements for jobs affect the race of who gets hired for both men and women, although women are overrepresented in jobs requiring some of these skills, such as customer contact and computer use, and underrepresented in others, such as specific experience and previous training. Black females are underrepresented relative to white females, and black males relative to white males in most categories (Holzer 1998a). Finally, because these skills and tasks are generally associated with higher wages, the tendency of blacks to be hired into fewer jobs that require them will generally affect their relative earnings as well as their employment rates. For instance, previous experience and vocational training are each associated with an increase in starting wages of 8 to 10 percent; reading/writing and computer use have similar effects of 7 to 8 percent and 3 to 6 percent respectively.

These results suggest that employers perceive a wide range of skill deficiencies among black applicants, beyond educational attainment. The results hold even when we control for the percentage of applicants at a firm that are black, which partly helps us to separate labor supply–driven from demand-driven factors. Are their perceptions of these deficiencies accurate or discriminatory? We cannot tell for sure from these data. The ability to perform certain tasks cannot be observed ex-ante, though employers often claim that they can make these inferences from previous jobs held, the quality of writing on an application, and the interview. Also, the gaps in test scores described above, even when controlling for educational attainment, suggest that these perceptions may, on average, be correct.

Of course, the required credentials are observable among individuals ex-ante. Although it is possible that employers are more willing to hire whites than blacks who do not meet the stated requirements, the data actually suggest the opposite (Holzer and Neumark 1999, forthcoming). This analysis also assumes that the stated requirements are in fact legitimately related to job performance, as required by law. While it is possible that hiring requirements are chosen that are unnecessary, it seems unlikely in most cases, given that they are associated with higher pay.[11] Thus, it seems as though deficiencies in both basic and job-related skill acquisition, along with the ability to signal such skill-acquisition to prospective employers, constitute major barriers to the employment of blacks, especially in high-paying jobs.

Two other findings about employer perceptions of worker quality are relevant here. First, over half of employers say that they are unwilling to hire workers with only temporary or part-time work experience, which they associate with employment instability (Ballen and Freeman 1986). Two-thirds claim they would not hire someone with a criminal record. Of course, most employers are never sure of an applicant's criminal record. While some applications request this information, there are obviously strong incentives for applicants with criminal records to lie since most employers do not actually check with government sources to determine if applicants have criminal backgrounds. Thus, it is quite possible that the mere suspicion of such activity could be a disadvantage to young blacks in the hiring process.

Informal Networks and Recruiting

Table 2.3 presents data on recruitment methods used by firms to fill their last available position, as well as the extent to which they hired blacks for these jobs. The methods are grouped as follows: informal referrals (solicited either through current employees or other acquaintances), responses to help-wanted signs or other direct walk-ins, responses to newspaper ads, use of private employment agencies, and use of state or community agencies. Once again, results are presented for all recently filled jobs and separately by educational requirements or occupation.

The results show that informal referrals are used to fill 35 to 40 percent of all new jobs and somewhat more in the less-skilled occupational categories. Other informal methods, such as help-wanted signs and walk-ins, are used to fill another 10 to 20 percent. So a majority of new jobs are filled by informal methods. Newspapers are also used in roughly 30 percent of all cases, while employment agencies and state/community agencies are used in somewhat smaller percentages of jobs.

Not surprisingly, the results also show that blacks are most likely to be hired when jobs are filled through state/community agencies, confirming the results of prior research (Holzer 1987b). They are also less likely to be hired when firms use informal referrals, as well as newspapers, compared to other methods. These results hold even when we control for a wide range of skill needs on jobs and other firm characteristics (Holzer 1996). However, this finding appears to reflect the fact that with the vast majority of jobs now located in suburban areas, informal referrals often will generate white applicants. When we look at jobs and firms located in central cities or heavily black areas, the use of informal referrals does not seem to create this disadvantage for blacks. Thus, the heavy reliance of many firms on informal referrals, especially in low-skill jobs, appears to constitute another barrier to employment opportunities for many blacks.

Spatial Imbalances

In the four metropolitan statistical areas (MSAs) of Atlanta, Boston, Detroit, and Los Angeles, most blacks live in the primary central cities.[12] Some also live in other municipalities that have been categorized as central cities, or in heavily black suburban areas located close to the central cities.[13] To what extent are these residential patterns mirrored in application and employment rates by geographic location within the MSA?

Table 2.4 presents data on this issue that show the percentage of job applicants who are black males, black females, Hispanics, and Asians in each of three types of locations: primary central cities, other urban areas (nonprimary central cities and other municipalities with a population that is at least 30 percent black), and suburbs. The table also gives the ratio of employees to applicants in each demographic category and location, as well as the ratio of new hires to applicants for each.

The extent of the difficulty that blacks may have in gaining access to suburban employers because of geography per se (including such associated problems as transportation and job information) should be reflected in fewer applications from blacks to these employers. The extent to which employers in any area have either discriminatory preferences or skill needs different from those of their black applicants should be reflected in lower ratios of employees or new hires to applicants among blacks.

The results show that establishments located in the primary central cities are roughly twice as likely to receive applications from blacks as are those located in the suburbs—roughly 40 percent versus 20 percent. Those in "other areas" have somewhat more black applicants than do suburban employers but less than those in the primary central cities. The patterns for Hispanic and Asian applicants are similar but with much smaller differences across geographic areas. These results parallel the distribution of residential locations among blacks and other minority groups (Frey and Farley 1993). Blacks remain far more residentially segregated than any other minority group.

Other recent work has also shown that the tendency of any establishment within central cities or suburbs to receive applications from blacks varies quite positively with location near a public transit stop and negatively with distance from the black residential population (Holzer and Ihlanfeldt 1996). Furthermore, the effect of an establishment's distance from the black population on the probability that it will have black applicants or employees is strongest when firms recruit informally, indicating that information networks are at least partly based on local geography. In contrast, the establishment's location has the smallest effect on race of employees when it recruits through newspaper advertisements, indicating that this recruitment method spreads information over wider areas more effectively than do others. Indeed, management choices over how to recruit may partly reflect their desires to recruit over narrower or broader geographic distances, with resulting effects on the demographics of the applicant pool.

Thus, the fact that most new employment growth is occurring in suburban areas, especially those located far from black residential areas, constitutes another barrier to improved employment opportunities for blacks. Transportation and informational problems seem to be part of the effects of local geography on employment outcomes by race.

Discrimination

Table 2.4 also presents the ratios of employees or new hires to applicants by race to allow consideration of potentially discriminatory preferences against blacks in hiring. These results show several interesting patterns: (1) The ratios are generally higher for Hispanics (and, to a lesser extent, for Asians) than they are for blacks; (2) they are higher for black females than for black males; and (3) they are generally higher for blacks in the primary central cities and other areas than for blacks in the suburbs.

Of course, these simple computations do not adjust for possible differences across employers in skill requirements and across job applicants for differences in skills or other relevant personal characteristics. Differences in skills across applicants might exist not only because of differences in the relevant population, but also because of differences in the self-selection processes by which workers judge where to apply for jobs. If applicants from one group are better matched to employers than those from another group in terms of skills, wage expectations, personal contacts, and other relevant characteristics, that will improve their relative tendencies to be hired from the applicant pool.

But many of these potential caveats are not relevant to the results presented here. For instance, average skill requirements are actually somewhat lower for jobs located in the suburbs than for those in the central cities, especially among those jobs that do not require college (Holzer 1996), and the skill levels of blacks who live in or commute to the suburbs, relative to comparable whites, are generally higher than those of blacks who live and work in the central cities. For instance, educational attainment among blacks is generally higher for suburban than for central-city residents, but the opposite is true among whites. Those central-city residents who commute to suburban jobs generally are higher-wage, higher-skill employees than those who work locally; the same is generally true for white suburban residents who commute to the central cities relative to those who stay closer to home. Thus, the racial gaps in worker quality faced by suburban employers actually should be lower than those faced by central-city employers.

Thus, the greater tendencies of central-city employers to hire from among their black applicants does not appear to reflect relative differences in the qualifications of applicants. More likely, it reflects greater discrimination on the part of suburban employers. Perhaps this is because of employer self-selection; that is, discriminatory employers may choose to live further from black populations. Or perhaps the relationship is practical—their distance from blacks may enable them to lower the risk of prosecution for violating EEO laws or it may allow them to maintain inaccurate stereotypes across groups.

Other recent analyses also suggest that the racial composition of customers, independent of location, has important effects on the tendencies to hire blacks, especially in jobs in which there is direct contact between employees and customers (Holzer and Ihlanfeldt 1998). Also, controlling for all observable characteristics of firms and jobs, smaller establishments are far less likely than large establishments to hire blacks (Holzer 1998b). This latter finding likely reflects greater concern with potential EEO violations on the part of larger establishments as well as their general use of more formal recruitment and hiring procedures that tend to be more objective. Thus, the results together suggest that blacks are most likely to face discrimination in hiring at smaller establishments, particularly those located in the suburbs and serving a predominantly white clientele.

The differences in ratios of hires to applicants between blacks and Hispanics are also open to various interpretations. They do not reflect higher skills among Hispanics; levels of educational attainment are clearly higher among blacks (Hauser and Phang 1993). Hispanics are even less likely than blacks to be hired into jobs that require cognitive or verbal skills (Holzer 1996). In contrast, Hispanic applicants are more likely than blacks to be hired for jobs requiring few skills, such as blue-collar and manufacturing jobs. Blacks were once overrepresented in these types of jobs but now are underrepresented relative to their presence in white-collar jobs or in the service sector. The wages received by Hispanics are also not appreciably lower than those of blacks, after controlling for job and worker quality. Thus lower wage expectations among Hispanics do not seem to be a major factor in their greater tendencies to be hired.

Instead, the results are somewhat more consistent with the notion of ethnic niches in particular industries. This theory suggests that co-ethnics of current employees are often recruited by employers who are pleased with their work (Waldinger 1996). The results also seem consistent with the stated preference among many employers for immigrants rather than native-born blacks in unskilled jobs, believing that the former have stronger work ethics and are more appreciative of the jobs that they have (Kirschenman and Neckerman 1991). In this case, the results might likely reflect discriminatory preferences and perceptions on the part of these employers, in addition to stronger employment networks and connections among Hispanics, and perhaps real differences in average employee attitudes as well. The ratio of Hispanic new hires to applicants is somewhat greater than the ratio of employees to applicants, especially relative to the same ratios for blacks. One possible interpretation of this is higher job turnover among Hispanics than among blacks. Alternatively, these results might indicate a shift over time in employment toward Hispanics (perhaps because of their growing presence in the labor market), so that they would be more visible among new than older employees.

Black females also are more likely than black males to be hired. Here, too, there is no evidence of greater skills among the former group. These results are also consistent with stated preferences among employers for black females and with greater fear of young black males (Kirschenman 1991). They also could reflect recent shifts in employment toward clerical, sales, and service occupations in which females have traditionally found relatively greater employment opportunities than men have. Indeed, these data suggest no preference for black female over black male applicants in construction/manufacturing or in blue-collar jobs, while such preferences are suggested in retail trade/service establishments and white-collar/service jobs.

While black men seem to face less wage discrimination today than do black females, the opposite seems to be true in terms of gaining employment. But the generally low wages and benefits obtained by both less-educated blacks and whites in new jobs are clearly apparent in the data on the wages and benefits of these new hires (Holzer 1996). Median starting wages in all jobs that do not require college degrees are generally in the range of $7.00 to $8.00 per hour, with about a third paying $6.00 an hour or less (as of 1994). Health benefits are not provided in about a quarter of all jobs, and employer contributions to pensions are not provided in about half.

Finally, with regard to the effects of affirmative action in limiting such discrimination, Holzer and Neumark (1999, forthcoming) found that minorities hired under affirmative action policies have weaker observable credentials, such as education, than their white counterparts, but are usually rated quite comparably by their supervisors in terms of job performance.

PUBLIC POLICIES FOR REDUCING EMPLOYMENT BARRIERS

The previous section provides evidence that blacks face major barriers in gaining employment, especially at relatively higher wages. These barriers are posed by the skills sought by employers (which are not consistent with the skill levels of blacks), by the use of informal recruitment patterns by employers (because of the weaker employment networks available to blacks), by employer geographic locations in suburban areas (because of the concentration of blacks in inner-city areas or nearby suburbs), and by discrimination. What policies are most likely to be successful in helping blacks to overcome these barriers in the labor market?

Education, Job Training, and Experience

The importance of improving basic cognitive and other job-related skills and credentials among blacks is certainly apparent from these results. This can be done in a variety of ways. For instance, while high school dropout rates among blacks have been brought down quite successfully in recent years, increases in levels of college enrollment have lagged behind those of whites. Making young blacks more aware of the importance of post-secondary education and of the availability of Pell grants and other means of financing should be a high priority, along with maintaining or even raising the funding of such programs.

Improving the basic skills of black high school graduates must also be stressed, even for those who choose not to obtain more education. Whether this can be best accomplished through special in-school programs, such as the recently acclaimed Quantum Opportunities program (Katz 1994), or various reform efforts such as those involving school finance, school choice, and curriculum development is an issue that is clearly beyond the scope of this paper, but which needs careful consideration.[14]

The problem of inadequate early work experience for blacks also needs to be addressed. School-to-work programs might be important in this regard. The links generated between employers and students in secondary school could benefit blacks in a variety of ways. For one thing, they might enable employers to more easily gauge the actual abilities of blacks who, on paper or in an interview, look somewhat weaker than their white counterparts. Furthermore, directly illustrating to students the importance of basic skills for the attainment of good jobs might improve incentives for young black students to perform well in the classroom.

Transportation, Job Search, and Job Placement

A variety of approaches are available to help overcome the barriers young blacks face in terms of spatial mismatch and weak informal networks. These include job search instruction, either in the schools or afterwards; transportation assistance; and job placement efforts. All of these approaches are much less costly than traditional education and training, and job search instruction is often one of the most cost-effective ways of helping disadvantaged or displaced workers (Lalonde 1995). Although transportation and placement efforts have been less frequently evaluated, one transportation assistance program called "Bridges-to-Work" is currently being analyzed by Public Private Ventures (PPV) Inc.[15]

But the limitations of these approaches must be stressed as well. For one thing, they are much more likely to be successful in tight labor markets than in slack ones. Since these approaches involve improving the matching processes between workers and jobs, they assume the existence of available jobs. Furthermore, these approaches are likely to be most successful with job candidates who are readily employable, that is, those whose basic skills and work experience are not extremely deficient. Indeed, placement agencies have strong incentives to skim from their available candidates in order to maintain credibility with their clients, the employers.

Enterprise Zones vs. Residential Mobility

Another way of bridging the gaps between inner-city workers and suburban employers is through the use of enterprise or empowerment zones, which give employers a variety of tax incentives for locating in areas with high concentrations of low-income residents. Most evaluations of earlier, state-level efforts have found that these are very expensive ways of bringing jobs back to central-city residents, as the credits and subsidies have rarely been tied to the actual employment of zone residents (Papke 1993).

Instead of bringing jobs back to the cities, another possibility would be to focus on bringing inner-city residents to the suburbs where the new jobs are increasingly located. This not only overcomes the spatial disadvantages of access to work, but also breaks down social isolation and the negative effects of residential segregation on young people as they grow up. Indeed, the results of the Gautreaux experiment seem to bear out this dual advantage. The employment prospects of adults and the educational outcomes for children both improved when low-income minorities were given housing vouchers and other assistance in order to relocate from low-income housing projects in the city of Chicago to elsewhere in the metropolitan area (Rosenbaum and Popkin 1991).

Thus, there are strong arguments for attacking housing market discrimination, such as discriminatory zoning provisions that limit the access of blacks and lower income groups to suburban neighborhoods, as well as for providing housing assistance through vouchers rather than constructing public housing units. Indeed, the primary costs of this approach are likely to be political, given the intense opposition that frequently exists to these efforts.

Another way of improving access that should be considered would be to improve the migration of minority workers across (as opposed to just within) metropolitan areas. These policies are important parts of labor market policy in some European countries, such as Sweden (Katz 1994), but to date, our experience with them in the United States has been limited.

Discrimination

Given the relatively strong evidence that discrimination persists in the labor market, the importance of maintaining antidiscrimination efforts seems clear. While some have recently questioned the efficacy of these policies in limiting discrimination in employment (Donohue and Siegelman 1991; Bloch 1994), their usefulness for expanding opportunities in some sectors (such as among large employers and those located in central cities) is strongly suggested here.

But how do we raise the pressure on suburban employers, or those in small establishments, to hire blacks? Given how few black applicants many have and the relatively low cost-effectiveness of monitoring these establishments, it is not obvious how to accomplish this goal. At some level, getting more black applicants to suburban job markets, either through residential relocation or better transportation, must be viewed as complementary to pressures on employers to hire them in greater numbers once they apply. Finally, in the face of the recent political assault on such efforts, we note the need to maintain affirmative action programs at the federal and state level.

Job Creation Efforts

Given the relative lack of jobs available for those with very poor cognitive and verbal skills and weak credentials, the need to create more jobs for these individuals, at least in the short-term, remains great. A variety of schemes have been devised to subsidize private-sector employers who hire these and other disadvantaged workers. The relative costs and benefits of targeting these groups—displacement of one group by another, windfalls to employers, and the like—are fairly well known at this point. However, at least some evidence suggests that these efforts might be useful in creating additional employment opportunities (Katz 1996). Alternatively, public service employment might be reconsidered as a way of generating employment for the very unskilled who are now expected to work, but who might lack the means of obtaining private-sector jobs (Gottschalk 1997).

Of course, the importance of maintaining tight labor markets in general (through macroeconomic policy) must be stressed as well. The relatively beneficial effects of a tight labor market, either at the national or local level, on job prospects of blacks has been clearly demonstrated in many contexts (Freeman 1991; Bartik 1992; Bound and Holzer 1996). In particular, employers seem less likely to discriminate and more willing to recruit their least-favored employees when they have some difficulty finding their most-preferred candidates for filling job vacancies. Furthermore, tight labor markets are likely to make all of the interventions mentioned above more successful than they would otherwise be, as employers who are anxious to find workers will be more amenable to special training or placement efforts by labor market intermediaries.

Wage Supplements

In addition to making jobs more generally available, the rewards of regular work, relative to those of illegal activities, for young blacks (especially males) need to be improved. While the surest way to do so is to improve their relative skills, other approaches might be considered in the short term. The recently enacted increases in the minimum wage represent one such approach; possible increases or extensions of the Earned Income Tax Credits are another.[16]

Strengthening Community Institutions and Mentoring

Despite the lengthy list of needed government efforts to reduce the barriers faced by blacks in the labor market, we must also acknowledge the constraints, in terms of both public funds and political will, that will certainly limit any such activity in the foreseeable future. Therefore, there is a need to stress a greater role for private groups and individuals, such as community organizations and mentors (Mincy 1994; Brown 1996; Freeman 1986).

Stronger community institutions might help to provide individuals with better links to employers and the outside community, as well as better resources for the community. Mentors might play similar roles and act as important role models. More discussion of their potential is certainly in order.

1. Juhn (1992) also suggests that labor force participation among less-educated males has declined in response to the wage declines generated by shifts in labor demand. But while employment declines among less-educated young white males can be fully accounted for by their wage declines, the declines among young blacks are too large to be fully explained in this manner.

2. Government monitoring of racial hiring practices at the firm level is generally accomplished through the requirement that firms file EEO-1 forms. But these are required only of establishments with 100 or more employees, and some (such as federal contractors or multi-establishment firms) with 50 or more.

3. See also Jencks and Mayer (1990a), Case and Katz (1991), and Borjas (1995) for evidence on neighborhood effects and outcomes by race/ethnic group.

4. Differential self-selection of individuals into neighborhoods is a problem that plagues much of this research, though it is somewhat less severe in various micro-level or panel studies.

5. Earlier evidence on differential treatment of job applicants by race can be found in Culp and Dunson (1986).

6. For instance, if employers are correct in believing that there are other unobserved characteristics of applicants in which whites, on average, outperform blacks, then interpreting these findings as statistical discrimination grows more plausible.

7. This work is part of a larger study in these areas, known as the Multi-City Study of Urban Inequality, sponsored by the Ford and Russell Sage Foundations.

8. See the appendix to Holzer (1996).

9. More complete discussions of many of these results can be found in my book (Holzer 1996) or in the particular articles that I cite in this section of the chapter. The differences between blacks and whites that are discussed in the chapter are all statistically significant at the .10 level or better.

10. This does not necessarily contradict Cameron and Heckman (1993), who find that GEDs are not rewarded as well as high school diplomas in terms of wages. It also does not necessarily contradict the findings of the National Center on the Educational Quality of the Workforce (1995), namely that the high school diploma is not viewed by most employers as a terribly important screen. Instead, our results suggest that the diploma is necessary, but hardly sufficient, for gaining many jobs.

11. This relates to the issue of hiring requirements and "disparate impact" that was first raised in the Supreme Court case of *Griggs* v. *Duke Power* (1971) and more recently in the Civil Rights Act of 1991.

12. The percentages of blacks in each area who live in the primary central city are 39, 63, 83, and 49 respectively in Atlanta, Boston, Detroit, and Los Angeles.

13. Census Bureau definitions of "central-city" are based on population size and ratios of jobs to residents. Other central cities in these metro areas include Marietta in the Atlanta MSA; Cambridge, Brockton, Framingham, Lawrence, Lowell, Salem, and Waltham in the Boston MSA; Dearborn and Pontiac in the Detroit MSA; and Long Beach, Pasadena, and Pomona in the Los Angeles MSA.

14. In general, programs for disadvantaged out-of-school youth (such as JTPA) have been largely unsuccessful in improving their labor market performance, though they have been somewhat more effective for adults, especially adult women (Lalonde 1995). Only very intensive and relatively expensive programs such as the Job Corps have shown generally positive effects on youth. On the other hand, improving the cognitive skills of in-school youth before they graduate might enable them to avoid the early employment problems that signal low quality to employers thereafter.

15. Other such local efforts are described in Hughes and Sternberg (1992).

16. Such increases and extensions are currently being implemented or are under consideration in several states, including Iowa, Minnesota, New York, and Wisconsin.

Badgett, M.V. Lee. 1994. "Rising Black Unemployment: Changes in Job Stability or Employability?" *Review of Black Political Economy* 22 (3, Winter):55–75.

Ballen, John, and Richard Freeman. 1986. "Transitions between Employment and Nonemployment." In *The Black Youth Nonemployment Crisis*, ed. R. Freeman and H. Holzer. Chicago: University of Chicago Press.

Bartik, Timothy. 1992. *Who Benefits from State and Local Economic Development Policies?* Kalamazoo, MI: W.E. Upjohn Institute for Employment Research.

Becker, Gary. 1971. *The Economics of Discrimination*. Chicago: University of Chicago Press.

Berman, Eli, John Bound, and Zvi Griliches. 1994. "Changes in the Demand for Skilled Labor Within U.S. Manufacturing: Evidence from the Annual Survey of Manufacturers." *Quarterly Journal of Economics* 109 (2, May): 367–397.

Blanchard, Olivier, and Lawrence Katz. 1992. "Regional Evolutions." *Brookings Papers on Economic Activity 1*. Washington, D.C.: Brookings Institution.

Bloch, Farrell. 1994. *Antidiscrimination Law and Minority Employment*. Chicago: University of Chicago Press.

Bluestone, Barry, Mary Stevenson, and Chris Tilly. 1992. "An Assessment of the Impact of Deindustrialization and Spatial Mismatch on the Labor Market Outcomes of White, Black and Hispanic Men and Women Who Have Limited Schooling." Working paper, University of Massachusetts–Boston.

Borjas, George. 1995. "Ethnicity, Neighborhoods, and Human Capital Externalities." *American Economic Review* 85 (3, June):365–390.

Borjas, George, Richard Freeman, and Lawrence Katz. 1997. "How Much Do Immigration and Trade Affect Labor Market Outcomes?" *Brookings Papers on Economic Activity* 1:1–67.

Bound, John, and Richard Freeman. 1992. "What Went Wrong? The Erosion of Relative Earnings and Employment for Blacks." *Quarterly Journal of Economics* 107 (1, February):201–232.

Bound, John, and Harry Holzer. 1993. "Industrial Structure, Skill Levels, and the Labor Market for Whites and Blacks." *The Review of Economics and Statistics* 75 (3, August):387–396.

Bound, John, and Harry Holzer. 1996. "Structural Changes, Employment Outcomes, and Population Adjustments: 1980–1990." Discussion paper, Institute for Research on Poverty, University of Wisconsin–Madison.

Brown, Prudence. 1996. "Comprehensive Neighborhood-Based Initiatives." *Cityscape* 2 (2, May):161–176 .

Browne, Irene, and Cynthia Hewitt. 1996. "Networks, Discrimination, or Location? Explaining Job Segregation among African-Americans." Unpublished paper, Emory University.

Cameron, Stephen, and James Heckman. 1993. "The Nonequivalence of High School Equivalents." *Journal of Labor Economics* 11 (1, January):1–47.

Card, David, and Thomas Lemieux. 1994. "Changing Wage Structure and Black-White Wage Differentials." *American Economic Review* 84 (2, May):29–33.

Case, Ann, and Lawrence Katz. 1991. "The Company You Keep: The Effects of Family and Neighborhood on Disadvantaged Youth." Working paper, Cambridge, MA: National Bureau of Economic Research.

Cawley, John, Karen Conneely, James Heckman, and Edward Vytlacil. 1996. "Measuring the Effects of Cognitive Ability." Working paper, Cambridge, MA: National Bureau of Economic Research.

Culp, Jerome, and Bruce Dunson. 1986. "Brothers of a Different Color: A Preliminary Look at Employer Treatment of White and Black Youth." In *The Black Youth Employment Crisis*, ed. R. Freeman and H. Holzer. Chicago: University of Chicago Press.

Cutler, David, and Edward Glaeser. 1997. "Are Ghettoes Good or Bad?" *Quarterly Journal of Economics* 112 (3, August):827–87.

Donohue, John, and Peter Siegelman. 1991. "The Changing Nature of Employment Discrimination Litigation." *Stanford Law Review* 43 (May):983–1033.

Ellwood, David. 1982. "Teenage Unemployment: Permanent Scars or Temporary Blemishes?" In *The Youth Labor Market Problem*, ed. R. Freeman and D. Wise. Chicago: University of Chicago Press.

Ferguson, Ronald. 1993. "New Evidence on the Growing Value of Skill and Consequences for Racial Disparity and Returns to Schooling." Unpublished paper, Harvard University.

Fernandez, Roberto. 1994. "Race, Space and Job Accessibility: Evidence from a Plant Relocation." *Economic Geography* 70 (October):390–416.

Fix, Michael, and Raymond Struyk, eds. 1994. *Clear and Convincing Evidence.* Washington, D.C.: The Urban Institute Press.

Freeman, Richard. 1973. "Relative Improvements in the Economic Status of Black Americans, 1948–1972." *Brookings Papers on Economic Activity*. Washington, D.C.: Brookings Institution.

Freeman, Richard. 1986. "Who Escapes? The Effects of Church-Going and Other Individual Characteristics on Outcomes of Inner-City Youth." In *The Black Youth Employment Crisis*, ed. R. Freeman and H. Holzer. Chicago: University of Chicago Press.

Freeman, Richard. 1991. "Employment and Earnings of Disadvantaged Young Men in Labor Shortage Economy." In *The Urban Underclass*, ed. C. Jencks and P. Peterson. Washington, D.C.: Brookings Institution.

Freeman, Richard. 1992. "Crime and the Employment of Disadvantaged Youths." In *Urban Labor Markets and Job Opportunities*, ed. G. Peterson and W. Vroman. Washington, D.C.: The Urban Institute Press.

Freeman, Richard. 1995. "Are Your Wages Set in Beijing?" *Journal of Economic Perspectives* 9 (Summer):15–32.

Freeman, Richard, and Harry Holzer. 1986. *The Black Youth Employment Crisis*. Chicago: University of Chicago Press.

Freeman, Richard, and James Medoff. 1984. *What Do Unions Do?* New York: Basic Books.

Frey, William, and Reynolds Farley. 1993. "Latino, Asian and Black Segregation in Multi-Ethnic Metro Areas: Findings from the 1990 Census." Population Studies Center, University of Michigan.

Friedberg, Rachel, and Jennifer Hunt. 1994. "The Impact of Immigrants on Host County Wages, Employment, and Growth." *Journal of Economic Perspectives* 9:23–42.

Gottschalk, Peter. 1997. "Public Service Employment." In *Demand-Side Strategies for Low-Wage Labor Markets*, ed. R. Freeman and P. Gottschalk. New York: Russell Sage Foundation.

Granovetter, Mark. 1974. *Getting a Job: A Study of Contacts and Careers*. Cambridge: Harvard University Press.

Grissmer, David, Sheila Kirby, Mark Berends, and Stephanie Williamson. 1994. *Student Achievement and the Changing American Family*. Los Angeles: Rand Corporation.

Harrell, Adele, and George Peterson, eds. 1992. *Drugs, Crime, and Social Isolation*. Washington, D.C.: The Urban Institute Press.

Hauser, Robert, and Hanam Samuel Phang. 1993. "Trends in High School Dropout Among White, Black and Hispanic Youth: 1973 to 1989." Discussion paper, Institute for Research on Poverty.

Heckman, James, and Brook Payner. 1989. "Determining the Impact of Federal Antidiscrimination Policy on the Economic Status of Blacks." *American Economics Review* 79 (1, March):138–177.

Holzer, Harry. 1987a. "Hiring Procedures in the Firm: Their Economic Determinants and Outcomes." In *Human Resources and Firm Performance*, ed. R. Block et al. Madison, WI: Industrial Relations Research Association.

Holzer, Harry. 1987b. "Informal Job Search and Black Youth Unemployment." *American Economics Review* 77 (3, June):446–452.

Holzer, Harry. 1991. "The Spatial Mismatch Hypothesis: What Has the Evidence Shown?" *Urban Studies* 28 (1, February):105–122.

Holzer, Harry. 1994. "Black Employment Problems: New Evidence, Old Questions." *Journal of Policy Analysis and Management* 13 (4, Fall): 699–722.

Holzer, Harry. 1996. *What Employers Want: Job Prospects for Less-Educated Workers.* New York: Russell Sage Foundation.

Holzer, Harry. 1997. "The Detroit Labor Market: A View from the Supply Side." Unpublished paper, Michigan State University.

Holzer, Harry. 1998a. "Employer Skill Needs and Labor Market Outcomes Across Racial and Gender Groups." *Industrial and Labor Relations Review* 52 (1, October): 82–98.

Holzer, Harry. 1998b. "Why Do Small Establishments Hire Fewer Blacks than Large Ones?" *Journal of Human Resources* 33 (4, Fall).

Holzer, Harry, and Keith Ihlanfeldt. 1996. "Spatial Factors and the Employment of Blacks at the Firm Level." *New England Economic Review* (May/June):65–82.

Holzer, Harry, and Keith Ihlanfeldt. 1998. "Customer Discrimination and the Employment of Blacks and Hispanics." *Quarterly Journal of Economics* 113 (3, August): 835–868.

Holzer, Harry, Keith Ihlanfeldt, and David Sjoquist. 1994. "Work, Search and Travel Among White and Black Youth." *Journal of Urban Economics* 35 (May):320–345.

Holzer, Harry, and David Neumark. 1999. "Are Affirmative Action Hires Less Qualified?" *Journal of Labor Economics*, forthcoming.

Hotz, V. Joseph, and Marta Tienda. 1994. "Education and Employment in a Diverse Society: Generating Inequality Through the School-to-Work Transition." Unpublished paper, University of Chicago.

Howell, David, and Edward Wolff. 1991. "Trends in the Growth and Distribution of Skills in the U.S. Workplace, 1960–1985." *Industrial and Labor Relations Review* 44 (3, April):486–492.

Hughes, Mark, and Julie Sternberg. 1992. "The New Metropolitan Reality: Where the Rubber Meets the Road in Antipoverty Policy." Washington, D.C.: The Urban Institute Press.

Hunt, Earl. 1995. *Will We Be Smart Enough?* New York: Russell Sage Foundation.

Ihlanfeldt, Keith. 1997. "Information on the Spatial Distribution of Job Opportunities within Metropolitan Areas." *Journal of Urban Economics* 41 (2, March):218–242.

Jencks, Christopher, and Susan Mayer. 1990a. "Residential Segregation, Job Proximity and Black Job Opportunities: The Empirical Status of the Spatial Mismatch Hypothesis." In *Inner-City Poverty in the United States*, ed. L. Lynn and M. McGeary. Washington, D.C.: National Academy Press.

Jencks, Christopher, and Susan Mayer. 1990b. "The Social Consequences of Growing Up in a Poor Neighborhood." In *Inner-City Poverty in the United States*, ed, L. Lynn and M. McGeary. Washington, D.C.: National Academy Press.

Johnson, James, and Melvin Oliver. 1992. "Structural Changes in the U.S. Economy and Black Male Joblessness: A Reassessment." In *Urban Labor Markets*, ed. G. Peterson and W. Vroman. Washington, D.C.: The Urban Institute Press.

Juhn, Chinhui. 1992. "Decline of Male Labor Force Participation: The Role of Declining Market Opportunities. *Quarterly Journal of Economics* 107 (1, February):79–122.

Juhn, Chinhui, Kevin Murphy, and Brook Pierce. 1993. "Wage Inequality and the Rise in the Returns to Skill." *Journal of Political Economy* 101 (2, June):410–442.

Kain, John. 1992. "The Spatial Mismatch Hypothesis Three Decades Later." *Housing Policy Debate* 3 (2):371–460.

Kane, Thomas. 1994. "College Entry by Blacks Since 1970: The Role of College Costs, Family Background and the Returns to Education. *Journal of Political Economy* 102 (October): 878–911.

Kasarda, John. 1995. "Industrial Restructuring and the Changing Location of Jobs." In *State of the Union*, Vol. 1, ed. R. Farley. New York: Russell Sage Foundation.

Katz, Lawrence. 1994. "Active Labor Market Policies." In *Reducing Unemployment: Current Issues and Policy Options*. Federal Reserve Bank of Kansas City.

Katz, Lawrence. 1996. "Wage Subsidies for the Disadvantaged." Working paper, Cambridge, MA: National Bureau of Economic Research.

Kirschenman, Joleen. 1991. "Gender Within Race in the Labor Market." Unpublished paper, University of Chicago.

Kirschenman, Joleen, and Katherine Neckerman. 1991. "We'd Love to Hire Them But ..." In *The Urban Underclass*, ed. C. Jencks and P. Peterson. Washington, D.C.: Brookings Institution.

Lalonde, Robert. 1995. "The Promise of Public Sector–Sponsored Training." *Journal of Economic Perspectives* 9 (Spring):149–168.

Leonard, Jonathan. 1990. "The Impact of Affirmative Action Regulation and Equal Opportunity Law on Black Employment." *Journal of Economic Perspectives* 4 (4, Fall):47–63.

Levy, Frank, and Richard Murnane. 1992. "U.S. Earning Levels and Earnings Inequality: A Review of Recent Trends and Proposed Explanations." *Journal of Economic Literature* 30 (3, December):1332–1381.

Massey, Douglas, and Nancy Denton. 1992. *American Apartheid*. Cambridge: Harvard University Press.

Meyer, Robert, and David Wise. 1982. "High School Preparation and Early Labor Force Experience." In *The Youth Labor Market Problem*, ed. R. Freeman and D. Wise. Chicago: University of Chicago Press.

Mincy, Ronald. 1994. *Nurturing Young Inner-City Black Males*. Washington, D.C.: The Urban Institute Press.

Moss, Phil, and Chris Tilly. 1992. "Why Black Men Are Doing Worse in the Labor Market: A Review of Supply-Side and Demand-Side Explanations." New York: Social Science Research Council.

Moss, Phil, and Chris Tilly. 1995. "Soft Skills and Race." Working paper, New York: Russell Sage Foundation.

Murnane, Richard, John Willett, and Frank Levey. 1995. "The Growing Importance of Cognitive Skills in Wage Determination." Working paper, Cambridge, MA: National Bureau of Economic Research.

National Center on the Educational Quality of the Workforce. 1995. "First Findings from the EQW National Employer Survey." University of Pennsylvania.

Neal, Derek, and William Johnson. 1996. "The Role of Pre-Market Factors in Black-White Wage Differences." *Journal of Political Economy* 104 (October):869–895.

Oettinger, Gerald. 1996. "Statistical Discrimination and the Early Career Evolution of the Black-White Wage Gap." *Journal of Labor Economics* 104 (October):869–895.

O'Neill, June. 1990. "The Role of Human Capital in Earnings Differences Between White and Black Men." *Journal of Economic Perspectives* 4 (4, Fall):25–45.

O'Regan, Katherine, and John Quigley. 1996a. "Spatial Effects upon Employment Outcomes: The Case of New Jersey Teenagers." *New England Economic Review* (May/June):41–57.

O'Regan, Katherine, and John Quigley. 1996b. "Teenage Employment and the Spatial Isolation of Minority and Poverty Households." *Journal of Human Resources* 31 (Summer): 692–702.

Papke, Leslie. 1993. "What Do We Know About Enterprise Zones?" Working paper no. 4251, January. Cambridge, MA: National Bureau of Economic Research.

Raphael, Stephen. 1996. "The Spatial Mismatch Hypothesis of Black Youth Unemployment: Evidence from the San Francisco Bay Area." University of California at San Diego. Photocopy.

Rees, Albert. 1996. "Information Networks in Labor Markets." *American Economic Review* 56 (2, May): 559–566.

Rivera-Batiz, Francisco. 1992. "Quantitative Literacy and the Likelihood of Employment Among Young Adults in the U.S." *Journal of Human Resources* 27 (2, Spring):313–328.

Rodgers, William, and William Spriggs. 1996. "What Does the AFQT Really Measure? Race, Wages, Schooling and the AFQT Score." College of William and Mary. Photocopy.

Rosenbaum, James, and Susan Popkin. 1991. "Employment and Earnings of Low-Income Blacks Who Move to Middle-Class Suburbs." In *The Urban Underclass*, ed. C. Jencks and P. Peterson. Washington, D.C.: Brookings Institution.

Ross, Stephen. 1996. "Racial Differences in Residential and Job Mobility: Evidence Concerning the Spatial Mismatch Hypothesis." University of Connecticut. Photocopy.

Shulman, Steven. 1987. "Discrimination, Human Capital, and Black-White Unemployment: Evidence from Cities." *Journal of Human Resources* 22 (3, Summer): 361–376.

Waldinger, Roger. 1996. *Still the Promised City? African-Americans and Immigrants in Post-Industrial New York*. Cambridge: Harvard University Press.

Wilson, William. 1987. *The Truly Disadvantaged*. Chicago: University of Chicago Press.

Yinger, John. 1995. *Closed Doors, Opportunities Lost*. New York: Russell Sage Foundation.

Zax, Jeffrey, and John Kain. 1996. "Moving to the Suburbs: Do Relocating Companies Leave their Black Employees Behind?" *Journal of Labor Economics* 14 (July):472–504.

Table 2.1

Daily Tasks and Required Credentials for Newly Filled Jobs, by Educational Labeling of Jobs
(In Percents)

	All	College Required	No College Required	
			White-Collar	Blue-Collar/Service
Newly Filled Jobs	100.0	24.6	45.8	29.6
Daily Tasks				
Customer Contact	72.9	81.9	82.2	51.4
Reading or Writing Paragraphs	68.4	90.6	67.4	51.3
Arithmetic	67.7	76.9	70.1	56.6
Computers	56.4	74.0	70.5	20.2
None of the Above	6.2	0.1	2.6	16.5
Required Credentials				
High School Diploma	78.4	100.0	82.2	54.7
GED Accepted	—	—	66.2	43.9
GED Not Accepted	—	—	15.9	10.8
General Work Experience	69.9	75.1	71.9	62.9
Specific Work Experience	64.2	74.1	64.4	56.0
Previous Training or Certification	42.5	55.6	39.3	37.4
None of the Above	8.8	0.0	7.4	17.7

Source: Author analyses.
Notes: All results are sample weighted. Credentials are considered "required" if they are "absolutely necessary" or "strongly preferred" at the time of hiring.

Table 2.2

Daily Tasks and Required Credentials for Newly Filled Jobs Held by Blacks, by Educational Labeling of Jobs
(In Percents)

New Jobs Held by Blacks	All New Jobs 21.5		College Required 11.4		No College Required			
					White-Collar 21.1		Blue-Collar/ Service 26.8	
	Yes	No	Yes	No	Yes	No	Yes	No
Daily Tasks								
Customer Contact	20.9	23.3	13.9	00.7	20.4	24.9	24.7	31.0
Reading or Writing Paragraphs	19.1	27.1	11.2	13.3	18.4	26.7	25.7	28.5
Arithmetic	17.3	30.9	8.9	19.4	17.5	30.1	22.0	33.8
Computers	18.8	25.5	12.8	7.4	19.6	25.0	24.5	28.2
Any of the Above	20.8	35.7	11.2	0.0	20.8	39.9	25.4	38.8
Required Credentials								
High School Diploma	19.1	32.2	11.4	—	19.6	28.9	25.0	31.8
GED Accepted	—	—	—	—	19.7	24.1	24.7	29.8
GED Not Accepted	—	—	—	—	18.9	21.5	26.2	26.9
General Work Experience	19.3	27.6	11.6	10.8	17.8	30.4	24.8	31.6
Specific Work Experience	18.7	27.1	11.1	12.6	17.6	27.1	24.9	30.1
Previous Training or Certification	17.8	24.6	12.1	11.4	15.1	25.1	23.6	29.4
Any of the Above	20.5	36.1	11.8	—	20.2	34.7	26.3	32.6

Source: Author analyses.

Notes: Sample consists of jobs filled by only whites or blacks. "Yes" and "No" refer to whether the skill or credential is required, rather than to whether blacks were hired.

Table 2.3

Recruitment Methods for All Newly Filled Jobs and for Those Filled by Blacks, by Method and by Educational Labeling of Jobs
(In Percents)

	All Jobs	College Required	No College Required	
			White-Collar	Blue-Collar/Service
Method Used (All Jobs)				
Informal Referrals	41.3	43.3	37.7	42.5
Signs/Walk-Ins	16.9	10.0	18.1	16.9
Newspaper Ads	30.5	35.7	32.5	28.2
Private Employment Agencies	6.7	8.6	7.3	5.4
State/Community Agencies	4.6	2.4	4.4	7.0
All Methods	100.0	100.0	100.0	100.0
Jobs Filled by Blacks by Method*				
Informal Referrals	18.3	9.7	17.7	25.2
Signs/Walk-Ins	33.2	19.6	35.6	32.7
Newspaper Ads	16.8	7.6	14.7	23.1
Private Employment Agencies	20.5	8.8	19.7	28.4
State/Community Agencies	40.2	12.3	30.3	45.9

Source: Author analyses.
* Columns for this lower half of the table do not sum to 100% because respondents were allowed to report more than one recruitment method.

Table 2.4

Applicants, Employees, and Newly Hired Workers, by Race, Gender, and Location of Jobs

	Primary Central City	Other Urban Areas	Suburbs
Percent of Applicants Who Are:			
Black Males	22.9	18.6	11.9
Black Females	18.9	14.5	9.3
Hispanics	15.1	13.0	13.7
Asians	5.7	4.7	5.8
Ratio of Employees to Applicants for:			
Black Males	.642	.640	.555
Black Females	.926	.751	.581
Hispanics	.974	.731	.993
Asians	.905	.548	.759
Ratio of New Hires to Applicants for:			
Black Males	.620	.640	.496
Black Females	.836	.786	.699
Hispanics	1.000	1.223	1.022
Asians	.930	.596	.690

Source: Author analyses.

Note: The employment and hires data refer only to jobs that do not require college graduates.

Job Creation for At-Risk African Americans Through Empowerment Zones and Enterprise Communities

William M. Rodgers III

Job creation strategies in economically distressed areas, as measured by persistently high unemployment and poverty rates, have been a major concern of researchers and policymakers for decades, with peaks in interest after periods of racial conflict. Past policy remedies, associated with different ideologies, can be sorted into three distinct types. The first, largely driven by liberal thought, focuses on providing resources via public expenditures to at-risk communities. The second, strongly supported by conservatives, focuses on providing market-based incentives to employers either to hire residents of at-risk communities, to relocate to at-risk communities, or to expand their facilities into at-risk communities. The current strategy, which is the focus of this chapter, pulls together these two methods and adds a strong community development component.

The success of market-based incentives to stimulate job creation in at-risk areas is mixed.[1] Most of the evidence comes from an examination of state enterprise zone programs that offer targeted tax, expenditure, and regulatory inducements, along with subsidies to start new businesses or to expand or relocate existing firms in a designated geographic area. Enterprise zones have been a part of state and local economic development strategies since the early 1980s. Currently, 37 states and the District of Columbia have some form of enterprise zone program. Since these programs are administered by states, they employ a wide variety of tax structures and incentives. When positive effects on zone employment, zone unemployment, and zone investment are found, they typically are small. Some researchers attribute this finding to the size of the subsidies, the criteria for success, and the methods of collecting and evaluating data.

The most recent job creation initiative for economically distressed areas seeks to facilitate employment growth in these areas by merging two strategies: (1) block grants and (2) tax credits for labor and capital. Communities, however, may choose to limit their involvement to the receipt of federal block grants. The new entities created by the legislation are called Empowerment Zones and Enterprise Communities.

This chapter provides some insight into how successful these programs may be in creating job opportunities for residents in economically distressed areas, particularly at-risk African Americans. I look at the effects on wages and employment of the current labor and capital subsidies in the nine federally designated Empowerment Zones, with an eye to answering the following questions. What are the wage and employment effects of the current 1 percent subsidy to zone labor and 12.5 percent subsidy to capital? What types of products are most likely to generate the greatest benefits for zone residents in terms of increased employment and wages? Are the federal wage and capital subsidies set at levels that maximize zone employment gains? If not, what mix of labor and capital tax subsidies would generate the greatest improvement in zone employment?

I begin with a historical overview of past policy initiatives for at-risk communities, including a detailed description of the current program. The next section provides a review of the evidence from state enterprise zones. This evidence, however, only provides lower-bound estimates because, along with the tax incentives, this latest program contains block grant and community development components, which may further increase wages and employment by lowering the actual and perceived costs of hiring zone residents and doing business in zone areas.

The third section describes the rationale for using tax incentives to create employment in economically and socially distressed areas. Based on the present subsidies to labor and capital of 1 percent and 12.5 percent, respectively, results are simulated for each federally designated Empowerment Zone using a modified version of Papke's (1993) partial equilibrium model. While the model distinguishes between black and white workers, it does not incorporate the block grants or the community development aspects of the current program. As with the evidence for the state enterprise zones, if these program features have sizable direct or secondary effects on zone wages and employment, then the estimates generated should only be viewed as lower bounds. The final section summarizes the results and offers policy recommendations for maximizing job creation for zone residents, a great many of whom are at-risk African Americans.

THE EVOLUTION OF DEVELOPMENT POLICIES FOR AT-RISK COMMUNITIES

Early efforts to create jobs in at-risk communities employed public funding. Recently, these more "liberal" efforts have been viewed very critically. During the 1980s, state governments shifted away from these public-spending initiatives and toward market-oriented programs that provide businesses with incentives to locate or expand into at-risk areas by offering subsidies to employers. The subsidies lower the costs of hiring zone residents, either by directly subsidizing the wages of zone employees or by subsidizing the purchase of equipment and machinery.

The latest round of federal attempts to foster job creation in economically depressed areas was spurred by the Los Angeles riots in April and May 1992. The 103rd Congress passed legislation to implement a tax incentive pilot program to establish fifty enterprise zones over a five-year period.[2] The legislation focused on lowering the costs of doing business in economically distressed areas relative to healthier areas.

The tax incentives included in the bill would have lowered the costs of capital more than the costs of labor. They included a 15 percent credit on wages paid to zone residents with a cap of $3,000 per worker annually, a 50 percent reduction in capital gains taxes on profits from investments held in a zone for at least five years,[3] a $20,000 immediate expense deduction for newly purchased capital equipment, and an annual deduction of up to $25,000 for purchases of stock in businesses investing in enterprise zones, up to $250,000 for each person. President Bush vetoed the legislation on November 4, 1992.

The next attempt to create a federal subsidy program came the following year. Congress passed and the President signed the Omnibus Budget Reconciliation Act (Title XIII, Chapter I), which established the funding, designation procedures, and eligibility criteria for the Empowerment Zone/Enterprise Community (EZ/EC) program. Under this legislation, an urban or rural area could be designated as an Empowerment Zone (EZ), Supplemental Empowerment Zone (SEZ), Enhanced Enterprise Community (EEC), or an Enterprise Community (EC).

The Empowerment Zones are similar to the enterprise zones envisioned by the 1992 legislation and to existing state enterprise zones. Employers in these designated areas receive subsidies on labor and capital for 10 years. The benefits are more generous than those of state enterprise zone benefits or those provided in the 1992 federal legislation. However, they are similar in that they also lower the costs of capital more than the costs of labor.

Table 3.1 presents the Empowerment Zone 10-year employment credit schedule. For the first seven years, from 1995 to 2002, employers can take a wage credit of up to $3,000 per year for each resident employee or new hire. After 2002, the credit starts to decline. In 2003, the maximum credit equals $2,250, $1,500 in 2004, and $750 in 2005. By 2006, the credit falls to zero.

The capital incentives are as follows: Employers can use the tax code's Section 179 provision to write off up to $37,500 a year on the purchase of depreciable, tangible property. This exceeds the basic Section 179 first-year write-off by $20,000. Finally, employers can use special low-interest, tax-exempt, privately issued bonds to finance new facilities or to renew or expand existing facilities. Both employee and capital credits are not indexed; thus, their real value will erode over time.

Block grants to designated areas are an additional feature of the program. Table 3.2 describes the size of the block grants that each type of designee received. Each urban Empowerment Zone received a block grant of $100 million; each rural Empowerment Zone received a block grant of $40 million. The two Supplemental Empowerment Zones and the four Enhanced Enterprise Communities were each awarded $300 million in Economic Development

Initiative grants. Each Enterprise Community received $3 million of Title XX funds from the Department of Health and Human Services. These very flexible grants can be used to fund a variety of economic, social, and community development activities. They are similar to first-generation efforts to create jobs in economically distressed areas. An additional feature of the current legislation is the return of the decision-making process to local communities.

On December 21, 1994, the Clinton Administration announced its first round of Empowerment Zone and Enterprise Community designations. Applications had been solicited from both urban and rural areas. The criteria for selection included population, geographic size, and level of economic distress. Urban areas are required to have a population between 50,000 and 200,000 residents or 10 percent of the population of the largest city located within the nominated area, whichever is greater. The urban zones can not be larger than 20 square miles. Rural areas can have a maximum of 30,000 residents and cover no more than 1,000 square miles.

Urban zones must have either a continuous boundary or consist of no more than three noncontiguous parcels. They may be located in no more than two contiguous states. Rural zones must be located entirely within no more than three contiguous states. Zones located in more than one state must have one continuous boundary. If located in one state, the zone can have no more than three noncontiguous parcels. However, each of the noncontiguous parcels must meet the poverty requirements. Rural and urban zones must be located completely within the jurisdiction of the local government unit applying for designation.

Both urban and rural areas must have pervasive, persistent poverty, as measured by the 1980 and 1990 decennial censuses. More specifically, within each census tract or census block numbering area within the zone, the poverty rate must exceed 20 percent. It must exceed 25 percent for at least 90 percent of the population census tracts and 35 percent for at least 50 percent of the population census tracts.

Urban zones also are required to have an unemployment rate not lower than the national unemployment rate. Evidence of high crime, narcotics use, homelessness, abandoned housing, deteriorated infrastructure, or substantial out-migration of residents will satisfy the condition of economic distress. Urban and rural zones cannot include any portion of a central business district, unless the poverty rate for each population census tract is at least 35 percent for an Empowerment Zone and 30 percent for an Enterprise Community. Rural zones cannot include any portion of an Indian reservation.

In constructing its application, each designated area was required to put together a strategic plan that stressed four key principles: (1) economic opportunity, (2) sustainable community development, (3) community-based partnerships, and (4) strategic vision for change. To promote economic opportunity, the zone's initiatives were supposed to create jobs within the community and throughout adjacent areas, provide opportunities for entrepreneurial initiatives and small business expansion, and create job training opportunities that place individuals on meaningful career ladders. To promote sustainable community development, the initiatives were evaluated based on their ability to create livable, vibrant communities through comprehensive approaches that coordinate economic, physical, environmental, community, and human development.

To create community-based partnerships, initiatives were supposed to involve political and government leaders, community groups, health and service groups, environmental groups, religious organizations, private and nonprofit firms, educational facilities, and individual citizens. Finally, zone initiatives were required to provide a strategic vision for change. More specifically, zone officials were asked to identify the objectives for the community and to provide a strategic map for its rejuvenation. This vision was to build on existing community resources and to respond to community needs in a holistic fashion. The plan also was required to have a reasonable set of goals, performance benchmarks on which to assess progress, and a framework for monitoring, evaluating, and modifying the zone's strategic plan.

Of the more than 500 rural and urban areas that submitted applications, 105 were designated as EZ/EC communities. Six urban and three rural areas were designated as Empowerment Zones (EZ)—Atlanta, Chicago, Baltimore, Detroit, Bronx (NY), Philadelphia-Camden (NJ), the Kentucky Highlands (portions of Clinton, Jackson, and Wayne Counties), the Mississippi Delta (portions of Bolivar, Holmes, Humphreys, Leflore, Sunflower, and Washington Counties), and the Rio Grande Valley (portions of Cameron, Hidalgo, Starr, and Willacy Counties, TX). Two urban areas were named Supplemental Empowerment Zones (SEZ), and four were designated Enhanced Enterprise Communities (EEC). The remaining 90 communities, one-third of which are rural areas, were designated as Enterprise Communities (EC). A complete list of the sites is presented in Appendix 3.1 at the end of this chapter.

Table 3.3 provides an overview of the size and conditions of the nine designated Empowerment Zones. Except for the Kentucky Highlands, all zones are small relative to the metropolitan or county area in which the zone is located. The Kentucky zone population comprises 71 percent of Clinton, Jackson, and Wayne Counties. In the other Empowerment Zones, resident population is no more than 14 percent of the population of the metropolitan area or county. Land area comparisons provide similar rankings.

As a share of zone population, African Americans living in the Detroit zone comprise 67 percent, the largest percentage among the seven zones. African Americans make up only 1 percent of zone population in the Rio Grande valley and 2 percent of the county population in the Kentucky Highlands. The zone labor market indicators measure each zone's level of economic and social distress. The unemployment and poverty rates are well in excess of their state rates. Detroit and New York's zone unemployment rates are 29 and 18 percent. In Atlanta, New York, and the Rio Grande, more than 50 percent of zone population lives in poverty.

THE EMPIRICAL EVIDENCE ON STATE ENTERPRISE ZONES

The many studies that assess the economic impact of state enterprise zones serve as valuable sources of information for evaluating the potential effects of this latest program. However, the accumulated evidence can only indicate a potential lower bound because the state programs only provide subsidies, not block grants, a key feature of the Clinton Administration's urban agenda. Researchers have used a variety of measures to assess the effectiveness of state enterprise zones, including employment and unemployment rates, and the value of depreciable personal property, inventories, investment, per capita income, and municipal property. Researchers also have used benefit-cost analysis to assess enterprise zone success.

The absence of data for zones before and after designation as well as for nonzone areas in these same periods has hampered attempts to estimate what their performance would have been in the absence of zone designation. Papke (1994) addresses these methodological issues in her study, however, by using data for the state of Indiana and comparing the change in zone outcomes to the change in nonzone outcomes. Her estimates indicate an initial reduction in the value of depreciable personal property by 13 percent, an increase in inventories by 8 percent, and a decrease in unemployment claims in the zone and surrounding community by 19 percent.

These results differ from those in Papke (1993). Using Indiana decennial census data for 1980 and 1990, this earlier paper finds no improvement in the economic status of zone residents. Comparisons of outcomes in zones and nonzones indicate that the zone per capita income fell relative to nonzone per capita income. Zone unemployment also fell relative to nonzone unemployment, but the difference was only 0.11 percentage points. The Papke studies indicate that enterprise zones attract investment, but it is unclear whether this investment is from new businesses or employers that are relocating and whether zone residents benefit disproportionately from the investment. Zone residents may receive little benefit because of poor infrastructure within the zone, such as the absence of well-developed roads and transit systems. Further, the preponderance of unskilled labor in zone areas may discourage investors.

Boarnet and Bogart (1996) come to a similar conclusion as Papke (1994). They follow 28 Northern and Central New Jersey municipalities from 1982 to 1990. Although all were eligible for designation, only 14 submitted applications, and seven were designated enterprise zones. Boarnet and Bogart find no positive effect of zone status on municipal employment, employment in various sectors, and municipal property values compared to nonzone municipalities. However, in their conclusion, Boarnet and Bogart do not completely reject the possibility that designation as an enterprise zone could have had positive effects.

Research also has focused on estimating enterprise zone cost-effectiveness. Direct spending and cost-per-job for zone residents (foregone revenue per job created) are the typical measures of cost-effectiveness. However, these calculations only capture the initial level of public investment required per zone job created and fail to capture any of the secondary effects such as reductions in the use of public assistance. This omission is quite important because, without accounting for these savings in government expenditures, estimates of the cost per job are clearly biased upward.

Papke's (1990) review finds that the average cost per job is $4,564 and about $31,113 per zone resident job annually. More recent cost-per-job estimates for New Jersey range from $8,000 to $13,000, well within the range found in other research (Papke 1993). Enterprise zone costs are comparable to those of other programs to generate jobs in distressed areas, even without taking into account such items as reductions in the use of public assistance.[4]

To assess whether zone residents and minorities disproportionately benefit from the presence of enterprise zones, I reviewed the literature cited in Papke (1993) and two recent empirical studies, Boarnet and Bogart (1996) and Papke (1994). The median share of jobs that go to residents is 37 percent, but varies across enterprise zones. Residents in the Madison (IN) and York (PA) enterprise zones received only 5 percent of the new jobs, while residents in the Chicago enterprise zone received 90 percent of the new jobs.

To assess whether minorities benefitted disproportionately, I searched for direct counts of minority zone job growth, but had little success. Few studies disaggregate job growth by race and ethnicity; consequently, I found only two studies that described the share of new zone jobs that went to minorities. Funkhouser and Lorenz (1987) document that 29 percent of the 205 new jobs in Maryland's seven enterprise zones went to minorities. The York (PA) enterprise zone, evaluated in HUD (1986), generated 620 jobs, with 60 percent going to minorities.

THE ECONOMICS OF ZONE WORKER AND CAPITAL SUBSIDIES

From the inception of these programs, all have had in common the idea that subsidies to employers to lower the costs of doing business in the zone relative to nonzone areas would cause them to alter their behavior in response. This section examines the likely responses to these subsidy incentives in terms of cost and the supply of labor and capital. Although employers have the incentive to increase output in the zone by using both inputs, that is, labor and capital, if one is relatively cheaper than the other, employers will favor it, thus biasing the benefits away from the other, which becomes relatively more expensive.

For example, a subsidy to employers that hire zone labor unambiguously raises the wages and employment of zone workers. If the labor supply response to a change in wages is small (as found in the literature), then the gains from the subsidies will tend to be in the form of higher wages rather than employment gains. If workers are motivated to work more for small wage increases, the gains will shift from wages to employment.

In reality, under the current program, the capital subsidy is 12.5 times the zone worker subsidy. Since their relative costs for zone workers are higher than the costs for capital, employers have an incentive as a result of the capital subsidy to substitute away from zone workers toward capital. Two effects determine whether zone workers' wages and employment increase or decrease. The shift away from zone labor because of the increase in its relative expense leads to a decline in zone wages and employment, while the increased need for workers to produce greater output leads to an increase in zone wages and employment. The net effect on zone workers depends on the responsiveness of consumer demand to changes in the product's price. If consumer demand is not sensitive to price changes (which might result from increased output), then the wages and employment of zone workers fall (because fewer are needed to produce the same output). If consumer demand is sensitive to price changes, then the wages and employment of zone workers increase.

An additional factor that researchers consider when attempting to assess the zone's impact is its size relative to the surrounding area. As the zone's relative size increases, the gains to zone workers increase. However, at some point, as the zone becomes larger with respect to the surrounding area and begins to trade with the surrounding markets, the wage and employment effects become difficult to predict. The net employment effects depend on the relative size of the zone, employers' ability to shift between workers and capital, consumers' ability to substitute zone and nonzone products in household consumption, and the economy-wide responsiveness of workers to small changes in wages.

Regardless of these relationships, as the number of areas designated as Empowerment Zones increases, the impact on zone wages decreases. As noted earlier, the subsidies in the Clinton Administration program are only one tool for providing incentives for employers to hire zone residents, expand their business in a zone, or relocate to a zone. So the overall impact will depend on the effect of the block grant programs on economic development as well.

SIMULATING THE EFFECTS OF THE CURRENT EMPOWERMENT ZONES

This section presents simulation results for each zone from a modified version of Papke's (1993) partial equilibrium model. I use the model to answer the following questions: What are the wage and employment effects of the current subsidies of 1 percent to zone labor and 12.5 percent to capital? What types of products are most likely to generate the biggest benefits for zone residents in terms of increased employment and wages? That is, how do products compare in their influence on wages and employment given their sensitivity or insensitivity to changes in price? The results from these simulations provide a lower-bound estimate of the impact of the program for two reasons. Block grants used to invest in services that increase the skills and reduce the costs of hiring minority zone residents may lead to wage and employment benefits in addition to those of the

Empowerment Zone's subsidies. If the block grants lead zone residents to increase their labor force participation, then the gains will be more in the form of employment than wages. The block grants also may lessen the uncertainty associated with hiring or doing business in a zone. Grants used to finance zone infrastructure or public safety projects that reduce the costs and risks of investing in Empowerment Zones may also lead to additional payoffs in the form of more jobs and higher wages.

The parameters for the model are constructed from the demographic data in Table 3.3 and presented in Table 3.4. The first column shows each zone's share of its metropolitan or county population. Kentucky is the largest zone relative to its surrounding economy, while Philadelphia/Camden and New York are the smallest. The table also reports the percentage of the zone's population that is African American. The African American population is proportionally the largest in the Detroit, Atlanta, and Baltimore zones and smallest in the Kentucky-Highlands and Rio Grande Valley zones. These population shares are used to generate estimates of nonzone, zone black, and zone white shares of income.

To do this, I assume that capital's share of income is 25 percent and labor's share of income (zone and nonzone) is 75 percent. Given this assumption about how income is split between capital and labor, I then solve for nonzone labor's share of income and the shares' of zone black and white income. The values of these parameters are in the last three columns of Table 3.4. The nonzone shares of income range from a low of 22 percent in Kentucky to highs of 73 percent in Philadelphia/Camden and New York. The zone's share of income in Kentucky is 53 percent and 2 percent in Philadelphia/Camden and New York. The share ranges from 5 to 10 percent in the other Empowerment Zones.

African Americans' shares of zone income are lowest in Kentucky, Philadelphia/Camden, and New York. This is the case for Kentucky because African Americans comprise such a small share of Kentucky's zone population. In the case of the Philadelphia/Camden and New York zones, the reason is that they are so small relative to the surrounding metropolitan area. In Atlanta, Detroit, and Baltimore, African American zone residents have higher shares of zone income than do white zone residents, while in Chicago, black and white zone residents split zone income virtually in half.

Using the parameters in Table 3.4, I simulate the impact that the wage and capital subsidies have on the use of zone labor and capital.[5] I assume that the responsiveness of zone black and white labor supply to wage changes equals 0.3, that is, a 1 percent increase in wages increases hours worked by 0.3 percent. This mild response to a wage change is found in the labor supply literature. I am not aware of any study that estimates the labor supply responses of residents in areas in severe economic distress. However, for residents of such severely distressed economic areas, this value may overstate the responsiveness to wage changes. The implication of assuming that labor is inelastically supplied is that the gains to zone workers will be in the form of increases in wages rather than employment.

I perform simulations over a range of consumer responses to changes in the

---

product's price to assess benefits from changes in product prices for zone wages and employment. A value of .5 implies that a 1 percent increase in price leads to a .5 percent decline in demand for the product. A value of 1.0 implies that a 1 percent change in the product's price is associated with a fall in demand of 1 percent, and a value of 1.5 indicates that a 1 percent change in price leads to a 1.5 percent reduction in product demand. The values from the simulations should be interpreted as the percentage change in wages or employment for a percentage change in the subsidy. For example, an estimate of .5 indicates that a 1 percentage point increase in the wage and a 12.5 percentage point capital subsidy (the level of the current program's subsidies) is associated with a 0.5 percent increase in wages. The detailed model is presented in the technical appendix.

The wage subsidy results for each Empowerment Zone are in Panel 1 of Tables 3.5a to 3.5g. The largest wage and employment gains are experienced by residents of Kentucky's zone, including African American residents even though they comprise only 1 percent of the zone's population. This is due to the zone's large size relative to the counties in which it is located. The gains are largest when consumer demand for the product is very sensitive to price changes. Under the 1 percent labor subsidy, the wages of black and white Kentucky zone residents increase by 0.79 to 0.91 percentage points, and employment increases by 0.24 to 0.27 percentage points. The wage increases of the black and white residents of the Detroit, Baltimore, and Atlanta zones range from 0.55 to 0.61 percentage points. Chicago, Philadelphia-Camden, and New York zone residents experience wage increases that range from 0.53 to 0.57 percentage points. For all zones except Kentucky, zone employment increases range from 0.16 to 0.18 percentage points.

The capital subsidy simulations, given in Panel 2 of Tables 3.5a to 3.5g, show that employers substitute away from zone (black and white) and nonzone labor when consumer demand is not sensitive to price changes. The basic result is that zone and nonzone workers only experience wage and employment gains when product demand is sensitive to price changes (elasticity of demand greater than 1.00). The magnitude of the changes is not sensitive to zone size relative to the surrounding labor market. More specifically, Kentucky's wage and employment results are not too different from the results in the six other zones.

When demand for the product is not very sensitive to price changes (elasticity of demand = .5), black zone wages fall 2.0 to 2.5 percentage points, and employment falls 0.60 to 0.74 percentage points. The losses to white zone workers are solely in the form of wages, which fall 2.7 to 3.6 percentage points. Nonzone wages and employment fall 1.7 and 0.5 percentage points. When product demand is highly sensitive to price changes (elasticity of demand = 1.5), black zone wages increase by approximately 1.1 percentage points, while employment increases by only 0.3 percentage points. White zone gains, which are solely in the form of wage increases, range from 1.2 to 2.0 percentage points. Nonzone wages and employment increase by 0.8 to 0.9 and 0.2 to 0.3 percentage points, respectively.

Another set of questions that the simulations seek to answer is whether the current federal wage and capital subsidies are the optimal mix. That is, do they maximize zone employment gains? If not, what mix of labor and capital tax incentives generates the greatest improvement in zone employment? Tables 3.7a to 3.7d present the tax experiments for Kentucky, the largest zone relative to its surrounding market, and Atlanta, a small zone relative to its metropolitan area. These two zones also differ in racial makeup. The Kentucky zone is virtually all white, while the Atlanta zone is 59 percent African American.

Tables 3.7a to 3.7d provide estimates of the employment change for given pairs of labor and capital subsidies. Each entry represents the change in employment for such a pair of subsidies. For each zone, I simulate the results for a product whose demand is not sensitive to price changes (elasticity of demand = .5) and for one whose demand is sensitive to price changes (elasticity of demand = 1.5). Three unambiguous results emerge from the analysis. First, if the demand for the product is not sensitive to price changes, then the government should set the capital subsidy equal to zero and set the labor subsidy as large as possible. Second, if the demand for the product is sensitive to price changes, then the government should make both subsidies as large as possible. Third, the fact that the employment gains are largest in Kentucky, the largest of the Empowerment Zones, implies that local governments should make their zones as large as possible. Further, the federal government should use zone size as a criterion in the designation process.

These results also suggest that in terms of maximizing zone employment growth, the Clinton Administration labor and capital subsidies of 1 and 12.5 percent are probably too low. For products that have demands that are very sensitive to price changes, employment growth under the Clinton labor subsidy is 2 to 3 percentage points less than it would be if labor and capital were both subsidized at 12 percent.

For products whose demand is not sensitive to price changes, the subsidies also are set too low. In fact, by itself, the Clinton Administration capital subsidy actually leads to a decline in zone employment. To increase Kentucky zone employment, the government could lower the capital subsidy to 8 percent or less and set the labor subsidy to 2 percent, or it could keep the capital subsidy at 12 percent but set the labor subsidy in excess of 2 percent. For the Atlanta zone, the government could lower the capital subsidy to no more than 6 percent and set the labor subsidy at 2 percent, or keep the capital subsidy at 12 percent and set the labor subsidy in excess of 4 percent.

SUMMARY AND CONCLUSIONS

This chapter attempted to determine the likely effects of the current labor and capital subsidies on wages and employment in the nine federal Empowerment Zones. The following questions were examined: What are the wage and employment effects of the current 1 percent subsidy to zone labor and 12.5 percent subsidy to capital? What types of products are most likely to generate the greatest benefits for zone residents in terms of increased employment and wages? Are the federal wage and capital subsidies set at levels that maximize zone employment gains? If not, what mix of labor and capital tax subsidies would generate the greatest improvement in zone employment?

The answers to these questions come from simulations of a modified version of Papke's (1993) partial equilibrium model. Under the 1 percent labor subsidy, the wages of black and white zone residents increase by 0.53 to 0.91 percentage points, and employment increases by 0.16 to 0.27 percentage points. Under the capital subsidy, if demand for the product is not very sensitive to price changes, zone wages and employment fall by 2.0 to 3.6, and 0.60 to 2.5 percentage points, respectively. However, if demand for the product is price-sensitive, then zone wages increase by 1.1 to 2.0, and employment increases by 0.3 percentage points. For both subsidies, the gains increase as the zone becomes larger relative to its surrounding metropolitan or county labor market, and the gains shift from wages to employment as zone workers' labor supply decisions become more responsive to small wage changes.

The labor market impact of the current round of Empowerment Zones will probably be larger than predicted because the model does not include the block grant, community-based partnership, and sustainable community development components. If these components lower the costs associated with hiring a zone worker, then the gains to black and white zone labor estimated for the nine Empowerment Zones will be even larger. Further, if these components raise the cost of remaining out of the labor force, then the labor market gains will shift toward employment. If, on the other hand, these initiatives lower the opportunity cost of remaining out of the labor force, then the labor gains will shift to wages.

The optimal tax simulations reveal that the current labor and capital subsidies of 1 and 12.5 percent, respectively, do not maximize zone employment growth. For products that have demands that are very sensitive to price changes, employment growth under the Clinton labor subsidy is 2 to 3 percentage points less than employment growth if labor and capital were both subsidized at 12 percent. For products whose demand is not sensitive to price changes, the subsidies also are not at an optimal level. In fact, by itself, the Clinton Administration capital subsidy actually leads to a decline in zone employment. The block grant and community development components, which are not explicitly included in the model, will probably help to narrow the gap.

To remove the gap, the government has several options. In zones that produce products with prices that are not sensitive to small price changes, the government should set the capital subsidy equal to zero and set the labor subsidy as large as possible. In zones with prices that are sensitive to price changes, the government should make both subsidies as large as possible.

On August 5, 1997, President Clinton signed the Taxpayer Relief Act, which establishes a second round of designations for 15 new Empowerment Zones. Applications for round two designations were received October 8, 1998. Designations were to be announced before January 1, 1999. The simulation results of this paper provide policymakers with several additional recommendations. First, in relation to their surrounding communities, zones should be as large as possible. Second, the subsidies and block grants should be structured such that they attract employers who produce products that are quite sensitive to price changes. Manufacturing goods are examples of such products. However, if the zone is faced with attracting employers whose products are not sensitive to price changes, then to maximize the employment benefits to zone workers, the subsidies and block grants should be structured such that they favor zone labor over capital. Finally, if maximizing employment growth is the policy goal, block grants should be given to programs in zones that attempt to make workers' labor supply decisions more sensitive to wage changes.

I wish to thank Margery Austin Turner, Wilhelmina A. Leigh, Margaret C. Simms, Edward Montgomery, Linda Paris, Edie Brashares, Linda Schakel, and William Spriggs for helpful comments and suggestions. I also want to thank Matthew Goette and Alison Spock for expert research assistance.

1. Several studies find little support for their use, while Bartik (1985, 1986) and Papke (1991) find that taxes play a role in determining a firm's geographic location.

2. See Lavation and Miller (1992) for a discussion of the proposals in 1992.

3. At the time the maximum rate was 28 percent.

4. The gross placement cost of the JOBS program during the late 1960s and early 1970s was $3,200 (1969 dollars) or $10,752 (1990 dollars) per hire. The costs per job in the Urban Development Action Grant Program was $11,570 ($17,058 in 1990 dollars), $13,000 ($19,110 in 1990 dollars) in the Business Loan Program of the Economic Development Administration, and $60,000 ($88,200 in 1990 dollars) per job in the local Public Works program of the Economic Development Administration (Bendick 1981). The reduction in public assistance payments resulting from increased employment is not incorporated in these calculations.

5. It is assumed that capital is able to move freely across areas. The substitution between capital and labor is assumed to equal 1. I also assume that white zone labor elasticity is always mildly responsive to wage changes (.3), and I allow the black zone labor supply elasticity to vary from 0 (perfectly inelastic) to .6. Thus, this set of parameters provides scenarios in which black zone labor supply is less responsive to wage changes than white labor supply responses and black zone labor supply is relatively more responsive to wage changes.

Advisory Council on Unemployment Compensation. 1995. *Unemployment Insurance in the United States: Benefits, Financing, Coverage.* Washington, D.C.

Bartik, T. J. 1985. "Business Location Decisions in the U.S.: Estimates of the Effects of Unionization, Taxes, and other Characteristics of States." *Journal of Business and Statistics* 3:14–22.

Bartik, T. J. 1986. "Neighborhood Revitalization's Effects on Tenants and the Benefit Cost Analysis of Government Neighborhood Programs." *Journal of Urban Economics* 19:234–248.

Bendick, M., Jr. 1981. "Employment, Training, and Economic Development." In *The Reagan Experiment,* ed. J.L. Palmer and I.V. Sawhill. Washington, D.C.: The Urban Institute.

Boarnet, Marlon G., and William T. Bogart. 1996. "Enterprise Zones and Employment: Evidence from New Jersey." *Journal of Urban Economics* 40:198–215.

Funkhouser, R., and E. Lorenz. 1987. "Fiscal and Employment Impacts of Enterprise Zones." *Atlantic Economic Journal* 15:62–76.

Lavation, S. A., and E. Miller. 1992. "Enterprise Zones are No Solution for our Blighted Areas." *Challenge* 35 (3):4–8.

Papke, J. A. 1990. "The Role of Market-Based Policy in Economic Development and Urban Revitalization: A Retrospective Analysis and Appraisal of the Indiana Enterprise Zone Program—Year Three Report." West Lafayette, IN: Center for Tax Policy Studies, Purdue University.

Papke, L. E. 1991. "Interstate Business Tax Differentials and New Firm Location: Evidence from Panel Data." *Journal of Public Economics* 45:47–68.

Papke, L. E. 1993. "What Do We Know about Enterprise Zones?" in *Tax Policy and the Economy*, ed. J.M. Poterba. Cambridge, MA: MIT Press.

Papke, L. E. 1994. "Tax Policy and Urban Development: Evidence from the Indiana Enterprise Zone Program." *Journal of Public Economics* 54:37–49.

U.S. Department of Housing and Urban Development. 1986. "State-Designated Enterprise Zones: Ten Case Studies." Washington, D.C.: The Office of Program Analysis and Evaluation.

U.S. General Accounting Office. 1982. "Enterprise Zones: Lessons from the Maryland Experience." Washington, D.C.: U.S. General Accounting Office.

Table 3.1

Empowerment Zone Employment Credit Schedule

Year	Percentage of First $15,000 in Wages	Credit
1995–2002	20	$3,000
2003	15	2,250
2004	10	1,500
2005	5	750
2006	0	0

Source: U.S. Department of Housing and Urban Development, *EZ/EC Implementation Guide.*

Table 3.2

Block Grant Awards

Type of Community	Value of Grant (in $ millions)
Urban Empowerment Zone	100
Rural Empowerment Zone	40
Supplemental Empowerment Zone	300
Enhanced Enterprise Community	300
Enterprise Community	3

Source: U.S. Department of Housing and Urban Development, *EZ/EC Fact Sheet.*

EMPOWERMENT ZONES AND ENTERPRISE COMMUNITIES

Table 3.3

Empowerment Zone and Metropolitan Area Characteristics

Panel A

Empowerment Zone	Population (in thousands)		Percentage Black		Land Area (square miles)	
	Zone	Metro or County	Zone	Metro or County	Zone	Metro or County
Atlanta	50	394	59	67.1	9.3	131.8
Baltimore	72	736	59	59.2	6.8	80.8
Chicago	200	2,784	39	39.1	14.3	227.2
Detroit	101	1,028	67	75.7	18.3	138.7
Kentucky	27	39	—	2.0	753.0	1,003.0
Mid-Delta	29	214	63	62.8	981.0	4,060.0
New York	199	7,323	—	28.7	7.6	308.9
Philadelphia/Camden	50	1600/87	—	39.9/56.4	4.4	135.1/8.8
Rio Grande	30	702	1	0.3	227.0	163.0

Panel B

Empowerment Zone	Unemployment Rate			Poverty Rate		
	Zone	Metro or County	State	Zone	Metro or County	State
Atlanta	—	9.2	5.7	57	27.3	14.7
Baltimore	—	9.2	4.3	—	21.9	9.2
Chicago	—	11.3	6.6	—	21.6	11.9
Detroit	29.0	19.7	8.2	47	32.4	13.1
Kentucky	—	10.0	7.4	39	38.0	19.0
Mid-Delta	14.5	12.4	8.4	45	39.0	25.0
New York	18.0	10.0	6.9	52	19.3	13.0
Philadelphia/Camden	—	9.7/16.3	6.0/5.7	—	20.3/36.6	11.1/7.6
Rio Grande	30.0	14.2	7.1	52	41.7	18.0

Source: 1990 Census.

Notes: Dash (—) indicates that zone statistic was not published in the Zone's Consolidated Executive Summary. Kentucky Highlands: Portions of Clinton, Jackson and Wayne Counties. Mid-Delta: Portions of Bolivar, Holmes, Humphreys, Leflore, Sunflower, and Washington Counties. Rio Grande Valley: Portions of Cameron, Hidalgo, Starr, and Willacy Counties.

Table 3.4

Simulation Parameters

Empowerment Zone	Zone Share of Metro or County Population (%)	Black Share of Zone Population (%)	a_n (%)	a_{zb} (%)	a_{zw} (%)
Kentucky	71	2*	22	1	52
Atlanta	13	59	65	6	4
Detroit	10	67	68	5	2
Baltimore	10	59	68	4	3
Chicago	7	39	70	2	3
Philadelphia/Camden	3	48*	73	0.96	1.04
New York	3	29*	73	0.6	1.4

Notes: Zone Share of metro/county population calculated from population values in Table 3.3, Panel A. Black Share of Zone Population is taken from Table 3, Panel A. The term a_n denotes the nonzone labor share of total income, and a_{zb} and a_{zw} are zone share of total income for black and white labor, respectively.

*Figures are percentage of metro/county population that is black since figures were not available for these zones. The Philadelphia/Camden number is an average of the two areas.

Table 3.5a

Simulations, Atlanta Empowerment Zone

Panel 1: Impact on the Wages and Employment of Zone and Nonzone Residents Due to a 1% Labor Subsidy for Zone Residents Only, by Elasticity of Product Demand

Elasticity of Product Demand	Change for Black Zone Residents (%)	Change for White Zone Residents (%)	Change for Nonzone Residents (%)
Wages			
0.0	0.56	0.56	0.00
0.5	0.59	0.59	0.02
1.0	0.60	0.60	0.03
1.5	0.61	0.61	0.04
Employment			
0.0	0.17	0.17	0.00
0.5	0.18	0.18	0.01
1.0	0.18	0.18	0.01
1.5	0.18	0.18	0.01

Panel 2: Impact on Wages and Employment of 12.5% Zone Capital Subsidy, by Elasticity of Product Demand

Elasticity of Product Demand	Change for Black Zone Residents (%)	Change for White Zone Residents (%)	Change for Nonzone Residents (%)
Wages			
0.0	-7.39	-11.51	-6.01
0.5	-2.09	-3.25	-1.70
1.0	0.00	0.00	0.00
1.5	1.12	1.74	0.91
Employment			
0.0	-2.22	0.00	-1.80
0.5	-0.63	0.00	-0.51
1.0	0.00	0.00	0.00
1.5	0.34	0.00	0.27

Notes: The elasticity of substitution between black and white zone labor is assumed to equal 1. Black and white zone resident labor supply elasticities equal .3.

Table 3.5b

Simulations, Baltimore Empowerment Zone

Panel 1: Impact on the Wages and Employment of Zone and Nonzone Residents Due to a 1% Labor Subsidy for Zone Residents Only, by Elasticity of Product Demand

Elasticity of Product Demand	Change for Black Zone Residents (%)	Change for White Zone Residents (%)	Change for Nonzone Residents (%)
Wages			
0.0	0.551	0.551	0.000
0.5	0.571	0.571	0.017
1.0	0.579	0.579	0.024
1.5	0.584	0.584	0.028
Employment			
0.0	0.165	0.165	0.000
0.5	0.171	0.171	0.005
1.0	0.174	0.174	0.007
1.5	0.175	0.175	0.008

Panel 2: Impact on Wages and Employment of 12.5% Zone Capital Subsidy, by Elasticity of Product Demand

Elasticity of Product Demand	Change for Black Zone Residents (%)	Change for White Zone Residents (%)	Change for Nonzone Residents (%)
Wages			
0.0	-7.186	-11.767	-5.907
0.5	-2.059	-3.371	-1.692
1.0	0.000	0.000	0.000
1.5	1.110	1.818	0.913
Employment			
0.0	-2.156	0.000	-1.772
0.5	-0.618	0.000	-0.508
1.0	0.000	0.000	0.000
1.5	0.333	0.000	0.274

Notes: The elasticity of substitution between black and white zone labor is assumed to equal 1. Black and white zone resident labor supply elasticities equal .3.

Table 3.5c

Simulations, Chicago Empowerment Zone

Panel 1: Impact on the Wages and Employment of Zone and Nonzone Residents Due to a 1% Labor Subsidy for Zone Residents Only, by Elasticity of Product Demand

Elasticity of Product Demand	Change for Black Zone Residents (%)	Change for White Zone Residents (%)	Change for Nonzone Residents (%)
Wages			
0.0	0.543	0.543	0.000
0.5	0.558	0.558	0.012
1.0	0.564	0.564	0.018
1.5	0.567	0.567	0.020
Employment			
0.0	0.163	0.163	0.000
0.5	0.167	0.167	0.004
1.0	0.169	0.169	0.005
1.5	0.170	0.170	0.006

Panel 2: Impact on Wages and Employment of 12.5% Zone Capital Subsidy by Elasticity of Product Demand

Elasticity of Product Demand	Change for Black Zone Residents (%)	Change for White Zone Residents (%)	Change for Nonzone Residents (%)
Wages			
0.0	-7.118	-12.101	-5.841
0.5	-2.051	-3.487	-1.683
1.0	0.000	0.000	0.000
1.5	1.110	1.888	0.911
Employment			
0.0	-2.136	0.000	-1.752
0.5	-0.615	0.000	-0.505
1.0	0.000	0.000	0.000
1.5	0.333	0.000	0.273

Notes: The elasticity of substitution between black and white zone labor is assumed to equal 1. Black and white zone resident labor supply elasticities equal .3.

Table 3.5d

Simulations, Detroit Empowerment Zone

Panel 1: Impact on the Wages and Employment of Zone and Nonzone Residents Due to a 1% Labor Subsidy for Zone Residents Only, by Elasticity of Product Demand

Elasticity of Product Demand	Change for Black Zone Residents (%)	Change for White Zone Residents (%)	Change for Nonzone Residents (%)
Wages			
0.0	0.551	0.551	0.000
0.5	0.571	0.571	0.017
1.0	0.579	0.579	0.024
1.5	0.584	0.584	0.028
Employment			
0.0	0.165	0.165	0.000
0.5	0.171	0.171	0.005
1.0	0.174	0.174	0.007
1.5	0.175	0.175	0.008

Panel 2: Impact on Wages and Employment of 12.5% Zone Capital Subsidy, by Elasticity of Product Demand

Elasticity of Product Demand	Change for Black Zone Residents (%)	Change for White Zone Residents (%)	Change for Nonzone Residents (%)
Wages			
0.0	-7.082	-11.597	-5.907
0.5	-2.039	-3.339	-1.701
1.0	0.000	0.000	0.000
1.5	1.103	1.807	0.920
Employment			
0.0	-2.125	0.000	-1.772
0.5	-0.612	0.000	-0.510
1.0	0.000	0.000	0.000
1.5	0.331	0.000	0.276

Notes: The elasticity of substitution between black and white zone labor is assumed to equal 1. Black and white zone resident labor supply elasticities equal .3.

Table 3.5e

Simulations, Kentucky Highlands Empowerment Zone

Panel 1: Impact on the Wages and Employment of Zone and Nonzone Residents Due to a 1% Labor Subsidy for Zone Residents Only, by Elasticity of Product Demand

Elasticity of Product Demand	Change for Black Zone Residents (%)	Change for White Zone Residents (%)	Change for Nonzone Residents (%)
Wages			
0.0	0.79	0.79	0.00
0.5	0.87	0.87	0.07
1.0	0.90	0.90	0.09
1.5	0.91	0.91	0.10
Employment			
0.0	0.24	0.24	0.00
0.5	0.26	0.26	0.02
1.0	0.27	0.27	0.03
1.5	0.27	0.27	0.03

Panel 2: Impact on Wages and Employment of 12.5% Zone Capital Subsidy, by Elasticity of Product Demand

Elasticity of Product Demand	Change for Black Zone Residents (%)	Change for White Zone Residents (%)	Change for Nonzone Residents (%)
Wages			
0.0	-11.49	-12.46	-7.99
0.5	-2.46	-2.67	-1.71
1.0	0.00	0.00	0.00
1.5	1.15	1.24	0.80
Employment			
0.0	-3.45	0.00	-2.40
0.5	-0.74	0.00	-0.51
1.0	0.00	0.00	0.00
1.5	0.34	0.00	0.24

Notes: The elasticity of substitution between black and white zone labor is assumed to equal 1. Black and white zone resident labor supply elasticities equal .3.

Table 3.5f

Simulations, New York (Bronx) Empowerment Zone

Panel 1: Impact on the Wages and Employment of Zone and Nonzone Residents Due to a 1% Labor Subsidy for Zone Residents Only, by Elasticity of Product Demand

Elasticity of Product Demand	Change for Black Zone Residents (%)	Change for White Zone Residents (%)	Change for Nonzone Residents (%)
Wages			
0.0	0.533	0.533	0.000
0.5	0.539	0.539	0.005
1.0	0.541	0.541	0.007
1.5	0.543	0.543	0.008
Employment			
0.0	0.160	0.160	0.000
0.5	0.162	0.162	0.002
1.0	0.162	0.162	0.002
1.5	0.163	0.163	0.003

Panel 2: Impact on Wages and Employment of 12.5% Zone Capital Subsidy, by Elasticity of Product Demand

Elasticity of Product Demand	Change for Black Zone Residents (%)	Change for White Zone Residents (%)	Change for Nonzone Residents (%)
Wages			
0.0	-6.828	-12.367	-5.744
0.5	-2.002	-3.626	-1.684
1.0	0.000	0.000	0.000
1.5	1.096	1.985	0.922
Employment			
0.0	-2.049	0.000	-1.723
0.5	-0.601	0.000	-0.505
1.0	0.000	0.000	0.000
1.5	0.329	0.000	0.277

Notes: The elasticity of substitution between black and white zone labor is assumed to equal 1. Black and white zone resident labor supply elasticities equal .3.

Table 3.5g

Simulations, Philadelphia/Camden Empowerment Zone

Panel 1: Impact on the Wages and Employment of Zone and Nonzone Residents Due to a 1% Labor Subsidy for Zone Residents Only, by Elasticity of Product Demand

Elasticity of Product Demand	Change for Black Zone Residents (%)	Change for White Zone Residents (%)	Change for Nonzone Residents (%)
Wages			
0.0	0.533	0.533	0.000
0.5	0.539	0.539	0.005
1.0	0.541	0.541	0.007
1.5	0.543	0.543	0.008
Employment			
0.0	0.160	0.160	0.000
0.5	0.162	0.162	0.002
1.0	0.162	0.162	0.002
1.5	0.163	0.163	0.003

Panel 2: Impact on Wages and Employment of 12.5% Zone Capital Subsidy, by Elasticity of Product Demand

Elasticity of Product Demand	Change for Black Zone Residents (%)	Change for White Zone Residents (%)	Change for Nonzone Residents (%)
Wages			
0.0	-6.785	-12.289	-5.744
0.5	-1.993	-3.610	-1.688
1.0	0.000	0.000	0.000
1.5	1.092	1.979	0.925
Employment			
0.0	-2.036	0.000	-1.723
0.5	-0.598	0.000	-0.506
1.0	0.000	0.000	0.000
1.5	0.328	0.000	0.277

Notes: The elasticity of substitution between black and white zone labor is assumed to equal 1. Black and white zone resident labor supply elasticities equal .3.

Table 3.6a

Simulation: Optimal Taxation and Labor Effects for Atlanta, With Product Elasticity of .5

	Capital Subsidy	Labor Subsidy: Zone Residents Only						
		0	2	4	6	8	10	12
Black Zone	0	0	0.354	0.708	1.062	1.416	1.77	2.124
	2	-0.097	0.257	0.611	0.965	1.319	1.673	2.027
	4	-0.194	0.16	0.514	0.868	1.222	1.576	1.93
	6	-0.291	0.063	0.417	0.771	1.125	1.479	1.833
	8	-0.388	-0.034	0.32	0.674	1.028	1.382	1.736
	10	-0.485	-0.131	0.223	0.577	0.931	1.285	1.639
	12	-0.582	-0.228	0.126	0.48	0.834	1.188	1.542
White Zone	0	0	0.354	0.708	1.062	1.416	1.77	2.124
	2	-0.097	0.257	0.611	0.965	1.319	1.673	2.027
	4	-0.194	0.16	0.514	0.868	1.222	1.576	1.93
	6	-0.291	0.063	0.417	0.771	1.125	1.479	1.833
	8	-0.388	-0.034	0.32	0.674	1.028	1.382	1.736
	10	-0.485	-0.131	0.223	0.577	0.931	1.285	1.639
	12	-0.582	-0.228	0.126	0.48	0.834	1.188	1.542
Nonzone	0	0	0.015	0.029	0.044	0.058	0.073	0.087
	2	-0.083	-0.068	-0.054	-0.039	-0.025	-0.01	0.004
	4	-0.166	-0.151	-0.137	-0.122	-0.108	-0.093	-0.079
	6	-0.249	-0.235	-0.22	-0.205	-0.191	-0.176	-0.162
	8	-0.332	-0.318	-0.303	-0.288	-0.274	-0.259	-0.245
	10	-0.415	-0.401	-0.386	-0.371	-0.357	-0.342	-0.328
	12	-0.498	-0.484	-0.469	-0.454	-0.44	-0.425	-0.411
Total	0	0	0.723	1.445	2.168	2.89	3.613	4.335
	2	-0.277	0.446	1.168	1.891	2.613	3.336	4.058
	4	-0.554	0.169	0.891	1.614	2.336	3.059	3.781
	6	-0.831	-0.109	0.614	1.337	2.059	2.782	3.504
	8	-1.108	-0.386	0.337	1.06	1.782	2.505	3.227
	10	-1.385	-0.663	0.06	0.783	1.505	2.228	2.95
	12	-1.662	-0.94	-0.217	0.506	1.228	1.951	2.673

Source: Author's calculations from simulation model. See text and appendix for details.

Table 3.6b

Simulation: Optimal Taxation and Labor Effects for Atlanta, with Product Elasticity of 1.5

	Capital Subsidy	Labor Subsidy: Zone Residents Only						
		0	2	4	6	8	10	12
Black Zone	0	0	0.365	0.729	1.094	1.459	1.823	2.188
	2	0.052	0.417	0.782	1.146	1.511	1.876	2.24
	4	0.105	0.47	0.834	1.199	1.564	1.928	2.293
	6	0.157	0.522	0.887	1.251	1.616	1.981	2.345
	8	0.21	0.575	0.939	1.304	1.669	2.033	2.398
	10	0.262	0.627	0.992	1.356	1.721	2.086	2.45
	12	0.315	0.679	1.044	1.409	1.774	2.138	2.503
White Zone	0	0	0.365	0.729	1.094	1.459	1.823	2.188
	2	0.052	0.417	0.782	1.146	1.511	1.876	2.24
	4	0.105	0.47	0.834	1.199	1.564	1.928	2.293
	6	0.157	0.522	0.887	1.251	1.616	1.981	2.345
	8	0.21	0.575	0.939	1.304	1.669	2.033	2.398
	10	0.262	0.627	0.992	1.356	1.721	2.086	2.45
	12	0.315	0.679	1.044	1.409	1.774	2.138	2.503
Nonzone	0	0	0.024	0.047	0.071	0.094	0.118	0.142
	2	0.045	0.069	0.092	0.116	0.139	0.163	0.187
	4	0.09	0.113	0.137	0.161	0.184	0.208	0.231
	6	0.135	0.158	0.182	0.206	0.229	0.253	0.276
	8	0.18	0.203	0.227	0.25	0.274	0.298	0.321
	10	0.225	0.248	0.272	0.295	0.319	0.343	0.366
	12	0.269	0.293	0.317	0.34	0.364	0.387	0.411
Total	0	0	0.754	1.505	2.259	3.012	3.764	4.518
	2	0.149	0.903	1.656	2.408	3.161	3.915	4.667
	4	0.3	1.053	1.805	2.559	3.312	4.064	4.817
	6	0.449	1.202	1.956	2.708	3.461	4.215	4.966
	8	0.6	1.353	2.105	2.858	3.612	4.364	5.117
	10	0.749	1.502	2.256	3.007	3.761	4.515	5.266
	12	0.899	1.651	2.405	3.158	3.912	4.663	5.417

Source: Author's calculations from simulation model. See text and appendix for details.

Table 3.6c

Simulation: Optimal Taxation and Labor Effects for Kentucky Highlands, with Product Elasticity of .5

	Capital Subsidy	Labor Subsidy: Zone Residents Only						
		0	2	4	6	8	10	12
Black Zone	0	0.000	0.524	1.049	1.573	2.097	2.621	3.146
	2	-0.112	0.412	0.937	1.461	1.985	2.509	3.034
	4	-0.224	0.300	0.825	1.349	1.873	2.397	2.922
	6	-0.336	0.188	0.713	1.237	1.761	2.285	2.810
	8	-0.448	0.076	0.601	1.125	1.649	2.173	2.698
	10	-0.560	-0.036	0.489	1.013	1.537	2.061	2.586
	12	-0.672	-0.147	0.377	0.901	1.425	1.950	2.474
White Zone	0	0.000	0.524	1.049	1.573	2.097	2.621	3.146
	2	-0.112	0.412	0.937	1.461	1.985	2.509	3.034
	4	-0.224	0.300	0.825	1.349	1.873	2.397	2.922
	6	-0.336	0.188	0.713	1.237	1.761	2.285	2.810
	8	-0.448	0.076	0.601	1.125	1.649	2.173	2.698
	10	-0.560	-0.036	0.489	1.013	1.537	2.061	2.586
	12	-0.672	-0.147	0.377	0.901	1.425	1.950	2.474
Nonzone	0	0.000	0.040	0.080	0.120	0.160	0.200	0.240
	2	-0.090	-0.050	-0.010	0.030	0.070	0.110	0.150
	4	-0.181	-0.141	-0.101	-0.061	-0.021	0.019	0.059
	6	-0.271	-0.231	-0.191	-0.151	-0.111	-0.071	-0.031
	8	-0.362	-0.322	-0.282	-0.242	-0.202	-0.162	-0.122
	10	-0.452	-0.412	-0.372	-0.332	-0.292	-0.252	-0.212
	12	-0.543	-0.503	-0.463	-0.423	-0.383	-0.343	-0.303
Total	0	0.000	1.088	2.178	3.266	4.354	5.442	6.532
	2	-0.314	0.774	1.864	2.952	4.040	5.128	6.218
	4	-0.629	0.459	1.549	2.637	3.725	4.813	5.903
	6	-0.943	0.145	1.235	2.323	3.411	4.499	5.589
	8	-1.258	-0.170	0.920	2.008	3.096	4.184	5.274
	10	-1.572	-0.484	0.606	1.694	2.782	3.870	4.960
	12	-1.887	-0.797	0.291	1.379	2.467	3.557	4.645

Source: Author's calculations from simulation model. See text and appendix for details.

Table 3.6d

Simulation: Optimal Taxation and Labor Effects for Kentucky Highlands, with Product Elasticity of 1.5

Labor Subsidy: Zone Residents Only

	Capital Subsidy	0	2	4	6	8	10	12
Black Zone	0	0.000	0.547	1.094	1.641	2.188	2.735	3.282
	2	0.054	0.601	1.148	1.695	2.242	2.789	3.336
	4	0.109	0.656	1.203	1.750	2.297	2.844	3.391
	6	0.163	0.710	1.257	1.804	2.351	2.898	3.445
	8	0.218	0.765	1.312	1.859	2.406	2.953	3.500
	10	0.272	0.819	1.366	1.913	2.460	3.007	3.554
	12	0.327	0.874	1.421	1.968	2.515	3.062	3.609
White Zone	0	0.000	0.547	1.094	1.641	2.188	2.735	3.282
	2	0.054	0.601	1.148	1.695	2.242	2.789	3.336
	4	0.109	0.656	1.203	1.750	2.297	2.844	3.391
	6	0.163	0.710	1.257	1.804	2.351	2.898	3.445
	8	0.218	0.765	1.312	1.859	2.406	2.953	3.500
	10	0.272	0.819	1.366	1.913	2.460	3.007	3.554
	12	0.327	0.874	1.421	1.968	2.515	3.062	3.609
Nonzone	0	0.000	0.058	0.117	0.175	0.234	0.292	0.351
	2	0.044	0.102	0.161	0.219	0.278	0.336	0.395
	4	0.088	0.146	0.205	0.263	0.322	0.380	0.439
	6	0.132	0.190	0.249	0.307	0.366	0.424	0.483
	8	0.176	0.234	0.293	0.351	0.410	0.468	0.527
	10	0.220	0.278	0.337	0.395	0.454	0.512	0.571
	12	0.264	0.322	0.381	0.439	0.498	0.556	0.615
Total	0	0.000	1.152	2.305	3.457	4.610	5.762	6.915
	2	0.152	1.304	2.457	3.609	4.762	5.914	7.067
	4	0.306	1.458	2.611	3.763	4.916	6.068	7.221
	6	0.458	1.610	2.763	3.915	5.068	6.220	7.373
	8	0.612	1.764	2.917	4.069	5.222	6.374	7.527
	10	0.764	1.916	3.069	4.221	5.374	6.526	7.679
	12	0.918	2.070	3.223	4.375	5.528	6.680	7.833

Source: Author's calculations from simulation model. See text and appendix for details.

Appendix 3.1

Empowerment Zones and Enterprise Communities

Empowerment Zones (EZ)
Georgia: Atlanta
Illinois: Chicago
Kentucky: Kentucky Highlands*
Maryland: Baltimore
Michigan: Detroit
Mississippi: Mid Delta*
New York: Harlem, Bronx
Pennsylvania/NJ: Philadelphia, Camden
Texas: Rio Grande Valley*

Supplemental Empowerment Zones (SEZ)
California: Los Angeles City and County
Ohio: Cleveland

Enhanced Enterprise Communities (EEC)
California: Oakland
Massachusetts: Boston
Missouri/Kansas: Kansas City, Kansas City
Texas: Houston

Enterprise Communities (EC)
Alabama: Birmingham
Alabama: Chambers County*
Alabama: Greene, Sumter Counties*
Arizona: Arizona Border*
Arizona: Phoenix
Arkansas: East Central*
Arkansas: Mississippi County*
Arkansas: Pulaski County
California: Imperial County*
California: Los Angeles, Huntington Park
California: San Diego
California: San Francisco, Bayview, Hunter's
  Point
California: Watsonville*
Colorado: Denver
Connecticut: Bridgeport
Connecticut: New Haven
Delaware: Wilmington
District of Columbia: Washington
Florida: Jackson County*
Florida: Miami, Dade County
Florida: Tampa

Georgia: Albany
Georgia: Central Savannah*
Georgia: Crisp, Dooley Counties*
Illinois: East St. Louis
Illinois: Springfield
Indiana: Indianapolis
Iowa: Des Moines
Kentucky: Louisville
Louisiana: Macon Ridge*
Louisiana: New Orleans
Louisiana: Northeast Delta*
Louisiana: Ouachita Parish
Massachusetts: Lowell
Massachusetts: Springfield
Michigan: Five Cap*
Michigan: Flint
Michigan: Muskegon
Minnesota: Minneapolis
Minnesota: St. Paul
Mississippi: Jackson
Mississippi: North Delta*
Missouri: East Prairie*
Missouri: St. Louis
Nebraska: Omaha
Nevada: Clarke County, Las Vegas
New Hampshire: Manchester
New Jersey: Newark
New Mexico: Albuquerque
New Mexico: Moro, Rio Arriba, Taos
  Counties*
New York: Albany, Schenectady, Troy
New York: Buffalo
New York: Newburgh, Kingston
New York: Rochester
North Carolina: Charlotte
North Carolina: Halifax, Edgecombe,
  Wilson Counties*
North Carolina: Robeson County*
Ohio: Akron
Ohio: Columbus
Ohio: Greater Portsmouth
Oklahoma: Choctaw, McCurtain Counties
Oklahoma: Oklahoma City
Oregon: Josephine*
Oregon: Portland
Pennsylvania: Harrisburg
Pennsylvania: Lock Haven*
Pennsylvania: Pittsburgh

Continued...

Rhode Island: Providence
South Carolina: Charleston
South Carolina: Williamsburg County*
South Dakota: Beadle, Spink Counties*
Tennessee: Fayette, Haywood Counties*
Tennessee: Memphis
Tennessee: Nashville
Tennessee/Kentucky: Scott, McCreary
  Counties*
Texas: Dallas
Texas: El Paso
Texas: San Antonio
Texas: Waco
Utah: Ogden
Vermont: Burlington
Virginia: Accomac*
Virginia: Norfolk
Washington: Lower Yakima*
Washington: Seattle
Washington: Tacoma
West Virginia: Huntington
West Virginia: McDowell*
West Virginia: West Central*
Wisconsin: Milwaukee

*Denotes a rural designee.

Production in the zone uses capital K, black zone resident labor L_{ZB}, white zone resident labor L_{ZW}, and labor from outside the zone L_N. The package of zone tax incentives may include a subsidy to capital τ_K, zone resident labor τ_Z, and/or nonzone labor τ_N expressed as percentages (in decimals) of factor cost.

The production process in the zone is described by

$$Q = F(K, L_{ZB}, L_{ZW}, L_N).$$ 1

The demand function for the zone product is described by

$$Q = f(P).$$ 2

The three labor supply equations are

$$L_{ZB} = g_{ZB}(w)$$ 3

$$L_{ZW} = g_{ZW}(w)$$ 4

$$L_N = g_N(w).$$ 5

Capital is assumed to be in infinitely elastic supply to the zone, or

$$r = r_o.$$ 6

Under the assumptions of perfect competition and profit maximization, the zone economy is summarized by the following equations:

$$\hat{Q} = (1 - a_{ZW} - a_{ZB} - a_N)\hat{K} + a_{ZW}\hat{L}_{ZW} + a_{ZB}\hat{L}_{ZB} + a_N\hat{L}_N$$ 7

$$\hat{Q} = -e_p\hat{P}$$ 8

$$\hat{K} - \hat{L}_{ZW} = \sigma_{ZW}(\hat{w}_{ZW} - d\tau_Z + d\tau_K - \hat{r})$$ 9

$$\hat{K} - \hat{L}_{ZB} = \sigma_{ZB}(\hat{w}_{ZB} - d\tau_Z + d\tau_K - \hat{r})$$ 10

$$\hat{L}_{ZW} - \hat{L}_{ZB} = \sigma_{Z,BW}(\hat{w}_{ZB} - \hat{w}_{ZW})$$ 11

$$\hat{K} - \hat{L}_N = \sigma_N(\hat{w}_N - d\tau_N + d\tau_K - \hat{r})$$ 12

$$\hat{P} = a_{ZW}(\hat{w}_{ZW} - d\tau_Z) + a_{ZB}(\hat{w}_{ZB} - d\tau_Z) + a_N(\hat{w}_N - d\tau_N) + (1 - a_{ZB} - a_N - a_{ZW})(\hat{r} - d\tau_K)$$ 13

$$\hat{L}_{ZW} = e_{ZW}\hat{w}_{ZW}$$ 14

$$\hat{L}_{ZB} = e_{ZB}\hat{z}_{ZB}$$ 15

$$\hat{L}_N = e_N\hat{w}_N$$ 16

$$\hat{r} = 0$$ 17

where $\hat{Q}, \hat{P}, \hat{K}, \hat{L}_N, \hat{L}_{ZW}, \hat{L}_{ZB}, \hat{w}_{ZW}, \hat{w}_{ZB}, \hat{w}_N,$ and $\hat{r}$ are the percentage changes in output, price of output, capital, nonzone resident labor, zone resident white labor, zone resident black labor, and their wages, respectively, and the after-tax rate of return on capital. The terms a_{ZW} and a_{ZB} are zone white and black labor's share of total income, a_N is the nonzone labor share of total income, e_{ZW}, e_{ZB}, and e_N are the elasticities of labor supply for the three types of labor, e_p is the price elasticity of demand, σ_{ZW}, σ_{ZB}, and σ_N are the elasticities of substitution between capital and the three types of labor, and $\sigma_{Z,BW}$ is the elasticity of substitution between black and white zone labor. Setting labor supply equal to labor demand, this system yields three equations, that express the relationship between the percentage change in wages of each type of labor in response to any of the subsidies.

Job Creation Through Improved Access to Markets for Minority-Owned Businesses

Timothy Bates

M inority-owned businesses have grown in size and scope since the 1970s, at a rate surpassing that of firms owned by non-Hispanic whites.[1] Increasingly open markets have allowed black firms to compete in the broader economy, selling to formerly inaccessible clients, such as corporations and governments. This expanding minority business enterprise (MBE) community has generated many new jobs, most of which have been filled by minority employees (Bates 1997). This study documents that jobs generated by black-owned businesses nationwide have grown rapidly and identifies the subset of firms most responsible for producing employment growth.

Creation of viable MBEs entails the following elements: (1) the involvement of talented and capable entrepreneurs, (2) access to financial capital for these entrepreneurs to invest in their business ventures, and (3) access to markets for the products of these enterprises (Bates 1993). Absence of one or more of these three elements of business viability has traditionally handicapped many MBEs. Public policies seeking to generate minority business growth and job creation are most effective when they aid firms capable of having all three elements of business viability in place.

MBEs with capable owners often face greater barriers in gaining access to financial capital and markets than do small firms owned by non-Hispanic whites. The findings reported in this chapter focus principally on the third element of viability, access to markets.[2] Among MBEs and white-owned firms of the same size and scope, MBEs are shown to have less access to government and business clients than do white-owned firms. Government policies helping MBEs to overcome these discriminatory barriers and compete freely in the marketplace are needed if MBE growth and job creation are to continue on a positive trajectory.

THE CHANGING NATURE OF THE BLACK BUSINESS COMMUNITY

According to Census Bureau statistics, the number of African American–owned businesses operating in the United States increased 46 percent, from 424,165 to 620,912 between 1987 and 1992 (U.S. Bureau of the Census 1996). Census Bureau statistics, furthermore, report an impressive increase in the number of workers employed by black-owned firms, up from 220,467 to 345,193 over the 1987 to 1992 period—an increase of 56.6 percent in a five-year period.[3] Actual increases in the employee rolls of black enterprises were even higher than census statistics suggest since the Census Bureau provides incomplete firm counts that often overlook corporations owned and operated by black Americans (Boston 1995).[4]

Flaws notwithstanding, census data document impressive job growth. An examination of the underlying data provides insights into the specific types of businesses that are particularly prone to create employment opportunities. In fact, less than 1 percent of the nation's black-owned businesses account for the majority of the 345,193 jobs that the Census Bureau attributes to black enterprise, and the employment share of that one percent is increasing. Looking solely at black firms grossing one million dollars or more in revenue annually, we find that these firms employed 167,676 workers in 1992, more than double the 78,890 employees of such firms in 1987 (U.S. Bureau of the Census 1996; U.S. Bureau of the Census, 1990). Being big is not synonymous with rapid job creation, but focusing on big firms gives us a good starting point for understanding the employment generation process.

Job growth is found disproportionately among younger firms. Table 4.1 compares young black-owned businesses having 10 or more employees in 1987 to the broader universe of young firms owned by black Americans. All the firms described in Table 4.1 were formed since 1979. Measured by sales revenues, the average young black firm with 10 or more employees is over 20 times larger than the average young black firm nationwide (sales of $1,406,977 versus $64,526). The young firms with 10 or more employees, furthermore, have nearly 10 times the startup capitalization of their smaller counterparts ($134,753 versus $14,226, see Table 4.1) and are much more likely to remain in business than the typical firm. Over the 1987–1991 time period, 26.4 percent of the black-owned businesses active in 1987 shut down (Table 4.1), while only 8.1 percent of the large employer firms discontinued operations. The typical large employer firm is much bigger and better capitalized than black firms generally, and the owner is likely to be highly educated. Of the hundreds of thousands of black-owned firms identified as active in 1992 by the Census Bureau, only 5,313 of them had 10 or more paid employees. Yet these 5,313 firms accounted for 65 percent of total employment by black businesses. An additional 59,165 black-owned firms reported employing from one to nine workers. Collectively, these businesses accounted for the remaining 35 percent of employment by black-owned firms. Most black firms were zero-employee operations.

An important trait of the black firms having 10 or more employees is that they often started out large. Initial financial capitalization averaging $134,753 among these employer firms reflects this fact. Significantly, these large employer firms also have a much different industry distribution from black businesses generally. Among black-owned firms having 10 or more employees, the most common type of firm operates in the business services field. This sector typifies the emerging lines of black enterprise that account for most of the job creation coming from black-owned businesses nationwide. Total employment among all black enterprises operating in the business services niche has grown explosively, from 12,432 employees in 1982 to 32,636 employees in 1987 to 72,130 employees in 1992. A decade of extremely rapid growth has enabled these firms to create nearly 60,000 new jobs, representing roughly a five-fold increase in the number of paid employees. The underlying causes of this rapid growth in business services are the same as those underlying job creation generally in the realm of black enterprise.

WHICH BLACK-OWNED FIRMS ARE GROWING?

Business services, however, is not the sector of black employers with the most rapid job growth. That distinction belongs to the finance, insurance, and real estate (FIRE) sector, which generated job growth of 518 percent during the 1982 to 1992 period (compared with 480 percent in business services). Some sectors of the black business community have generated almost no job growth whatsoever. While the total number of employees of black firms in the FIRE sector increased from 2,851 in 1982 to 17,606 in 1992, black-owned food stores nationwide generated fewer than 1,000 net new jobs. Health service employment tripled (9,280 paid employees in 1982 and 29,578 in 1992), but employment in black-owned barbershops actually declined.

What accounts for these huge differences? Two traits powerfully delineate the types of firms that are rapidly expanding their employee numbers from those in laggard fields where job creation is either weak or entirely lacking. First, the growing fields have attracted more highly educated and skilled business owners than have the stagnant lines of business. The growing fields, furthermore, are much more oriented toward serving a racially diverse clientele, including corporate and government clients. The stagnant fields, in contrast, are typically traditional neighborhood personal service and "mom-and-pop" retail businesses serving a predominantly minority clientele. These dual patterns of rapid growth in some industry sectors and stagnation in others have profoundly transformed the black business community since the 1970s.

Rapid growth areas dominated by highly educated black entrepreneurs include skill-intensive service industries: finance, business services, and various professional services. Both of the forces propelling growth in black enterprise exist in the business services sector; that is, most firm owners are highly educated, and their clientele largely consists of other businesses and government units.

However, not all growth areas have both traits. Construction has been a growth area, but owners of construction firms have typically not been college educated. However, the construction sector does have the second characteristic: it has been very heavily oriented toward serving mainstream markets, particularly government clients (Boston 1997a). These sectors of rapid growth are commonly referred to as emerging lines of minority enterprise because minority ownership in these industries historically has been minimal. This all-important transformation—away from the declining traditional fields, toward these emerging lines of minority entrepreneurship—is more pronounced in the black business community than among other racial or ethnic minority groups. Firms owned by Korean and Chinese immigrants in particular have clung to traditional lines of minority enterprise (Bates 1997).

What accounts for the decline in the traditional strongholds? The large traditional sector of the black business community developed under pervasive racial segregation. Partial desegregation in housing, the workplace, commercial establishments, and public accommodations has contributed to the decline of these firms as it widened the range of retail and service markets accessible to black consumers. Desegregation did not, however, lead to significant white patronization of traditionally black-owned businesses. Many of these businesses were ill-equipped to exploit the new opportunities desegregation offered, and most whites remained unwilling to patronize businesses located in black neighborhoods (Bates 1993).

Growing numbers of experienced, financially sophisticated black entrepreneurs are thrusting some enterprises into the corporate mainstream. For example, businessman J. Bruce Llewellyn and former professional basketball player Julius Erving own the Philadelphia Coca Cola Bottling Company (Jaynes and Williams 1989). The largest black enterprises of the mid-twentieth century catered exclusively to minority clients, flourishing in market niches that were generally overlooked by corporate America. Since the 1960s, black-owned businesses reliant on these traditional markets have experienced growing competition from mainstream corporate America (Weems 1994). Their changing fortunes stem from the same social forces that have permitted emerging black-owned firms to compete successfully in the general marketplace.

In 1972, *Black Enterprise* magazine published its first listing of the top 100 black firms, ranked according to sales revenue. Total sales for the 100 firms were $473 million (Jaynes and Williams 1989, p. 181). By 1997, total sales for the largest 100 black-owned firms exceeded $10 billion. The ranks of the largest 100 black enterprises in the 1970s were dominated by firms catering to black households. Of the top 100 black-owned businesses, only two were in business services. By 1997, few of the top 100 black-owned businesses were in retailing: most were in manufacturing or business services. The business services sector, in turn, was dominated by computer software firms whose clients were commonly other businesses or government agencies, not individual consumers.

MINORITY-OWNED FIRMS AS EMPLOYERS: HOW MANY JOBS FOR WHOM?

The simple and powerful truth, demonstrated repeatedly in recent studies, is that MBEs hire a predominantly minority labor force (Bates 1993; Turner 1997; Boston and Ross 1997; Simms and Allen 1997). A growing local minority business community generates jobs that are captured disproportionately by minority employees. Given the high rates of unemployment and underemployment and the low rates of labor force participation experienced by minorities in most parts of the nation, promoting MBE growth has been recognized as a highly effective strategy for alleviating minority disadvantage in the labor market (Bates 1994; Sawicki and Moody 1997; Boston 1997b). Preferential procurement programs are particularly effective policy tools for cities seeking to generate private-sector job opportunities for minority residents (Boston and Ross 1997).

Boston and Ross (1997) examined workforce racial composition for black-owned businesses using data drawn from the Office of Contract Compliance certification records for the city of Atlanta and Fulton County. Among this group of large scale, generally successful black firms—all of which were actual or potential participants in public-sector procurement—Boston and Ross found that over 77 percent of their employees were African American (1997). Among the black-owned firms located in poor Atlanta-area communities, 81.8 percent of all employees were black; those located in affluent communities employed a workforce that was 77.1 percent black. Regardless of firm location—whether in a high-, low-, or middle-income area—black-owned firms largely employed blacks (Boston and Ross 1997). Summarizing the totality of employment pattern evidence, Boston stated, "the conclusion is that if the government or society wishes to increase African American employment and reduce the economic distress of inner-city neighborhoods, the most effective way to accomplish this is by promoting the growth of African American–owned businesses" (1997b, 21).

Utilizing data from the Characteristics of Business Owners (CBO) data base on black-business employment patterns in 28 very large metropolitan areas, I found that urban black employers in 1987 were employing a largely minority workforce (Bates 1993). Only 2.2 percent of black-owned firms in these metropolitan areas had an all-white workforce. In contrast, nearly 60 percent of the white-owned small businesses in the same urban areas employed all-white workforces. The predominant pattern, again, was one of whites hiring whites and blacks hiring blacks.

The location of small businesses within urban areas shaped hiring patterns somewhat, but the race of the firm owner was the major influence. Among white-owned firms operating in minority communities, 37.6 percent relied on minorities for at least 50 percent of their workers. Among black firms operating in predominantly white urban areas, 86.7 percent relied on minorities for at least 50 percent of their workers (Bates 1993). Plainly, white firms located in minority communities up their minority hiring somewhat, but they still rely largely on white employees. Simply luring more small businesses into urban minority communities, these statistics suggest, will create some jobs for minorities, but the employment impact will be vastly more beneficial to minority job seekers if the firms are black-owned. The white-owned firm located in the middle of a depressed minority community is much less likely to employ minorities than a black-owned enterprise located in an affluent white suburb.

In addition, a 1993 study by the Joint Center for Political and Economic Studies to identify the types of black-owned firms most likely to employ minorities found that "very few of these firms are located in high poverty areas" (Simms and Allen 1997, 215). This seems to confirm that the minority employment benefits derived from an expanding MBE community are maximized by encouraging firms to locate where they can best reach their customers and control their costs (Boston and Ross 1997). The poorest city neighborhoods may not be ideal locations for MBEs.

The relevance of social networks to job access helps to explain why the black-business workforce differs so profoundly from the employee racial makeup commonly observed in white-owned small firms (Granovetter 1994). Small firms heavily draw their employees from family-based networks, and networks of family and friends among white Americans commonly are made up of whites, and vice versa for black family-based networks.

The finding that white firms most often employ whites while black firms are more likely to employ blacks is consistent with the hypothesis that network hiring propensities tend to define workforce racial composition. When most of the jobs available in the small-business sector are found in white-owned firms, and most of the white owners prefer to hire family members, other relatives, friends, and friends of friends, it follows that black job seekers will do poorly (Bates 1994). A small business world of network hiring in which job accessibility is largely a function of the race of the owner is a world in which rapid growth of black-business employers is essential if black Americans are to expand their employment prospects. Fortunately, the rapid growth trajectory of black-owned businesses is rooted in factors that cannot easily be reversed.

Updating the MBE labor force composition data to 1992, nationwide statistics reveal that most black-owned businesses with payrolls rely on workforces comprised of 90 percent or more minority employees (Table 4.2). Other MBEs—largely those owned by Asians and Hispanics—also rely on a predominantly minority workforce, but their relative reliance on minority workers is somewhat less than that of black-owned businesses. Not every MBE hires a labor force that is predominantly minority, but MBE hiring patterns are nonetheless strikingly different from those observed among nonminority-owned small businesses. For example, the statistics in Table 4.2 indicate that 13.4 percent of black-owned firms rely on a workforce that is only 25 percent or less minority. The corresponding figures for nonminority and other minority firms are 77.1 percent and 26.1 percent, respectively.

As stated at the beginning of this chapter, figures from the Census Bureau show that the number of workers employed by black-owned firms increased 56.6

percent between 1987 and 1992. We know that employee rolls of the largest black businesses are actually increasing much faster than this, but these large firms are most commonly corporations, the group that is systematically, and hugely, undercounted by the census. This same problem plagues employment statistics for all MBE groups—Latinos, Native Americans, and Asian Americans, as well as blacks.[5] Complementary studies by Boston and Ross (1997), Simms and Allen (1997), and myself (Bates 1993; Bates 1994) also provide extensive evidence of (1) rapid growth in MBE employee numbers, (2) active hiring in inner-city minority neighborhoods by MBE employers, and (3) the high propensity of MBEs to employ minority workers.

Types of Firms Most Likely to Employ Minorities

The above evidence on MBE employment patterns does not address several issues that have particularly concerned government policymakers seeking to revitalize poor inner-city minority communities. Popular policies such as Enterprise Communities and Empowerment Zones are not usually aimed at improving minority employment specifically; rather, they seek to produce job opportunities in low-income neighborhoods. The 1993 analysis by the Joint Center for Political and Economic Studies, noted above, identified the types of firms that were likely to employ minority workers from low-income communities. The study focused explicitly on large-scale MBEs concentrating in emerging lines of business. More than 2,500 MBEs affiliated with regional councils of the National Minority Supplier Development Council in the states of Illinois, California, Florida, and Texas were surveyed.[6] This produced a high representation of non-black MBEs since the majority of Asian- and Hispanic-owned firms operating in the United States are located in these four states. Black business representation in the study was substantially increased by adding to the survey the nearly 600 black-owned firms surveyed by *Black Enterprise* magazine to construct its annual listing of the 100 largest black-owned industrial/service firms. Finally, 2,000 nonminority firms similar in size and industry distribution to the MBEs were surveyed to generate a comparison group.

The Joint Center survey responses indicated, as expected, that MBEs were more likely than nonminority firms to employ minority workers. Slightly over half of the MBEs responded that they recruited employees in low-income neighborhoods. MBE construction firms were most active in low-income neighborhood recruiting: 74.6 percent of them actively recruited employees in poor neighborhoods. The MBE business service firms ranked second: 66.7 percent of them recruited in poor areas. MBEs in manufacturing were in third place, with 62.8 percent of them recruiting actively in low-income neighborhoods. It is noteworthy that government procurement dollars targeted to MBEs flow most often to construction firms; business services rank second in sales to government; and MBE manufacturing has an above-average reliance on government clients. Thus, the types of MBEs that are most active in government procurement are the lines of business that are most actively seeking to hire minorities who reside in poor neighborhoods (Simms and Allen 1997).

For governments concerned about generating jobs for minority residents, the above studies collectively provide a compelling rationale for assistance programs that target viable MBEs. First, the targeted firms are already growing rapidly and generating many jobs, most of which are filled largely by minority employees. Furthermore, the types of MBEs active in government procurement—particularly construction firms—are precisely the firms that are most actively seeking to hire workers in low-income minority communities. Preferential procurement, in short, is potentially a powerful tool for increasing employment opportunities in depressed urban minority communities.

THE EFFECT OF DECLINING BARRIERS ON THE DEVELOPMENT OF HUMAN CAPITAL

Gains in higher education show how reductions in discriminatory barriers are translated into significant progress in the minority business community. Fewer than 300,000 African Americans were enrolled nationwide in colleges and universities in 1965. By 1980, corresponding enrollment figures for blacks had risen to 1,107,000 (Carter and Wilson 1992; Carter and Wilson 1995). In less than one generation, college enrollment nearly quadrupled, and the fields of concentration pursued by African American college students shifted dramatically toward business and technical fields.

The educational gains that took place a generation ago are particularly relevant to understanding present-day trends in the black business community. Self-employment is rarely pursued full-time by recent college graduates. Entry into small business is most widespread among persons in their late thirties and in their forties who possess 15 to 20 years of work experience (Bates 1995a). Thus, the full impact of the educational gains of the late 1960s and 1970s is reflected in the number and nature of the business startups undertaken by African Americans in the 1980s and 1990s.

The framework for identifying viable MBEs put forth at the beginning of this chapter attributed three traits to viable firms—capable owners (human capital), adequate financing (financial capital), and access to markets. The human capital element is the strongest single factor driving MBE growth in sales and employment. Highly educated owners experienced in business operations have been entering self-employment in large numbers, producing substantial gains in the entrepreneurial human capital underpinnings of the minority business community (Bates 1993; Bates 1997). The human capital piece of the MBE growth equation is far from perfect, however. In specific areas—construction, for example—major barriers continue to block both potential and actual minority business owners from acquiring the skills and experience needed to build strong firms (Bates and Howell 1998; Waldinger and Bailey, 1991). Nonetheless, the human capital basis for sustained MBE growth is already in place. Consequently, policy interventions seeking to sustain MBE growth are probably needed least in this area. The greater challenge is to insure that these well-educated, experienced, capable minority business owners have sufficient access to financial capital and market opportunities to sustain future growth of the minority business community.

ACCESS TO MARKETS: CONTESTED TERRAIN

Vast segments of the many markets in which goods and services are bought and sold have traditionally been closed to MBEs, mostly because of a racial caste system that continued to shape the minority business community well into the twentieth century. African Americans who attended college were particularly hemmed in by white social attitudes about which occupations were appropriate for blacks and made rational economic decisions based on this reality. Between 1912 and 1938, 73 percent of black college graduates nationwide became either teachers or preachers (Holsey 1938). The few entering into other professions— law, medicine, dentistry—served an all-black clientele. Shoeshine stand operators, caterers, even barbers might serve a white clientele, but black college graduates did not. When minority entrepeneurs ventured into the broader marketplace, they were constrained to function only in those capacities that white society felt were consistent with their inferior status. Traditional servant occupations, such as ironing shirts, shining shoes, and preparing and serving meals, were commonly deemed suitable by the dominant society. When the range of alternatives open to persons entering careers is greatly reduced, the size of the middle class is artificially restricted, and the nature of the resultant small business community is severely circumscribed. It is this hemming-in process that shaped and narrowed the African American small business community during this period.

This tradition was still profoundly shaping the nature of the minority-business community in 1960, leading college-educated blacks to avoid self-employment. But the traditional minority business community entered the 1960s as a fading relic of a declining era. In fact, a new age was dawning. The years of great growth were about to begin for minority-owned businesses. During the 1960s, increased loan availability became the focus of black business promotion efforts. In the late 1970s the use of procurement dollars and set-asides targeted to minority firms by corporations and government units was the major force promoting business growth. The rise of black political power in many big cities, particularly the election of black mayors, also helped open up important new markets into which MBEs expanded rapidly (Bates and Williams 1993).

Market Access: Selling to Public Clients

African American–owned firms historically have not been involved in the contracting and procurement activities of government agencies and authorities. In Atlanta, Georgia, in 1973, black-owned firms received only one-tenth of 1 percent of Atlanta's procurement business even though the majority of the population was African American. Atlanta became a pioneer in seeking to expand MBE presence in public procurement, and by 1976, with the city's MBE program fully operational, the minority share of contracting and procurement had risen to 19.9 percent. By 1978, the city boasted of having achieved 38.5 percent minority participation (Boston 1997a). Actual percentages were below these claims, but the minority share had grown significantly, accounting for over 15 percent of all contract dollars awarded by the city of Atlanta over the 1979–1989 period (Boston 1997a).

Penetration of the public marketplace has permitted MBEs to grow and diversify while increasing numbers of highly qualified minorities have been drawn into entrepreneurship (Bates 1993). By 1987, over 10 percent of the minority-owned firms operating nationwide sold goods and services to state and local governments (Bates and Williams 1995). With the opening of this multi-billion dollar market, employment soared in the impacted sectors. Most of the additional employees were minorities (Bates 1993). Challenges to the constitutionality of minority business assistance programs, however, threaten to reverse the process of broadening the range of markets served by black-owned enterprises. Minority business set-asides are being cut back due to the judicial constraints imposed by the U.S. Supreme Court rulings in *Richmond* v. *Croson* (1989) and *Adarand* v. *Peña* (1995). Within two years of the *Croson* ruling, for example, 33 of the nation's 200-plus preferential minority-business procurement programs at state and local levels had been disbanded, with another 65 undergoing re-evaluation (Boston 1997a).

Are Black Businesses Reliant on Government Sales?
In the process of constructing the Characteristics of Business Owners (CBO) data base, the Census Bureau asked tens of thousands of small business owners, roughly 60 percent of whom were minorities, to identify the types of clients (households, business, government) from which their sales were derived. Table 4.3 presents data describing these firms, disaggregated by the presence or absence of sales to government clients. All of these statistics are weighted to be representative of small firms nationwide that were operating in 1987.[7] Relative to their numbers nationwide, minority-owned businesses are underrepresented in the ranks of government vendors. Among the small businesses operating nationwide in 1987, 15.0 percent of the white-owned firms and 12.2 percent of the minority-owned establishments reported selling goods or services to federal, state, or local governments, including authorities and special districts. Among the large MBEs studied by the Joint Center, about 7 percent of the firms received at least 50 percent of their revenues from sales to government. Thus, neither study supports the view that most MBEs are dependent on government contracts. The reliance of young firms (i.e., firms starting in the 1979–1987 period) with paid employees, whether white- or black-owned, on government clients is pronounced: 20.9 percent of young white-owned firms nationwide were selling to the government in 1987; for young black-owned firms the percentage was 17.5 percent.

Minority business penetration in public procurement has been controversial.

The media and others often portray images of heavy reliance on government contracts that are quite inconsistent with the above statistics. Writing about black-owned businesses, for example, Dinesh D'Souza asserts that "a large proportion of its receipts come from the government; many black businesses would collapse without government contracting preferences and set-asides" (1995, 33).

Why are perceptions so out of touch with reality? Analysis of data for large cities with black mayors and preferential procurement efforts targeting minority vendors provides an explanation of this controversy. In fact, the minority business share of public-sector procurement is extremely small nationwide, but substantial gains have been achieved in a few large cities that have or have had minority mayors (Bates 1997). Minority-owned firms operating in the nation's largest urban areas are much more likely to sell to state and local government clients than are cohort firms located elsewhere, and selling to government by minority businesses is most prevalent in cities with black mayors (Bates and Williams 1993). Nearly 14 percent of the minority businesses in 15 very large metropolitan areas sold goods and services to state and local governments in 1987.

Disparity: A Lack of Capacity or Exclusion by Old-Boy Networks?
As minority-owned firms have penetrated the broader national marketplace, serving corporate and government markets, the question of capacity has surfaced. Particularly in government markets, the claim is that MBEs tend to be smaller, younger firms than nonminority-owned firms and, hence, often lack the capacity to compete effectively. A counterclaim, generally put forth by proponents of preferential procurement programs in government and corporate America, is that entrenched "old-boy networks" want to block MBE expansion into mainstream markets. Which is true: Do the entrenched status quo networks really thwart MBEs, or do they simply lack the capacity to compete?

Many government entities have commissioned studies of MBE involvement in public-sector procurement, commonly referred to as "disparity" studies. A frequent finding is that MBEs in a particular geographic area, such as a state, receive a disproportionately small share of government procurement dollars. For example, in New Jersey in the early 1980s, MBEs accounted for roughly 7 percent of the state's businesses, but received less than 1 percent of the procurement dollars flowing to business vendors from New Jersey state government (Bates 1995c). Hence, the claim of disparity is based on the difference between the MBEs' percentage of the businesses and their percentage of the dollars going to businesses.

Professor George La Noue has spearheaded a powerful attack against the disparity concept that has rationalized preferential procurement programs benefitting MBEs. "Ignoring company size constitutes a major methodological flaw in disparity studies," notes La Noue (1994, 500). Most minority-owned firms have zero employees: is it realistic to assume that such tiny firms have the ability to compete for government procurement contracts? How many of these firms are really ready, willing, and able to sell to government clients? These and related complaints have been leveled at existing studies of the involvement of minority- and women-owned businesses in government procurement. "Most disparity studies ignore firm size and include as equally available for even the largest, most complex contracts every business in the census or on some list, whether it is a part-time casual activity or a multi-national corporation," continues La Noue (1994, 499).

In short, La Noue asserts that MBEs are commonly not available to compete for government procurement dollars because they lack the capacity to sell goods and services to government. Government cannot be expected to utilize MBEs incapable of selling to public-sector clients; therefore, the whole disparity concept is rejected as a rationale for affirmative government efforts to buy goods and services from minority-owned businesses. Because of the supposed lack of capacity typifying MBEs, preferential procurement programs, according to La Noue, in fact amount to preferential treatment of minorities, which violates the Equal Protection Clause of the Fourteenth Amendment.

Recent rulings in U.S. District courts in Florida, Ohio, and other states have embraced La Noue's assertions about the weak factual underpinnings used to justify government preferential procurement. Court rulings in 1996 declaring preferential procurement unconstitutional include *Associated General Contractors of America* v. *City of Columbus* (case # 94-1848-CIV) and *Engineering Contractors Association of South Florida* v. *Metropolitan Dade County* (case # 94-1848-CIV). La Noue has not offered comprehensive evidence to support his hypothesis of MBE lack of capacity, but the courts have not required such evidence. Rather, the burden of proof is on defenders of preferential procurement to demonstrate that La Noue is off-base. This study now turns to the task of addressing La Noue's concerns.

The relevance of the MBE capacity issue transcends questions about the legality of preferential procurement programs run by governments. If MBE growth is reliant on preferential treatment—sheltered markets, noncompetitive bids that receive preferential breaks, and the like—then the ability of MBEs to operate in the broader economy is questionable. Government-run preferential procurement programs are in retreat nationwide (Boston 1997a). Programs run by large corporations targeting procurement spending to MBEs have been heavily shaped by public-sector preferential procurement efforts. Will these programs too back away from MBE vendors as affirmative action efforts lose favor in the government arena? Private businesses, after all, buy much more from MBEs than do government clients, and MBEs in emerging industries would be devastated by the loss of their corporate customers. The crux of the matter is capacity: tiny startup firms operating in personal services industries sell little that government and business clients wish to buy. It is the larger scale, more established firms that are expected to sell, most often, to these clients.

Yet MBEs nationwide are clearly a younger, smaller group of firms than white-owned small businesses, and they are underrepresented in industries, such as manufacturing and wholesaling, that often sell to corporate and government clients. One of the reasons that MBEs are smaller, on average, than white-owned firms is the presence of discriminatory barriers such as "old boy" networks that constrain the ability of MBEs to get work. A government entity attempts to remedy this discriminatory barrier by adopting a preferential procurement program seeking to increase access to work for MBE construction firms. Dr. La Noue then urges the courts to declare programs unconstitutional unless the MBEs can show that they have the capacity of the white-owned firms, which they probably don't. If they did have the same capacity as the white-owned firms, then the preferential procurement program would have been unnecessary in the first place. The issue raised by La Noue, nonetheless, needs to be addressed, in light of the tendency of federal courts to embrace his objection to preferential procurement programs. So the question is: Without preferential treatment, do MBEs have the capacity to compete for government and corporate clients?

Table 4.3 uses nationwide small business data from the Census Bureau to compare the size and scope of MBEs and white-owned small firms. Many of the MBEs thus described are tiny, zero employee operations, which gives rise to La Noue's complaint that broad, across-the-board firm counts are grossly inadequate measures of the number of MBEs that are "ready, willing, and able" to sell to government or corporate clients. How is "ready, willing, and able" to be measured? "Ready and willing" traits describe the state of mind of the owner of the firm; "able" is directly determined by the client. A firm is not "able" unless the government client is satisfied that the firm is offering suitable goods and services. These "ready/willing/able" traits are not clearly defined and have a distinctly intangible element. The ready trait, for example, may change week by week, depending on the state of the firm's activities and opportunities. A construction firm fully booked with private-sector business this year may not be ready or willing to sell to government; next year, it may be ready and willing. Because they reflect an intangible, fluctuating set of circumstances, ready, willing, and able are only meaningful, measurable firm traits in hindsight: if a firm actually sold to government in 1987, it was obviously ready, willing, and able to do so. Using this measure of availability, 12.2 percent of MBEs, and 15.0 percent of nonminority firms, are ready, willing, and able to sell to government, as evidenced by their past actions (Table 4.3). Similarly, 30.2 percent of MBEs and 43.7 percent of nonminority firms are ready, willing, and able to sell to other businesses.

Consider two distinct measures of MBE availability: (1) MBEs as a percentage of all firms, and (2) MBEs as a percentage of firms ready, willing, and able to sell to government. The CBO data indicate that MBEs are 8.3 percent of all firms and 6.8 percent of the firms actually selling to government. This pattern could be interpreted as evidence that MBEs have less capacity than nonminority firms to sell to government clients (La Noue 1994). Alternatively, it may reflect the presence of discriminatory barriers that have produced a disparity between MBE availability to service government customers and the actual utilization of MBEs by governments seeking to purchase goods and services from private enterprise. This pattern of restricted MBE access to the government marketplace is consistent with the hypothesis that entrenched networks of suppliers tend to cut off MBEs from their potential customers.

Of course, there is the alternative explanation that firms that sell to government are the larger-scale, more established businesses that are overrepresented in industries such as wholesaling where MBE presence is minimal. Table 4.3 data demonstrate that white businesses selling to government (mean sales = $397,522) are larger than other small businesses and over two times larger than the average minority firm that sells to government (mean sales = $174,561). Perhaps most MBEs, because of their relative smallness and newness, simply lack the capacity to sell to government. These two conflicting hypotheses—entrenched networks keep out MBEs versus lack of capacity keeps out MBEs—are tested econometrically in Table 4.4.

The objective of the logistic regression equations in Table 4.4 is to introduce three measures of firm capacity—size (gross receipts), age, and industry—into a regression analysis delineating firms that sell to government from firms that do not. The dependent variable "government vendor" is a binary variable equal to one for firms selling to government clients and zero otherwise.

Model one (Table 4.4) demonstrates that small businesses that sell to government clients are disproportionately the established, larger-scale, white male–owned firms. Controlling for firm size and age, as well as owner gender, MBEs are less likely to sell to government than are white-owned firms, and this difference in market penetration is highly statistically significant. In other words, among two firms of equal size and age, the minority firm is less likely to sell to government than is the nonminority firm. Also noteworthy is the relevance of owner gender. Consistent with the hypothesis of entrenched networks keeping out women, firms having women owners, other things equal, are much less likely to sell to government clients than are male-owned small businesses (Table 4.4).

Model two (Table 4.4) introduces variables that identify the firm's industry affiliation, which turns out to be an important factor for delineating firms selling to government from those that do not. Controlling for other capacity measures, firms in wholesaling and retailing are found to be most likely to sell to government; firms in transportation are least likely. The hypothesis of MBEs being blocked by restrictive networks rather than lack of capacity is, once again, supported in model 2. Controlling for firm capacity, MBEs are still much less likely than white-owned firms to sell to government. This difference in market access is statistically highly significant. Controlling for all three capacity measures—firm size, age, and industry—the MBE is clearly less likely than the white-owned firm to sell to government (Table 4.4, model 2). Among firms of identical capacity, in other words, the MBEs nationwide would increase their aggregate sales if they had the same access to government clients as do white-owned small businesses. La Noue's objection to preferential procurement fails the test of empirical scrutiny.

Market Access: Selling to Private Business

Cities and states that run substantial, large-scale preferential procurement programs invariably find that very large increases in MBE bidding for city contracts accompany their affirmative efforts to increase purchases from MBE vendors. Myers and Chan (1996) report that "the set-aside era was accompanied by a significant increase in the numbers of bids submitted by MBEs" (213-14) in the State of New Jersey. Despite a substantial increase in awards to MBEs, New Jersey's preferential procurement actually produced a decline in the success rate of MBEs receiving contract awards; this occurred because the number of bids submitted by MBEs grew even faster than the number of awards they received. Among MBEs competing for state of New Jersey business, "the ratio of contracts awarded to bids offered declined from 34 percent before set-asides to 27 percent during set-asides" (Myers and Chan 1996, 213).

Why do MBEs respond so aggressively to set-aside opportunities? Government work is attractive, in part, because MBEs often have extreme difficulty penetrating the mainstream business community market. Other businesses traditionally bought few goods and services from MBEs. Among the small businesses analyzed in Tables 4.3 and 4.4, white-owned firms were much more likely than MBEs to sell to other firms: 43.7 percent of white-owned firms sell to other businesses compared with 30.2 percent of MBEs that do so (Table 4.5).

In fact, increased access to the mainstream marketplace of business clients since the 1970s has been a major factor fueling MBE growth in industries such as business services. The activities of the National Minority Supplier Development Council (NMSDC) have been enormously helpful in allowing MBEs to sell to corporate America. The efforts of corporate America to develop and cultivate MBE suppliers are often coordinated through the NMSDC. In 1997, the NMSDC, through its 43 affiliated councils throughout the United States, had 3,500 corporate members, including most of the nation's large corporations and more than 15,000 MBE members. Large corporations seeking to expand their networks of MBE suppliers most often do so by using NMSDC as the vehicle for announcing their intentions to buy various specific products from MBEs. The MBE members, in turn, use the NMSDC to publicize the products they would like to sell to business clients. They also use NMSDC information to seek out corporations that have specific demands for goods and services that overlap with products they are selling. MBEs active in the NMSDC are disproportionately the large-scale employer firms identified earlier in this chapter as the primary source of jobs nationwide from the minority business community.

Ford Motor Company in 1996 purchased an estimated two billion dollars in goods and services from minority suppliers. According to Renaldo Jensen, director of minority supplier development at Ford, the initial steps, which necessitated shaking up existing supplier relations, were the most difficult part of integrating MBE suppliers into Ford's operations. "It's difficult to get buyers within a company to accept new suppliers," stated Jensen (Minority Supplier News 1997, 3).

Jensen's experience is the crux of the problem that MBEs face as they attempt to become suppliers to other businesses. The status quo networks, which have traditionally excluded minority businesses, tend to resist change. An alternative explanation for low MBE participation, paralleling La Noue's explanation of low MBE involvement in government procurement, is that minority firms lack the capacity to sell to other businesses. Among small businesses nationwide, MBEs on average are a smaller, younger group than other small businesses. Table 4.5 reveals that average revenues among MBEs selling to other businesses were $157,049 in 1987, less than half the corresponding sales figures ($320,362) reported by white-owned firms.

Does lack of capacity, rooted in smaller average firm size, younger firm age, and peculiar industry distribution, explain the fact that MBEs are much less likely than nonminority firms to sell to other businesses? Regression models that are the mirror image of those found in Table 4.4 were used to delineate firms with sales to other businesses from all other firms. The dependent variable, "business vendor," was a binary variable equal to one for firms selling to business clients and zero otherwise. The findings, which are not reported here, closely resemble those reported in Table 4.4. Controlling for firm age and size, MBEs are shown to have a significantly lower probability than white-owned firms of selling to business clients. Adding industry variables to this econometric exercise reveals that small businesses in manufacturing and wholesaling are the ones most prone to sell to other businesses; retail firms are the least likely to sell to business clients. Controlling for capacity differences does not erase the glaring fact that white male–owned small firms of identical industry, size, and age are much more likely than MBEs and women-owned firms to sell to other businesses. Entrenched networks, not firm capacity differences, are at the root of these large differentials in market access.

CONCLUSIONS

Opening up mainstream markets to MBEs has generated rapid growth in sales and the number of firms and paid employees. The findings of this chapter indicate that further opening up markets would lead to very substantial gains for MBEs. Opening markets for selling to other businesses has the greatest potential for generating MBE growth in sales, employment, and number of firms. Extension of the successful NMSDC model to a broader segment of the nation's business community would generate a large potential payoff. If MBEs and white-owned firms having equal capacity also enjoyed equal access to the business supplier market, the resultant growth opportunities for minority business would be enormous. If the barriers can be removed by shaking up the entrenched networks, then rapid MBE growth and job creation will continue into the future.

Providing MBEs and white-owned firms equal access to government clients would also generate a large boost in MBE sales and employment totals. However, even if the entire government sector became a race-neutral purchaser of goods and services (instead of its 1987 status of limited market access for MBEs), it would still be playing the role of a passive participant in private business–sector processes that limit MBE market access. A more affirmative effort to buy from MBE vendors would be necessary to offset private-sector discriminatory processes that reduce the size and scope of the minority business community. This would potentially reduce the limited access to markets that is constraining MBE growth. Yet only a few cities have attempted to move boldly to equalize opportunities for MBEs (Bates 1997).

Simply stated, the crux of the matter is this: among two construction firms of identical size and age, the MBE has somewhat less access to government work and much less access to the private-business marketplace than does the white-owned firm. That is why programs that seek to expand MBE access to partially closed markets are of such importance to firm growth and job generation. Opening up mainstream markets generates rapid growth in numbers of MBEs as well as substantial employment and revenue growth. Also the MBEs serving mainstream markets are precisely the firms that are most likely to hire actively in low-income minority communities.

Rulings by the federal judiciary are seriously threatening this trend toward expanded market access. In part, the rulings use concepts, such as limited MBE capacity, that are not based on facts. MBE progress is not predicated on preferential access. What is needed is a removal of the barriers that disproportionately handicap MBEs. If government were simply to achieve a state of equal opportunity in the sense that MBEs and white-owned firms of equal capacity enjoyed equal access to all classes of clients—households, governments, and business—then MBEs would be assured a future trajectory of rapid sales growth and job generation.

1. Throughout this chapter, the term "minority" refers to blacks, Hispanics, Asians, Pacific Islanders, and Native Americans. The term "white" or "non-minority" refers to non-Hispanic whites.

2. For discussion of access to capital, see Bates 1993 and Bates 1997.

3. It should be noted that the Census Bureau time-series statistics have a certain randomness in them, due to inconsistencies in the way the Bureau collects data. Thus, the growth in jobs in the black business sector between 1987 and 1992 is more accurately thought of as an increase to 345,193, with a margin of error of 7,000 jobs.

4. Census Bureau survey estimates of MBE firm numbers include subchapter S corporations but exclude subchapter C corporations.

5. Regarding black businesses only, concrete data for Atlanta provide insights into how severe this undercount may be. Boston and Ross estimate that, by omitting subchapter C corporations from its survey universe, census data underestimated the employment of Atlanta area black-owned firms by as much as 50 percent (1997, 342). Because Atlanta's black business community ranks as one of the nation's most sophisticated and rapidly growing (Boston 1997a), the employee undercount applicable to Atlanta may be relatively larger than the black business employee undercount nationwide. The range into which the undercount can reasonably be assumed to fall is 25 to 50 percent. This implies that black firms, nationwide, had between 431,491 and 517,790 paid employees.

6. The response rate in the Joint Center study was 20%.

7. "Weighted" firm statistics are reported throughout this chapter, meaning that the numbers cited are representative of "all" small firms operating in 1987 in the United States. Mean overall MBE sales reported in this chapter are higher than those reported in applicable Census Bureau publications. The restrictive editing practices applied to the CBO data base, which account for this result, are described in detail in Bates (1997). Briefly, Census Bureau publications count a person as a "small business" if that person filed an income tax return showing gross self-employment revenues of $500 or more. This study tries to lessen the presence of casual self-employment in the small business data by applying a higher gross revenue cutoff: small businesses included in tables one through five of this chapter are always taken from Census Bureau sources, but they include only those firms reporting gross revenues $5,000 or more in 1987. Further, all of these firms filed a small business income tax return with the IRS in 1987, either as proprietorship, a partnership, or a corporation. (Also see Nucci 1992.)

Bates, Timothy. 1993. *Banking on Black Enterprise.* Washington, D.C.: Joint Center for Political and Economic Studies.

Bates, Timothy. 1994. "Utilization of Minority Employees in Small Business: A Comparison of Nonminority and Black-Owned Urban Enterprises." *The Review of Black Political Economy* 23 (1, Summer):113–121.

Bates, Timothy. 1995a."Self-Employment Across Industry Groups." *Journal of Business Venturing* 10 (6, January):143–156.

Bates, Timothy. 1995b. "Small Businesses Appear to Benefit from State and Local Government Economic Development Assistance." *Urban Affairs Review* 31 (2, November):206–225.

Bates, Timothy. 1995c. "Why Do Minority Business Development Programs Generate So Little Minority Business Development?" *Economic Development Quarterly* 9 (1, February):3–14.

Bates, Timothy. 1997. *Race, Upward Mobility, and Self-Employment: An Illusive American Dream.* Baltimore: Johns Hopkins University Press.

Bates, Timothy, and David Howell. 1998. "The Declining Status of African American Men in the New York Construction Industry." *Economic Development Quarterly* 12 (1, February):88–100.

Bates, Timothy, and Darrell Williams. 1993. "Racial Politics: Does It Pay?" *Social Science Quarterly* 74 (3 September):507–522.

Bates, Timothy, and Darrell Williams. 1995. "Preferential Procurement Programs and Minority-Owned Businesses." *Journal of Urban Affairs* 17 (1):1–17.

Boston, Thomas. 1995. "Characteristics of Black-Owned Corporations in Atlanta with Comments on the SMOBE Undercount." *The Review of Black Political Economy* 23 (4, Spring):85–99.

Boston, Thomas. 1997a. *Strict Scrutiny: Minority Set-Asides and African American Entrepreneurship.* New York: Routledge.

Boston, Thomas. 1997b. "Black Business Can Make the Difference." *Black Enterprise* 27 (8, March):21.

Boston, Thomas, and Catherine Ross. 1997. "Location Preferences of Successful African American-Owned Businesses in Atlanta." In *The Inner City,* ed. Thomas Boston and Catherine Ross. New Brunswick, NJ: Transaction Publishers.

Carter, D., and R. Wilson. 1992. *Minorities in Higher Education*. Washington, D.C.: American Council on Higher Education.

Carter, D., and R. Wilson. 1995. *Minorities in Higher Education*. Washington, D.C.: American Council on Higher Education.

D'Souza, Dinesh. 1995. "Work and the African American." *The American Enterprise* 6 (5, October):33–34.

"Ford Purchases from MBEs Reach a Record $2 Billion." 1997. *Minority Supplier News.* Winter:1, 3.

Granovetter, Mark. 1994. *Getting a Job: A Study in Careers and Contracts.* Chicago: University of Chicago Press.

Holsey, Albon. 1938. "Seventy-Five Years of Negro Business." *Crisis* 45 (7):241–242.

Jaynes, Gerald, and Robin Williams. 1989. *A Common Destiny: Blacks and American Society.* Washington, D.C.: National Academy Press.

La Noue, George. 1994. "Standards for the Second Generation of *Croson*-Inspired Disparity Studies." *The Urban Lawyer* 26 (3, Summer): 485–540.

Myers, Samuel, and Tsze Chan. 1996. "Who Benefits from Minority Set-Asides? The Case of New Jersey," *Journal of Policy Analysis and Management* 15 (2):202–226.

Nucci, Alfred. 1992. "The Characteristics of Business Owners Data Base." Discussion paper, U.S. Bureau of the Census Center for Economic Studies.

Sawicki, David, and Mitch Moody. 1997. "Deja-vu All Over Again: Porter's Model of Inner City Redevelopment." In *The Inner City*, ed. Thomas Boston and Catherine Ross. New Brunswick, NJ: Transaction Publishers.

Simms, Margaret, and Winston Allen. 1997. "Is the Inner City Competitive?" In *The Inner City*, ed. Thomas Boston and Catherine Ross. New Brunswick, NJ: Transaction Publishers.

Turner, Susan. 1997. "Barriers to a Better Break: Wages, Race and Space in Metropolitan Detroit." *Journal of Urban Affairs* 19 (2):123–141.

U.S. Bureau of the Census. 1990. *Survey of Minority-Owned Business Enterprises: Black.* Washington, D.C.: U.S. Government Printing Office.

U.S. Bureau of the Census. 1996. *Survey of Minority-Owned Business Enterprises: Black.* Washington, D.C.: U.S. Government Printing Office.

Waldinger, Roger, and Thomas Bailey. 1991. "The Continuing Significance of

Race: Racial Conflict and Racial Discrimination in Construction." *Politics and Society* 19 (3):291–321.

Weems, Robert. 1994. "A Crumbling Legacy: The Decline of African American Insurance Companies in Contemporary America." *The Review of Black Political Economy* 23 (2, Fall): 25–38.

Table 4.1

Black-Owned Businesses Formed Nationwide from 1979 to 1987

	Young Firms Having 10 or More Paid Employees	All Young Firms
1987 Sales (mean)	$1,406,977	$64,526
Number of Employees in 1987 (mean)	27.1	0.7
Total Financial Capital* (mean)	$134,753	$14,226
Still Operating in Late 1991	91.9%	73.6%
With College-Educated Owners	66.6%	54.1%

Source: Characteristics of Business Owners data base.
*At date of firm start-up.

Table 4.2

Minority Composition of Labor Force for Small Businesses With Paid Employees, 1992

	Black-Owned Firms (%)	Other Minority-Owned Firms (%)	Majority-Owned Firms (%)
Minority Percentage of Employees			
90 percent or more	67.9	47.6	9.9
51 percent or more	79.1	61.7	15.8
26 percent or more	86.6	73.9	22.9
25 percent or less	13.4	26.1	77.1

Source: Characteristics of Business Owners data base.

Table 4.3

Sales to Governmental Units by Small Businesses, by Race of Firm Owner

	All	With Sales to Government	No Sales to Government
Minority-Owned Firms			
1987 Sales (mean)	$102,024	$174,561	$91,956
Started in 1986, 1987	37.5%	35.6%	37.7%
Still Operating in Late 1991	79.4%	85.7%	78.5%
With Sales to Other Firms	30.2%	63.1%	25.7%
With Sales to Government	12.2%	100%	0
Male-Owned	72.7%	76.7%	72.2%
White-Owned firms			
1987 Sales (mean)	$210,578	$397,522	$177,822
Started in 1986, 1987	31.7%	26.9%	32.5%
Still Operating in Late 1991	80.9%	89.3%	79.4%
With Sales to Other Firms	43.7%	73.9%	38.3%
With Sales to Government	15.0%	100%	0
Male-Owned	75.9%	81.9%	74.9%

Source: Characteristics of Business Owners data base.

Table 4.4

Differences Between Firms That Sell to Government Clients and Those That Do Not: Logistic Regression

	Model #1 Regression Coefficient (standard error)	Model #2 Regression Coefficient (standard error)	Variable Mean
Constant	-1.984* (.030)	-2.052* (.036)	—
1987 Sales	.0006* (.0001)	.0005* (.0001)	20.163
Young Firm	-.237* (.028)	-.239* (.028)	.322
Minority Owner	-.207* (.030)	-.220* (.049)	.083
Male Owner	.387* (.031)	.430* (.032)	.757
Construction	—	-.177* (.043)	.139
Manufacturing	—	.127 (.068)	.035
Wholesale	—	.378* (.061)	.038
Transportation	—	-.386* (.061)	.045
Retail	—	.444* (.036)	.173
Skilled Services	—	-.115* (.034)	.300
n	52,491	52,491	
-2 Log L	43,563	43,182	
Chi Square	367.0	748.2	

Notes: *1987 Sales:* This variable measures 1987 gross sales revenues of firms, divided by 10,000. Thus "1987 sales = 20.163" means that gross sales were $201,630. *Young Firm:* Firms in operation for two years or less. *Skilled Services*—This includes firms operating in professional service fields, finance, insurance, real estate, and business services areas. Business service firms are those selling services that are often bought by other businesses; common examples include ad agencies, computer software firms, personnel firms, and protective service vendors.
*Statistically significant at the .05 level.

Table 4.5

Sales to Other Businesses for Small Businesses Nationwide, by Race of Firm Owner

	All	With Sales to Other Firms	With No Sales to Other Firms
Minority-Owned firms			
1987 sales (mean)	$102,024	$157,049	$78,161
Started in 1986, 1987	37.5%	38.3%	37.1%
Still Operating in late 1991	79.4%	84.5%	77.2%
With Sales to Other Firms	30.2%	100%	0%
With Sales to Government	12.2%	25.4%	6.5%
Male-Owned	72.7%	79.6%	69.7%
White-Owned Firms			
1987 Sales (mean)	$210,578	$320,362	$125,794
Started in 1986, 1987	31.7%	32.1%	31.4%
Still Operating in Late 1991	80.9%	84.6%	78.1%
With Sales to Other Firms	43.7%	100%	0%
With Sales to Government	15.0%	25.4%	6.9%
Male-Owned	75.9%	81.8%	71.4%

Source: Characteristics of Business Owners data base.

The Impact of Economic Development Policy on Black-Owned Enterprises

Randall W. Eberts and Edward B. Montgomery

This chapter addresses the issue of whether economic development incentives affect the location and expansion of black-owned businesses, and thus whether this form of government assistance is effective for promoting black employment and entrepreneurship.[1] We explore various issues regarding the number of jobs generated by black-owned businesses, the determinants of job creation by black-owned firms in metropolitan areas, and the propensity of black-owned firms to locate in central cities versus suburbs.

Successful black-owned enterprises benefit the communities in which they are located in several ways. Black-owned firms hire black workers, upwards of 90 percent of their employees according to Bates (1994). Black-owned businesses located in neighborhoods with high concentrations of African Americans constitute an important source of jobs for these residents.[2] The presence of successful locally controlled black-owned firms in black neighborhoods also may offer residents the opportunity to take greater control of the economic future of their neighborhoods and communities by creating wealth that can be re-invested locally. One source of assistance to these businesses is the tax incentives and other subsidies that many state and local governments offer to attract businesses. To the extent that this form of government assistance nurtures the startup and growth of black-owned businesses, it can also benefit the neighborhoods in which these businesses are located.

We begin with a description of the types of government assistance to small businesses. Following that is a review of the literature that evaluates the effect of economic development on business location and expansion decisions. In the next section, we describe the two major data sets used to analyze the trends in and determinants of black-owned business formation and employment growth. Next, we provide an overview of the characteristics of black-owned businesses nationwide and by state and metropolitan area and examine various factors that affect the distribution of black-owned businesses among and within metropolitan areas. We then estimate the effect of various state and local characteristics on the employment of black-owned businesses in metropolitan areas, compared with their effects on other small businesses in these same areas. Finally, we discuss the implications of these results for the creation of economic development incentives.

GOVERNMENT ASSISTANCE TO SMALL BUSINESSES

Government assistance to small businesses takes two basic forms. The first is business-specific in that assistance is extended to small businesses with little regard for where they are located. This assistance comes primarily from federal programs administered by the Small Business Administration (SBA). The SBA offers loans and technical assistance to all eligible small businesses regardless of the race or ethnicity of the owners. Technical assistance may include specialized training, professional consultant assistance, and high-level executive development. In addition to small businesses that meet the general qualification criteria, special consideration is given to small disadvantaged businesses, low-income individuals, and small businesses in labor-surplus areas or areas with a high proportion of low-income individuals (U.S. SBA 1997).

The SBA also administers the Minority Enterprise Development Program (MED), a program that specifically targets minority-owned businesses. MED, sometimes referred to as the 8(a) program, allows minority-owned small businesses to receive government contracts on a sole-source or limited competition basis. Since its inception in 1968, the 8(a) program has awarded approximately 460,296 contracts worth about $73 billion dollars. During the 1997 fiscal year alone, 6,183 minority-owned businesses received $2.7 billion in 8(a) funds, accounting for 42 percent of their total revenue. State and local governments also provide contracting and procurement opportunities for minority-owned businesses.[3]

The second source of government assistance to black-owned businesses, and the focus of this chapter, consists of the economic development initiatives offered by state and local governments. Most economic development programs do not target minority businesses, but provide assistance to any business that meets their criteria. Economic development incentive programs are much more site- or area-specific than are the previously described SBA programs. A major goal of state and local government programs is to create and attract good jobs to their jurisdictions, regardless of whether these jobs are generated by minority businesses. These programs offer tax breaks, publicly subsidized worker training programs, loans, and a host of other incentives.

The last two decades have witnessed an explosion in the number of economic development instruments and the amount of public dollars used to assist businesses. State appropriations peaked in 1988 at nearly $1 billion, and this figure does not even include local government expenditures (National Association of State Development Agencies 1988). The incentives for attracting large companies have become increasingly large. Recently, Mercedes Benz was reportedly given $250 million to locate a plant in Alabama, and BMW was courted by South Carolina with incentives worth $130 million to locate a facility there. Some of these packages amount to more than $100,000 per job created, usually over a twenty-year program horizon.

A popular concept used to rejuvenate high unemployment areas is enterprise zones. Nearly 3,000 enterprise zones have been established in 37 states. In addition, the federal government has created 11 Empowerment Zones and 99 Enterprise Communities with the passage of the Empowerment Zone and Enterprise Community Act in 1993 (Wilder and Rubin 1996).

Whether enterprise zones effectively stimulate economic development in distressed areas as intended is not clear from the few evaluations that have been conducted. The results vary by program and evaluation methodology. For example, Papke (1994) found that enterprise zones in Indiana reduced unemployment claims and increased business investment. Alm and Hart (1998) concluded that the enterprise zone program in Colorado tended to improve employment conditions and increase the level but not the growth rate of per capita income in zone areas. However, effects were mixed across zones as some counties saw a general improvement while others did not. Using a survey method, Rubin (1990) examined the extensive enterprise zone program in New Jersey and found it to be highly successful in that the benefits from tax revenues exceeded the program costs. However, Boarnet and Bogart (1996), examining the same data but using a different methodology, found no evidence that the urban enterprise zone program had a positive effect on total municipal employment, employment in various sectors, or municipal property values.

The effectiveness of economic development programs in creating jobs in general and in assisting black-owned businesses in particular depends on satisfying several conditions. First, the business costs that are affected by economic development incentives, such as property taxes, training costs, and infrastructure costs, must be large enough relative to other costs to influence business location. For example, Bartik (1991) shows that businesses pay 14 times more for labor than they spend on state and local taxes. Furthermore, Bartik demonstrates that regional variations in construction, energy, and labor costs are often larger than variations in state and local taxes and incentives. Therefore, economic development initiatives that target only taxes, such as local property tax abatement, will have much less influence than those that help reduce labor costs.

Second, the business must be in an industry that is targeted by economic development efforts. In most cases, economic development assistance is targeted to export-based businesses—those that bring dollars into a region by selling products or services outside the region. Manufacturing is considered the primary export-based activity, although some services, such as tourism and extra-regional legal and medical organizations, also may be included. As shown later in this chapter, the percentage of black-owned firms in these activities is quite small;[4] consequently, on this basis alone, black-owned firms will have a small chance of receiving economic development assistance.

Third, businesses must be located in areas subject to economic development initiatives. Given the objective of economic development programs to stimulate economic growth in lagging areas, it is reasonable to assume that greater efforts would be exerted in more distressed areas. However, in recent years, many growing areas have also pursued active economic development initiatives so as not to fall behind other regions, resulting in intense competition among some states and localities. Burstein and Rolnick (1995) have criticized what they have called the "economic war among the states." Therefore, whether or not economic development efforts are concentrated in distressed areas remains an open issue. The results of the literature are mixed. Several studies, including Fosler (1988), Eisinger (1988), and Clarke (1986), to name a few, conclude that economic development efforts are concentrated in areas with higher unemployment, lower per capita income, and significant hardships due to economic restructuring. Yet, even within the group of studies that focus on government expenditures on economic development efforts, there is disagreement about whether economic conditions and economic development initiatives are related. Grady (1987) and Hanson (1993) found little correlation between changes in the level of economic distress and expanded use of economic development incentives at the state level, and Green and Fleischman (1991) found no such correlation for central cities.

The fourth condition for economic development efforts to affect business decisions, and thus effectively assist businesses, is for the combination of state and local incentives received by a firm to have a net positive effect on its internal rate of return. Fisher and Peters (1998) evaluate the effectiveness of taxes and incentives from the perspective of the firm's balance sheet. In addition, unlike most econometric studies that examine the effect of fiscal variables on business costs, they include both the tax side of government and the incentive side. Their method is based on a hypothetical firm's actual income by replicating operating ratios, balance sheets, and income and tax statements.

Using their hypothetical firm approach, Fisher and Peters address two questions: (1) how substantial is the regional variation in taxes and incentives, and (2) do states and cities attempt to design fiscal packages that offset the consequences of economically distressed areas. The second question goes beyond the studies that look only at the distribution of government expenditures and considers the net effect of these expenditures on a firm's profits. These two questions are pertinent for understanding how economic development efforts may affect black-owned businesses located in economically distressed areas.

With respect to the first question, Fisher and Peters find substantial variation among states and cities in returns on investment after including basic taxes and incentives. They report that the tax burden on manufacturers was three times as large in the highest tax state as in the lowest tax state. On the incentive side of the equation, several states offered substantial investment or job tax credits, as high as 45 percent of the before-incentive state and local tax burden. Yet, despite the potentially offsetting effect, they show that incentives generally do not reduce regional variation, but accentuate it. Fisher and Peters conclude that there is sufficient variation in taxes and incentives to figure into a business's location decisions.

With respect to the second issue, Fisher and Peters find no evidence that state taxes and incentives favor businesses in high unemployment areas. On the contrary, they find that state tax systems yield higher returns to firms in states with lower unemployment. This rather perverse effect of state taxes from an economic development policy perspective is largely offset by state tax credits and by local taxes and tax incentives. The authors conclude: "The end result is a spatial pattern of returns on new investment that has little or no bearing to the spatial pattern of unemployment among cities" (Fisher and Peters 1998, 200).

Based on these four conditions and the general findings from previous studies, it appears that even if black-owned firms were concentrated in high unemployment areas, economic development policies as they now stand would not necessarily target these businesses for favorable fiscal incentives over similar businesses in low unemployment areas. This is not to say that black-owned businesses would not receive favorable tax breaks or job tax credits if they chose to move into an enterprise zone, for example. Furthermore, regardless of whether more assistance is available in distressed areas, Fisher and Peters show that if a firm received the full package of economic incentives from each state, it would find that locating in a high unemployment area versus a low unemployment area would make little difference to its internal rate of return.

Consideration of these four conditions and the studies that relate to them is helpful in anticipating the effects of state and local fiscal structures on the behavior of firms. To explore the relationship between economic development initiatives and the behavior of black-owned businesses, one would ideally like information on how these tax and incentive packages actually affect the costs and profits of specific firms. Absent these data, we estimate the effect of various business costs, such as labor and energy costs and taxes, on black-owned business growth vis-à-vis overall small business growth. If these factors are statistically related to employment change, then state and local policies designed to reduce these costs may be effective. If these factors have little effect on business performance, then taxes and incentives would not have much effect. We compare the estimated effects of these factors on black-owned businesses versus all businesses.

DATA

The study uses the Survey of Minority-Owned Business Enterprises (SMOBE) and the Characteristics of Business Owners (CBO) survey for both 1987 and 1992 to examine the characteristics of black-owned businesses and their relationship to local economic factors. The SMOBE is a survey of the self-employed and smaller establishments that comprise about 30 percent of the nation's self-employed and payroll workers.[5] This data set identifies the ownership of companies by minority status. The 1992 survey, released in 1996, provides the most recent picture of the characteristics of black-owned businesses. Data from the CBO is used to compile a group of businesses of comparable size and type to those in the SMOBE, but without regard to the characteristics of the owners. Combining the SMOBE with the CBO permits the comparison of black-owned businesses to all businesses of similar size and type. For both data sets, only small businesses with fewer than 300 employees are included in the analysis.

The analysis focuses on the performance of black-owned firms with paid employees within metropolitan areas. We consider those with paid employees instead of self-employed persons because businesses with employees are more likely to create additional jobs within the metropolitan area and to be influenced by variations in economic development incentives and in business costs across markets. The business decisions of the self-employed appear to be guided more by personal concerns. Studies of the self-employed suggest that age, education, and years of experience in the industry in which they start their businesses are major characteristics of those who start small businesses (Fairlie and Meyer 1994). These attributes have little to do with economic incentives and even with local cost advantages. Metropolitan areas are used as the unit of analysis because they approximate more than any other geographical definition the characteristics of local labor markets and thus local economies.

The 1992 and 1987 SMOBE and CBO surveys are merged to assess net changes in various measures of activities of black-owned companies at the metropolitan level. These changes in black-owned companies are then related to attributes of the metropolitan area in which they are located. As a means of comparing the relative magnitudes of the effect of these factors on black-owned businesses, we also estimate the effect of these factors on employment changes in all firms of comparable size and type.

CHARACTERISTICS OF BLACK-OWNED FIRMS

National Perspective

Before focusing on businesses within metropolitan areas, we consider the characteristics and spatial distribution of black-owned businesses nationally. Throughout this chapter, unless otherwise specified, "small businesses" are those with the same characteristics as the SMOBE firms (i.e., proprietorships, partnerships, and subchapter S corporations) with paid employees. The survey reveals that blacks own a disproportionately small share of businesses of all sizes with payrolls and that these businesses are typically smaller, pay lower salaries to their employees, and are less capitalized than similar businesses owned by nonblacks. The 1992 survey reports that blacks were the primary owners of 64,478 firms with 345,193 paid employees,[6] which accounts for about 2 percent of all similarly defined businesses. This proportion falls short of blacks' 10 percent share of total payroll employment and their 11 percent share of the working age population. In fact, among the major minority groups, blacks are least represented in business ownership. Of the 345,105 minority-owned firms with paid employees in 1992, 20 percent were owned by blacks, 37 percent by Hispanics, and 43 percent by Native Americans, Asians, and Pacific Islanders combined. When self-employed entrepreneurs are included, the percentage of minority-owned firms owned by blacks increases to 31 percent.

Black-owned small businesses comprise an even smaller share of the total employees, sales, and payroll of all small businesses. While 2.06 percent of all small firms are owned by blacks, only 1.26 percent of all employees of small firms work for black-owned firms, and they receive only 0.92 percent of all payroll (table 5.1). The average number of employees in black-owned companies is 5.35, while the average number in all companies is 8.74 (table 5.2). Pay per employee is also less for black-owned firms than for all firms. Black-owned firms pay $13,924 per employee, which is 72 percent of the average amount paid by all companies. Sales per employee of black-owned firms are also smaller than the average for all firms. They average $65,440, which is 62 percent of the $106,084 received by all firms.

The representation of black-owned firms varies by industry (as shown in Table 5.2), but in none of the major one-digit sectors are blacks on a par with the overall sample.[7] Black-owned businesses in the retail sector hire the largest staff of the major one-digit sectors, averaging 6.86 employees and slightly edging out manufacturing. Black-owned firms in the wholesale sector have the highest payroll and sales per employee, paying out $23,533 per employee and bringing in $317,425 per employee. The wholesale sector has the narrowest gap in average compensation and average sales between black-owned firms and firms generally. Black-owned firms pay their employees 88 percent of the average and receive in sales per employee 85 percent of the average.

The largest percentage of black-owned firms is found in the services sector, as shown in table 5.3. In 1992, 46.7 percent of black-owned firms operated in that sector.[8] Within the services sector, business services had the highest concentration of black-owned firms, accounting for 23 percent of all black-owned firms and 42 percent of all employment in black-owned firms. Health services accounted for 21 percent of the firms, 30 percent of sales, but only 17 percent of employment. Black-owned wholesale businesses, which paid the highest salary per employee, accounted for only 2.3 percent of black-owned firms and 2.5 percent of the paid employees of black-owned firms.

The number of black-owned firms as a percentage of all firms increased slightly between the two survey years, from 1.84 percent in 1987 to 2.06 in 1992 (table 5.1). However, this increase in share does not reflect an increase in the number of black-owned businesses. Rather, both the total number of firms and the number of black-owned firms (with paid employees) declined during the five-year period, but the decrease was smaller for black-owned firms (9.0 percent versus 18.5 percent) (table 5.4). At the same time, employment in black-owned firms increased 56.6 percent, and employment in all firms increased 38.0 percent. The rate of increase in employment for black-owned businesses during the 1987-1992 period was the largest recorded by the census since it began keeping such records in 1972.

Between 1987 and 1992, the finance, insurance, and real estate (FIRE) sector had the largest increase both in the number of black-owned firms (32.3 percent) and in employment by these firms (196.5 percent) (table 5.4). The transportation, communications, and public utilities sector (TCPU) also experienced significant job growth for black-owned firms. The number of employees of black-owned firms increased by 104.9 percent in this sector, a faster growth rate than that of all firms in this category.

States and Metropolitan Areas

As a percentage of total employment, employment in black-owned firms is concentrated in the South and in California. The states along the Atlantic Ocean from Maryland to Florida and then along the Gulf of Mexico to Louisiana claim 40 percent of all employees of black-owned firms. The concentration of black-owned firms, that is the ratio of black-owned firms to all comparable firms, within these states ranges from 6.4 percent in Maryland to 1.6 percent in North Carolina. Michigan, Texas, and California are next highest in concentration of firms and, because of their large populations, account for 25 percent of the employees of black-owned firms.

To examine more closely the correlation between the concentration of black-owned firms and demographic characteristics, we calculated the ratio of the number of employees of black-owned firms to the number of employees in all comparable firms and used this ratio with two population measures: total population of the metropolitan area and the black share of total metropolitan population. The analysis was carried out for all metropolitan statistical areas (MSAs) defined in 1992. We found that the black share of the population far outweighed population size in explaining differences across MSAs in the percentage of businesses that were black-owned (table 5.5). For all industries, a one standard deviation increase in the percentage of an MSA's working age population (ages 16-65) that is black raises the percentage of businesses that are black-owned 10 times more than does a one standard deviation increase in population size.[9] Black population share explained more of the variation in the percentage of black-owned firms than did population size for each major sector, although the relative magnitudes varied across sectors. Neither percentage black nor population size explained the relative incidence of black-owned manufacturing and wholesaling. On the other hand, retailing was the only sector in which there was a statistically significant relationship between population size and the share of black-owned firms, which may reflect the importance of the overall market size to the retail businesses.

Central City–Suburban Patterns of Black-Owned Businesses

To examine the geographical distribution of black-owned firms within metropolitan areas, we focused on 21 of the largest MSAs. Examining the difference in the concentration of black-owned firms between central cities and suburbs within MSAs allows us to gain additional insight into the relationship between the location of black-owned businesses and local economic conditions. We used a measure of the relative concentration of black-owned firms within central cities and suburbs. The relative concentration ratio is calculated as the ratio of black-owned firms to all firms in the central city divided by black-owned firms as a percentage of all firms in the suburbs. The employment concentration ratio is the same except that we substituted paid employment for number of firms. A relative firm concentration ratio greater than one indicates that the percentage of black-owned firms in the central city is larger than the percentage in the suburbs, reflecting a greater concentration of black-owned firms in central cities.

As shown in table 5.6, the concentration ratio is larger when measured as the number of firms than when measured as the number of employees. In the 21 MSAs examined in 1992 (table 5.6), black-owned firms had a concentration ratio of 2.25, indicating that they are 2.25 times more concentrated in central cities than in suburbs. Yet, the central city's ratio of employees of black-owned firms to employees of all firms was more on a par with the suburbs' ratio, being only 1.14 times more concentrated. The two concentration ratios are explained by the fact that black-owned firms located in central cities on average hire fewer employees than do black-owned firms in the suburbs. Central-city black-owned businesses have an average of 5.87 employees on their payrolls, while suburban black-owned firms average 7.86 employees.

The concentration of black-owned firms varies widely among the selected MSAs. Detroit has the highest concentration of black-owned firms and employment by black-owned firms of any of the central cities included in the sample. Within the Detroit MSA, the ratio of the number of black-owned firms to the number of all comparable firms is 12 times higher in the central city than in the suburbs. For employment of black-owned businesses, the ratio is five times higher in Detroit's central city than outside it. Even with these large spatial differences, the percentage of black-owned firms is still relatively small, and their share of employment is even smaller. Twenty percent of firms in the city of Detroit were owned by blacks and accounted for 8 percent of employment.[11] Metropolitan statistical areas, such as Chicago and St. Louis, have more modest concentration ratios of less than five, but these MSAs still exhibit a wide gap in the share of black-owned businesses in inner versus outer cities. In a few MSAs—for example, Houston, Miami, and Baltimore—employees of black-owned firms are relatively more prevalent in suburbs than in central cities, although black ownership in these MSAs is still more concentrated in the central cities.

During the five-year period between 1987 and 1992, black-owned firms became less concentrated in several of the 21 central cities, suggesting that black-owned firms are becoming more established in the suburbs. For the overall sample, the concentration ratios for both black-owned firms and employees of black-owned firms declined over the time period. With respect to individual MSAs, the concentration ratios of the number of firms declined for 13 of the 21 MSAs, and the concentration ratios for the number of employees of black-owned firms declined for 11 MSAs. In Detroit, the concentration ratio declined slightly for black-owned firms, from 16 to 12, and substantially, from 11 to 5, for employment of black-owned firms. Of those MSAs that did not experience a decline in the concentration ratios, few showed any substantial increase in the prevalence of black-owned firms in central cities. The exception was Philadelphia, which experienced one of the largest gains in concentration of employees of black-owned firms, with an increase in the concentration ratio from 1.85 to 3.06.

The findings suggest that black-owned businesses and jobs for blacks have moved away from central cities to suburbs, while at the same time blacks, particularly those who are economically disadvantaged, remain highly concentrated in central cities.[12] These results are consistent with the trends that have led to the concern about spatial mismatch and the decline of jobs for inner-city residents.

Before examining the spatial distribution of black-owned firms between central cities and suburbs, we first consider whether black businesses are more prevalent in more distressed areas. If indeed economic development efforts are directed more toward areas with higher unemployment and lower per capita income, as some studies have shown, then a higher concentration of black-owned businesses in these areas would give them more opportunity to receive economic development assistance. Using the sample of 21 MSAs, we regress the ratio of black-owned firms to all firms against the unemployment rate, the black share of total population, average per capita income, and the population size (table 5.7). Results from this simple regression suggest that the prevalence of black business ownership, measured either by the share of firms or the share of employees, is not related to the unemployment rate or to the per capita income, for this sample of MSAs.[13] Only the black share of total MSA population was related to the concentration of black ownership with any reasonable level of statistical confidence. Therefore, even if more distressed MSAs offered more economic development incentives than less distressed areas, black-owned firms would be in no better position to receive this assistance.

We next examine whether the spatial distribution of black business ownership within MSAs, specifically between central cities and suburbs, can be explained by similar factors. We compare the relative concentration of black-owned firms in central cities and suburbs to the central-city-to-suburbs ratio of unemployment rates, number of blacks, and concentration of blacks.[14] As shown in table 5.8, these three variables explained 73 percent of the variation in the relative concentration of black-owned firms in central cities versus suburbs and 39 percent of the variation in the share of employees working for black-owned firms. We find that in both cases the relative unemployment rates between central cities and suburbs and the relative share of blacks in the central city and suburban populations are positively related to the prevalence of black-owned enterprises. Furthermore, these factors have the same effect on the percentage of employees of black-owned businesses as they do on the percentage of firms that are black-owned. Referring to the beta coefficients shown in parentheses in table 5.8, we find that an increase of one standard deviation in the unemployment rate in central cities over suburbs is associated with an increase of 0.367 standard deviations in the concentration of employment in black-owned businesses. A one standard deviation increase in the ratio of the black share of central city population to the black share of suburban population is associated with an increase of 0.390 standard deviations in the relative concentration ratio. However, with respect to the percentage of black-owned firms, an increase in black population share in the central city vis-à-vis the suburbs has twice the effect on the prevalence of black-owned firms in central cities as does the relative unemployment rate.

Consequently, although there appears to be no correlation between the concentration of black ownership and economic conditions across metropolitan areas, it does appear that black-owned firms are more likely to be concentrated in central cities with relatively high unemployment rates and larger concentrations of blacks. If economic development efforts are concentrated in distressed central cities, then black-owned businesses could have a better opportunity to receive assistance from these programs.

DETERMINANTS OF BLACK-OWNED BUSINESS GROWTH IN METROPOLITAN AREAS

Seven years ago, Bates (1991) compiled a bibliography of more than 50 articles and related studies on characteristics of minority-owned businesses and the factors affecting them. Since that time, many more articles have appeared in scholarly journals. The studies, as reported by Bates, suggest that emerging black-owned firms are commonly started by educated blacks, many with college degrees, who require substantial financial investments to launch their ventures. This group of entrepreneurs contrasts sharply with the more traditional black entrepreneurs whose small scale establishments are oriented more toward retail or personal services and require relatively little capital investment (Bates 1991, 23). To be successful today, black-owned businesses increasingly need access to capital along with better educated owners, managers, and workers.

The issues facing black business people are consistent with issues confronting small business owners in general. A recent survey of small business owners in a medium-size Midwestern metropolitan area revealed that the major obstacles to starting a business were: (1) identification of the appropriate customer base, (2) access to start-up and cash-flow financing, (3) personal problems, (4) government regulations and taxes, and (5) finding qualified workers. Respondents to the survey were asked to rank these issues, and the results were tallied by the number of years the business had been in operation. Those just starting out ranked these issues in the order listed above. Those who had been in business for more than three years had a completely different ranking. They placed government regulation and taxes at the top of the list and personal problems at the bottom. Financing issues were second from the bottom and finding qualified workers was second from the top. Therefore, the factors affecting small business startup and expansion differ.[15]

As discussed in the first section of the chapter, economic development initiatives typically attempt to reduce the cost of doing business in specific locales. Thus, in order for black-owned businesses to benefit from these initiatives, the businesses must be sensitive to cost factors in their location and expansion decisions. Our analysis then relates the growth rates of employment in black-owned firms within metropolitan areas, aggregated at the one-digit industry level, to various factors that affect business costs within these areas. For comparison purposes, we used the same explanatory variables to explain net employment growth of all small firms. In this way, we can determine the relative importance of various factors to black-owned firms versus their importance to the overall group of small businesses. A more thorough investigation would take the next step and collect information about state and local economic development initiatives and relate this information to outcomes for black-owned firms. However, that effort is beyond the scope of this chapter.

Local economic conditions and attributes conducive to economic development are measured by several variables: population size, population change, state output growth, wage rates, state tax rates, educational outcomes, unionization, and public capital stock. (Table 5.1 in the appendix to this chapter contains descriptions and summary statistics of the variables.) The reasons for including these variables are self-evident, except perhaps for public capital stock. Public capital is entered to represent the services that businesses receive from access to the highway system and water and sewer services. Public infrastructure is crucial for the operation of most businesses, and expenditures for public capital typically comprise a large part of the incentives that local governments make available to attract and keep businesses.

Separate estimates are obtained for several major industry divisions and for all industries combined. The sample of MSAs varies by industry because of the occurrence of missing values. Only MSAs with a total of 20 or more paid employees of black-owned firms were included, in order to avoid large values of net percentage employment change due to small numbers.

The estimation results shown in tables 5.9 and 5.10 reveal that very few of these variables show a statistically significant relationship to the net percentage change in either all firms or in black-owned firms. Yet, these variables taken together explain as much as 76 percent of the variation in the dependent variable, which is the case for black-owned firms in the manufacturing sector. Focusing on manufacturing, which one would expect to show the highest level of sensitivity to business costs because a plant's location is not directly tied to a specific market, we find that black-owned businesses are more sensitive to the set of explanatory variables than are the sample of all firms, as judged by the R-squared. Furthermore, for most variables, the coefficients associated with black-owned firms are larger than those for all firms. For example, in the manufacturing sector, taxes appear to have nearly four times the effect on black-owned firms that they have on all firms. The presence of unions and access to public infrastructure appear to have nearly five times the effect on black-owned firms versus all firms. The coefficients for hourly wages also show a large differential between black-owned firms and all firms. However, one would expect the coefficients on wages to be negative, not positive, particularly since we have controlled for unions and educational achievement. Thus, it is difficult to attribute much meaning to this variable.

While this analysis is preliminary, it does suggest that black-owned firms are at least as sensitive to cost-related factors as are comparable firms. Consequently, economic development initiatives, to the extent to which they are offered to small businesses, could have more value to black-owned firms than to all comparable firms in reducing business costs, since it appears that business costs affect the growth rate of black-owned firms more than they affect the growth rate of firms generally. However, the analysis needs considerable refinement before these conclusions can be presented with any reasonable degree of confidence.

SUMMARY OF FINDINGS AND IMPLICATIONS FOR DEVELOPMENT OF ECONOMIC POLICY INITIATIVES

We have explored job creation by black-owned businesses and considered whether black-owned businesses can benefit from economic development policy. Since we are aware of no comprehensive data set that records which businesses actually receive assistance from economic development programs, we pursued an indirect approach. We asserted that four conditions must be met in order for businesses to receive assistance from economic development programs and for these programs to have an effect on business decisions: (1) the business costs affected by economic development incentives must be large enough to affect business location, (2) the business must be one that is targeted by the program; (3) the business must be located in an area subject to the economic development initiative; and (4) the package of state and local incentives must have net positive effect on the business' internal rate of return. With respect to these conditions, we found that across metropolitan areas the prevalence of black-owned businesses is not correlated with the economic conditions of the metropolitan area. However, within metropolitan areas, black-owned businesses are concentrated primarily in the central cities, particularly those central cities that are relatively more distressed than their suburban neighbors. Furthermore, in recent years, there has been a noticeable shift of black-owned businesses toward suburban locations. We also found that black-owned businesses in manufacturing are more sensitive to cost factors than are businesses overall. We stress that all these results are merely suggestive, and the analysis needs refinement. Yet, even if refinement to the analysis supports these preliminary results, it must be recognized that only a very small percentage of black-owned firms and employees (3.04 percent and 3.76 percent, respectively) are in the manufacturing sector. Thus, black-owned firms are grossly underrepresented in the industry that displays the greatest sensitivity to the most commonly provided economic development incentives. This fact alone would suggest that black-owned firms would not have much access to and thus would not benefit much from economic development programs.

Until it is possible to make an accurate accounting of which firms receive economic development assistance from state and local governments and how much they have benefitted from it, the question of whether this form of government assistance meets the needs of black-owned businesses will remain unanswered. According to the analysis presented in this chapter, it appears that black-owned firms do not meet all the criteria necessary to benefit as fully as possible from these programs. Consequently, it is important that other programs, such as the SBA programs that offer loans, technical assistance, and procurement set asides, are in place to assist the growth of black-owned small businesses.

The authors thank Susan Bellers, Ken Kline, Kris Kracker, and Phyllis Molhoek for their expert assistance.

1. Several studies have examined minority self-employment: characteristics, trends, financial and other barriers to starting up businesses (e.g., Bates 1993; Meyer 1990; and Fairlie and Meyer 1994).

2. Bates (1994) attributes the dominance of blacks on the payrolls of black-owned enterprises to the extensive use of informal networks to obtain jobs. It would follow then that many of these workers live in or near the neighborhoods in which the establishments are located.

3. In chapter 4 of this volume, Timothy Bates discusses the use of these programs by black-owned enterprises.

4. The database used in this study may underestimate the presence of black-owned enterprises in export-based industries since it excludes "C" corporations. Nonetheless, the overall number of minority firms, as compared to nonminority firms in these industries is still quite small.

5. Included in the universe of this survey is any activity for which an IRS form 1040, Schedule C (individual proprietorship or self-employed person); 1065 (partnership); or 1120S (subchapter S corporation) was filed. A subchapter S corporation is a special IRS designation for legally incorporated businesses with 35 or fewer shareholders. Subchapter S corporations are typically small companies, averaging 5 employees and ranging from zero to more than 300 employees. Business owners with no employees report an annual payroll, but do not report any workers on their payroll during the specified period of time (U.S. Bureau of the Census 1992).

6. The survey also shows that 556,434 blacks were self-employed, bringing the total of black-owned businesses in 1992 to 620,912.

7. These comparisons are based on the ratio of black-owned statistics to the overall sample statistics.

8. An even higher percentage, 54.4 percent, of self-employed blacks were found in the service sector.

9. Other explanatory variables, including the number of years of education of whites and blacks and the percentage change in population, were used as explanatory variables, but none was statistically significant and thus is not reported in the table.

10. The central city was defined as the largest city or cities within the MSA. For instance, Cleveland is the central city of the Cleveland-Lorain-Elyria MSA;

Chicago is the central city for the Chicago MSA.

11. It should be mentioned that the three large auto makers would not be included in this sample since they are C corporations.

12. The SMOBE is a survey of firms, not establishments, and thus may not provide a completely accurate measure of the location of the place of work. The survey was sent to the address of the owners of the business, which is not necessarily the address of the place where the work is performed. Consequently, we are not sure that the employment attributed to the place the survey was sent is the actual place that employees report to work. It may be the case that successful owners have moved their residence from the central city to the suburbs, while still keeping the place of work in the central city. It may also be the case that they took their place of work with them to the suburbs.

13. Baltimore turns out to be an outlier in the sample, with employees of black-owned firms accounting for 10 percent of total employment of comparable firms. With Baltimore included in the regression, the unemployment rate is negatively and statistically significantly related to the share of employment in black-owned firms. With Baltimore excluded, there is no statistically significant relationship.

14. The relative concentration of blacks in central cities relative to suburbs is measured as the ratio of the black share of central city population to the black share of suburban population. This measure may appear at first to be highly correlated with the ratio of the number of blacks in the central city to the number of blacks in suburbs. However, the correlation is small, with a coefficient of only 0.24. The second variable (the ratio of the number of blacks in the central city to the number of blacks in the suburbs) is included to measure the relative size of the black population in central cities versus suburbs, which is different from the relative concentration of blacks in the two areas. The means of the two variables show that while blacks are four times more concentrated in central cities than in suburbs, blacks in central cities outnumber blacks in suburbs by only 2.5 to 1.

15. W. E. Upjohn Institute for Employment Research, 1996.

Alm, James, and Julie Ann Hart. 1998. "Enterprise Zones and Economic Development in Colorado." Presented at the 1998 ASSA meetings in Chicago, Ill.

Bartik, Timothy J. 1991. *Who Benefits from State and Local Economic Development Policies?* Kalamazoo, MI: W.E. Upjohn Institute for Employment Research.

Bartik, Timothy J. 1993. "The Effects of Local Labor Demand on Individual Labor Market Outcomes for Different Demographic Groups and the Poor." W. E. Upjohn Institute for Employment Research Working Paper No. 93-0233.

Bates, Timothy. 1991. *Major Studies of Minority Business: A Bibliographic Review.* Washington, D.C.: Joint Center for Political and Economic Studies.

Bates, Timothy. 1993. *Banking on Black Enterprise.* Washington, D.C.: Joint Center for Political and Economic Studies.

Bates, Timothy. 1994. "Utilization of Minority Employees in Small Business: A Comparison of Nonminority and Black-Owned Urban Enterprises." *The Review of Black Political Economy* 23 (1, Summer):113–121.

Boarnet, Marlon G., and William T. Bogart. 1996. "Enterprise Zones and Employment: Evidence from New Jersey." *Journal of Urban Economics* 40 (2, September): 198-215.

Burstein, Melvin L., and Arthur J. Rolnick. 1995. "Congress Should End the Economic War among the States." Federal Reserve Bank of Minneapolis 1994 Annual Report. *The Region* 9 (1): 3-20.

Clarke, Marianne K. 1986. *Revitalizing State Economies.* Washington, D. C.: National Governor's Association.

Eisinger, Peter. 1988. *The Rise of the Entrepreneurial State.* Madison: University of Wisconsin Press.

Fairlie, Robert W., and Bruce D. Meyer. 1994. "The Ethnic and Racial Character of Self-Employment." National Bureau of Economic Research Working Paper No. 479 1, July.

Fisher, Peter S., and Alan H. Peters. 1998. *Industrial Incentives: Competition among American States and Cities.* Kalamazoo, MI: W.E. Upjohn Institute for Employment Research.

Fosler, R. Scott. 1988. *The New Economic Role of American States: Strategies in a Competitive World Economy.* New York: Oxford University Press.

Grady, Dennis. 1987. "State Economic Development Incentives: Why Do States Compete?" *State and Local Government Review* 19 (Fall): 86-94.

Green, Gary, and Arnold Fleischman. 1991. "Promoting Economic Development: A Comparison of Central Cities, Suburbs, and Nonmetropolitan Communities." *Urban Affairs Quarterly* 27 (September): 145-154.

Hanson, Russell. 1993. "Bidding for Business: A Second War between the States?" *Economic Development Quarterly* 7 (2): 183-198.

Meyer, Bruce. 1990. "Why Are There So Few Black Entrepreneurs?" Working Paper No. 3537, National Bureau of Economic Research.

National Association of State Development Agencies (NASDA). 1988. *1988 NASDA State Economic Development Expenditure and Salary Survey.* Washington, D.C.: NASDA.

Papke, Leslie E. 1994. "Tax Policy and Urban Development: Evidence form the Indiana Enterprise Zone Program." *Journal of Public Economics* 54 (1):37–49.

Rubin, Marilyn M. 1990. "Urban Enterprise Zones: Do They Work? Evidence from New Jersey." *Public Budgeting and Finance* 10: 3-17.

U.S. Bureau of the Census, 1992. *Survey of Minority-Owned Business Enterprises.* Washinton, D.C.: U.S. Government Printing Office.

U.S. Small Business Administration (SBA), Office of Minority Enterprise Development. 1997. *A Report to the U.S. Congress on Minority Small Business and Capital Ownership Development for Fiscal Year 1997.*

Wilder, Margaret G., and Barry M. Rubin. 1996. "Rhetoric versus Reality: A Review of Studies on State Enterprise Zone Programs." *Journal of the American Planning Association* 62 (4): 473-491.

W. E. Upjohn Institute for Employment Research. 1996. "Assessment of the Importance of Small Business to Kalamazoo County's Economy and the Adequacy of Services to Nurture Small Business Formation." Kalamazoo, MI, October.

Table 5.1

Black-Owned Firms as a Percentage of Total Firms, by Industry Category, 1992 and 1987

Category	1992					1987				
	Self-Employed	Firms	Value	Employees	Payroll	Self-Employed	Firms	Value	Employees	Payroll
All	3.94	2.06	0.78	1.26	0.92	3.59	1.84	0.83	1.11	0.92
Mining	0.32	0.40	0.17	0.19	0.16	0.25	0.36	0.37	0.40	0.28
Construction	2.57	1.83	0.75	1.25	0.85	2.36	1.96	0.87	1.45	1.09
Manufacturing	2.41	1.19	0.26	0.35	0.29	2.03	1.57	0.42	0.56	0.51
TCPU[a]	7.72	3.52	1.20	1.68	1.22	6.96	3.75	1.31	1.44	1.24
Wholesale	1.64	0.88	0.44	0.50	0.43	1.81	0.87	0.42	0.53	0.45
Retail	4.25	1.68	0.84	1.19	0.91	3.73	1.68	0.98	1.06	1.00
FIRE[b]	2.22	1.34	1.20	1.01	0.90	2.44	1.10	0.52	0.61	0.51
Services	4.54	2.70	1.28	1.83	1.37	3.81	2.45	1.17	1.42	1.19

Source: Survey of Minority-Owned Business Enterprises, 1987, 1992.

Notes: Firms are defined as partnerships and subchapter S corporations with paid employees. Some caution should be used in comparing 1987 and 1992 because of changes in the collection of the data and changes in tax laws affecting the formation of subchapter S corporations.

a Transportation, Communications, and Public Utilities
b Finance, Insurance and Real Estate

Table 5.2

Characteristics of All Firms and of Black-Owned Firms, 1992

Category	Average No. of Employees per Firm		Average Pay per Employee ($)		Average Sales per Employee ($)		Average Ratio of Pay to Sales ($)	
	All	Black	All	Black	All	Black	All	Black
All	8.74	5.35	19,105	13,924	106,084	65,440	0.18	0.21
Mining	12.43	5.75	26,496	22,027	174,302	156,996	0.15	0.14
Construction	4.73	3.24	22,960	15,672	114,397	68,759	0.20	0.23
Manufacturing	22.50	6.63	23,779	19,366	119,970	89,004	0.20	0.22
TCPU[a]	10.48	4.99	20,927	15,184	90,059	64,264	0.23	0.24
Wholesale	10.05	5.73	27,374	23,533	359,479	317,425	0.08	0.07
Retail	9.64	6.86	11,987	9,164	95,530	67,423	0.13	0.14
FIRE[b]	7.27	5.51	24,431	21,586	133,248	157,420	0.18	0.14
Services	8.28	5.63	18,953	14,142	57,060	40,023	0.33	0.35

Source: Survey of Minority-Owned Business Enterprises, 1992.

Notes: Firms are defined as partnerships and subchapter S corporations with paid employees.

[a] Transportation, Communications, and Public Utilities

[b] Finance, Insurance, and Real Estate

Table 5.3

Relative Distribution of Black-Owned Firms Among Industries, 1992 and 1987

(In percents)

Category	1992					1987				
	Self-Employed	Firms	Value	Employees	Payroll	Self-Employed	Firms	Value	Employees	Payroll
Mining	0.08	0.08	0.20	0.08	0.13	0.08	0.07	0.33	0.18	0.25
Construction	6.22	13.64	8.69	8.27	9.31	7.27	15.65	11.81	12.44	15.38
Manufacturing	1.53	3.04	5.11	3.76	5.23	1.53	3.69	6.56	6.21	8.84
TCPU[a]	8.09	6.32	5.78	5.88	6.42	9.05	7.04	5.56	4.50	5.58
Wholesale	1.09	2.34	12.15	2.51	4.23	1.52	1.77	8.28	2.79	4.20
Retail	13.43	18.76	24.75	24.02	15.81	14.70	20.18	34.40	28.36	20.70
FIRE[b]	6.78	4.95	12.27	5.10	7.91	6.95	3.41	3.29	2.69	3.43
Services	54.44	46.65	29.99	49.03	49.80	50.82	42.31	27.52	40.69	39.02

Source: Survey of Minority-Owned Business Enterprises, 1987, 1992.

Notes: Firms are defined as partnerships and subchapter S corporations with paid employees. Some caution should be used in comparing 1987 and 1992 because of changes in the collection of the data and changes in tax laws affecting the formation of subchapter S corporations.

a Transportation, Communications, and Public Utilities

b Finance, Insurance, and Real Estate

Table 5.4

Percentage Change in Number of Firms, Number of Black-Owned Firms, and Numbers of Employees of Each, by Industry Category, Between 1987 and 1992

	Self-Employed		Firms with Paid Employees		Employees	
	All	Black	All	Black	All	Black
All	43.36	57.47	-18.52	-8.95	38.03	56.57
Mining	27.86	60.22	-5.56	6.25	54.76	-26.93
Construction	24.09	34.66	-14.71	-20.60	20.18	4.08
Manufacturing	32.89	57.84	-1.70	-25.04	52.08	-5.17
TCPU[a]	26.93	40.82	-13.23	-18.35	76.41	104.92
Wholesale	24.30	12.62	19.03	20.22	47.14	40.50
Retail	26.35	43.92	-15.27	-15.37	17.32	32.63
FIRE[b]	68.87	53.53	-8.95	32.31	78.53	196.50
Services	41.40	68.67	-8.68	0.39	46.57	88.68

Source: Survey of Minority-Owned Business Enterprises, 1987, 1992.

Notes: Firms are defined as partnerships and subchapter S corporations with paid employees. Some caution should be used in comparing 1987 and 1992 because of changes in the collection of the data and changes in tax laws affecting the formation of subchapter S corporations.

[a] Transportation, Communications, and Public Utilities

[b] Finance, Insurance, and Real Estate

Table 5.5

Relationship Between Share of Black-Owned Businesses and Selected Variables, Metropolitan Areas, 1992

Variables	Black Population Shares (ages 16-64)	Population Size	R-square
All Industries	0.64[**]	0.06	0.42
Construction	0.75[**]	-0.12	0.56
Manufacturing	0.11	-0.03	0.01
TCPU[a]	0.22[**]	0.09	0.06
Wholesale	0.11	0.09	0.02
Retail	0.57[**]	0.26[**]	0.41
FIRE[b]	0.27[**]	0.07	0.08
Services	0.55[**]	0.08	0.31

Source: Survey of Minority-Owned Business Enterprises and selected Census sources; see Appendix Table 5.1.

Note: Beta coefficients are reported. Beta coefficients measure the change in the explained variable (in standard-deviation units) for a change of one standard deviation in each explanatory variable.

[**] Denotes statistical significance at the .05 confidence level.

[a] Transportation, Communications, and Public Utilities

[b] Finance, Insurance, and Real Estate

Table 5.6

Concentration of Black-Owned Firms in Central Cities, 1987 and 1992
(In Percents)

	1987		1992	
	Firms	**Employees**	**Firms**	**Employees**
Atlanta	3.63	2.63	3.11	1.33
Baltimore	4.07	1.58	3.50	0.25
Chicago	4.74	3.42	3.52	3.02
Cleveland-Lorain-Elyria	4.87	2.62	4.00	2.00
Dallas	3.72	1.76	2.27	2.61
Detroit	15.97	10.56	12.05	5.22
Houston	2.30	1.25	1.58	0.60
Los Angeles-Long Beach	1.22	1.16	1.15	1.60
Miami	0.98	0.95	1.15	0.69
Minneapolis-St. Paul	4.00	2.82	4.80	2.50
New York	1.59	0.53	1.65	0.93
Newark	4.11	2.39	4.29	5.07
Philadelphia	3.72	1.85	4.23	3.06
Phoenix-Mesa	1.89	2.16	2.03	2.38
Pittsburgh	5.24	2.54	3.82	1.46
Portland-Vancouver	7.87	2.73	2.80	3.11
Riverside-San Bernardino	1.90	1.85	1.39	1.34
St. Louis	4.41	2.85	4.40	2.53
San Diego	2.45	0.76	2.49	1.11
Seattle-Bellevue-Everett	3.67	1.02	3.07	1.69
Tampa-St. Petersburg-Clearwater	4.24	2.30	3.64	3.16
Sample Average	2.36	1.57	2.25	1.14

Source: Survey of Minority-Owned Business Enterprises, 1987, 1992.
Notes: The firm concentration ratio is calculated as black-owned firms as a percentage of all firms in the central city divided by black-owned firms as a percentage of all firms in the outer area of the MSA. The employment concentration ratio is the same except that we substitute paid employment for number of firms. A firm concentration ratio greater than one indicates that the percentage of black-owned firms in the central city is larger than the percentage in the outer areas. Firms are defined as partnerships and subchapter S corporations with paid employees. Some caution should be used in comparing 1987 and 1992 because of changes in the collection of the data and changes in tax laws affecting the formation of subchapter S corporations.

THE IMPACT OF ECONOMIC DEVELOPMENT POLICY

Table 5.7

Effect of Economic Factors on the Share of Black-Owned Businesses in Metropolitan Areas

	Including Baltimore		Excluding Baltimore	
	Ratio of Black-Owned Firms to All Firms	Ratio of Black-Owned Firms' Employees to All Firms' Employees	Ratio of Black-Owned Firms to All Firms	Ratio of Black-Owned Firms' Employees to All Firms' Employees
Percent of MSA Population That Is Black	.0014**	.0018**	.0015**	.0006**
MSA Per-Capita Income	-1.60	-3.75	-1.71	-9.67
MSA Unemployment Rate	-.001	-.010*	-.0014	-.0014
MSA Population	-2.25	1.02	-2.05	5.09
Intercept	.037	.106	.040	.026
R-Square	.77	.43	.76	.45

Note: The dependent variable is the ratio of black-owned businesses to all comparable businesses in the MSA. The largest 21 MSAs are included in the regression.
** Denotes statistical significance at the 0.05 level.
* Denotes statistical significance at the 0.10 level.

Table 5.8

Effect of Economic and Demographic Factors on the Relative Concentration of Black-Owned Businesses in Central Cities and Suburbs

	Means	Concentration Ratio	
		Number of Firms	Number of Employees
Ratio of Central City Unemployment Rate to Suburban Unemployment Rate	1.87	1.15** (.349)	.692* (.367)
Ratio of Black Share of Central City Population to Black Share of Suburban Population	4.68	.464** (.677)	.152* (.390)
Ratio of Black Population in Central City to Black Population in Suburbs	2.58	-.158 (-.219)	-.098 (-.231)
Intercept		-.610	.333
R-Square		.73	.39

Notes: The dependent variable for the number of firms is the ratio of the number of black-owned firms to the number of all comparable firms in the central city divided by the ratio of the number of black-owned firms to all comparable firms in the suburbs. The dependent variable for the number of employees is the same except that the number of firms is replaced by the number of employees. The sample includes 21 of the largest MSAs. Numbers in parentheses are beta coefficients.

** Denotes statistical significance at the .05 level.
* Denotes statistical significance at the .10 level.

Table 5.9

Effect of Economic Factors on Employment Change, for All Firms and for Black-Owned Firms, 1987–1992

	SMOBE/CBO	
Variables	**Net Change in Employees for All Firms**	**Net Change in Employees for Black-Owned Firms**
Intercept	-10.071	85.715
Pop89	0.086**	0.146
% chgpop	0.273	-2.994
% chgGSP	0.914*	1.345
Hourly Wage	-0.372	-0.344
Years of Education, Whites	1.496	0.166
Years of Education, Blacks	0.686	0.012
Black % Pop 16+	-0.062	0.056
% Union	0.011	-0.025
SAT Scores	0.010	-0.164
Public Capital/Pop	-187.0	674.0
Tax/GSP	-12.271	-65.682
R-Square	0.2147	0.0472

Source: Survey of Minority-Owned Business Enterprises.
Note: For definition of variables, see Appendix Table 5.1.
** Denotes statistical significance at the .05 confidence level.
* Denotes statistical significance at the .10 confidence level.

Table 5.10

Effect of Economic Factors on Net Employment Change in Manufacturing, Wholesale, and Services Industries, 1987, 1992

Variable	Manufacturing		Wholesale		Services	
	All Firms	Black-Owned Firms	All Firms	Black-Owned Firms	All Firms	Black-Owned Firms
Intercept	-15.145	149.954	75.319	-56.985	17.448	13.487
Pop89	0.140	0.468	0.154	0.525	0.106*	-0.033
% chgpop	-1.543	-15.001*	-1.991	1.192	0.493	6.833
% chgGSP	-1.167	-7.060	2.018	19.568	0.711	-2.667
Hourly wage	0.187	8.722**	3.921*	-0.262	-0.004	-1.731
Black % Pop 16+	-0.054	-0.935	0.003	-0.463	-0.167	1.273**
% Union	-1.337**	-6.858***	-1.142	0.568	-0.225	0.431
SAT Scores	0.041	0.321	0.169	0.233	0.002	-0.144
Public Capital/Pop	6708.0***	33195.0***	-2197.0	-4899.0	-1149.0	3293.0
Tax/GSP	-1089.663***	-3901.700***	360.740	1262.345	80.886	374.503
R-Square	0.5795	0.7587	0.5040	0.2980	0.1994	0.1333

Source: Survey of Minority-Owned Business Enterprises and other sources. See Appendix 5.1.
Note: For definitions of variables, see Appendix Table 5.1.
*, **, *** Denote statistical significance at the .10, .05, and .01 levels, respectively.

THE IMPACT OF ECONOMIC DEVELOPMENT POLICY

Appendix 5.1

Variable Descriptions and Summary Statistics

Variable Name	Description	Mean	Standard Deviation	Source
Pop89	MSA population in hundreds	12639.69	15691.66	BEA Regional Economic Information System data
% chgpop	Percentage change in MSA population	1.57	1.16	BEA Regional Economic Information System data
% chgGSP	Percentage change in gross state product	1.51	1.42	BEA Regional Economic Information System data
Black % pop 16+	Black percentage of pop., 16 years and older	12.30	9.45	1990 Census of the Population
Hourly Wage	Nominal average hourly wage by industry	10.88	1.50	Census CPS files
Years of Education, Whites	Weighted average years of education for whites	12.99	.74	Census CPS files
Years of Education, Blacks	Weighted average years of education for blacks	12.47	1.01	Census CPS files
% Union	Percentage of workforce in unions	15.30	7.15	Census CPS files
SAT Scores	Average of verbal and math SAT scores	461.65	26.04	Digest of Education Statistics
Tax/GSP	State and local tax revenue as proportion of GSP	0.09	0.01	BEA Regional Economic Information System data
Public Capital/Pop	Dollars of public capital stock per person	10844.59	1771.98	Author derivation of Census data

Civilians Employed in Professional/Managerial and Technical, Sales, and Administrative Support Occupations, by Industry and Race, 1985

Industry & Race	In All Occupations		In Professional/Managerial				In Technical, Sales, & Administrative Support				
	No. (000s)	All (%)	No. (000s)	All (%)	Executive, Admin. & Managerial (%)	Professional Specialty (%)	No. (000s)	All (%)	Technical & Related Support (%)	Sales (%)	Admin. Support (%)
Whites											
Agriculture	2,936	100	115	3.9	1.9	2.0	128	4.4	0.8	0.4	3.2
Mining	895	100	225	25.1	15.0	10.2	163	18.2	4.9	1.6	11.7
Construction	6,409	100	926	14.4	12.4	2.0	541	8.4	0.8	1.1	6.6
Manufacturing	18,219	100	3,678	20.2	11.9	8.3	3,638	20.0	3.6	3.7	12.6
Durable Goods	11,120	100	2,398	21.6	12.1	9.5	2,105	18.9	4.3	2.6	12.0
Nondurable Goods	7,096	100	1,280	18.0	11.6	6.4	1,534	21.6	2.6	5.5	13.5
Transportation and Public Utilities	6,414	100	1,119	17.4	11.3	6.2	2,149	33.5	3.2	4.4	25.9
Wholesale/Retail	19,965	100	2,054	10.3	8.4	1.9	10,562	52.9	0.4	42.1	10.5
Wholesale Trade	4,017	100	507	12.6	11.1	1.5	2,426	60.4	0.8	40.6	19.0
Retail Trade	15,948	100	1,547	9.7	7.7	2.0	8,136	51.0	0.3	42.4	8.3
Finance, Insurance and Real Estate	6,262	100	1,670	26.7	24.5	2.2	4,191	66.9	1.7	25.2	40.0
Services	28,483	100	12,275	43.1	11.4	31.7	6,863	24.1	5.1	2.2	16.8
Private Household	873	100	9	1.0	0.1	0.9	14	1.6	0.5	0.1	1.0
Other Services Industries	27,610	100	12,266	44.4	11.8	32.7	6,849	24.8	5.3	2.2	17.3
Professional Services	18,480	100	9,874	53.4	9.9	43.6	4,793	25.9	6.5	0.6	18.8
Public Administration	4,155	100	1,501	36.1	22.2	13.9	1,317	31.7	4.7	0.5	26.5

Continued...

Appendix Table A.1 (Continued)

Industry & Race	In All Occupations No. (000s)	All (%)	In Professional/Managerial No. (000s)	All (%)	Executive, Admin. & Managerial (%)	Professional Specialty (%)	In Technical, Sales, & Administrative Support No. (000s)	All (%)	Technical & Related Support (%)	Sales (%)	Admin. Support (%)
Blacks											
Agriculture	189	100	2	1.1	0.5	0.5	2	1.1	*	0.5	0.5
Mining	32	100	3	9.4	6.3	3.1	9	28.1	6.3	*	21.9
Construction	473	100	24	5.1	4.7	0.4	20	4.2	0.6	0.4	3.2
Manufacturing	2,085	100	117	5.6	3.2	2.4	255	12.2	2.3	1.3	8.6
Durable Goods	1,086	100	69	6.4	3.6	2.8	131	12.1	2.9	0.6	8.6
Nondurable Goods	1,000	100	48	4.8	2.8	2.0	123	12.3	1.6	2.0	8.7
Transportation and Public Utilities	947	100	75	7.9	5.4	2.5	347	36.6	1.8	1.9	32.9
Wholesale/Retail	1,658	100	103	6.2	5.4	0.8	687	41.4	0.2	32.2	9.0
Wholesale Trade	236	100	15	6.4	5.1	1.3	83	35.2	1.3	15.3	18.6
Retail Trade	1,422	100	88	6.2	5.4	0.8	606	42.6	*	35.0	7.5
Finance, Insurance, and Real Estate	548	100	82	15.0	13.5	1.5	383	69.9	1.1	11.1	57.7
Services	3,879	100	935	24.1	5.9	18.2	803	20.7	4.8	1.2	14.6
Private Household	350	100	2	0.6	*	0.6	4	1.1	0.9	*	0.3
Other Services Industries	3,529	100	933	26.4	6.5	19.9	797	22.6	5.2	1.3	16.0
Professional Services	n.a.	100	802	n.a.	n.a.	n.a.	609	n.a.	n.a.	n.a.	n.a.
Public Administration	690	100	174	25.2	16.4	8.8	279	40.4	3.5	0.9	36.1

Source: *Employment and Earnings*, January issue, 1986.
Notes: * indicates less than 0.05 percent.; *n.a.* indicates not available.

Employed Civilians in Professional/Managerial and Technical, Sales, and Administrative Support Occupations, by Industry and Race, 1990

Industry & Race	In All Occupations		In Professional/Managerial				In Technical, Sales, & Administrative Support				
	No. (000s)	All (%)	No. (000s)	All (%)	Executive, Admin. & Managerial (%)	Professional Specialty (%)	No. (000s)	All (%)	Technical & Related Support (%)	Sales (%)	Admin. Support (%)
Whites											
Agriculture	2,974	100	170	5.7	3.0	2.7	153	5.1	0.9	0.8	3.4
Mining	682	100	169	24.8	16.1	8.7	106	15.5	4.3	1.3	10.0
Construction	7,047	100	1,108	15.7	14.1	1.7	531	7.5	0.8	1.0	5.7
Manufacturing	18,338	100	4,033	22.0	13.1	8.9	3,512	19.2	3.6	4.0	11.5
Durable Goods	11,060	100	2,553	23.1	13.1	10.0	2,013	18.2	4.2	2.9	11.1
Nondurable Goods	7,278	100	1,480	20.3	13.0	7.3	1,499	20.6	2.7	5.8	12.0
Transportation and Public Utilities	6,772	100	1,252	18.5	12.4	6.1	2,293	33.9	4.0	4.5	25.3
Wholesale/Retail	21,400	100	2,304	10.8	8.8	2.0	11,332	53.0	0.6	42.3	10.1
Wholesale Trade	4,233	100	573	13.5	11.7	1.8	2,523	59.6	1.0	41.9	16.7
Retail Trade	17,166	100	1,729	10.1	8.0	2.1	8,809	51.3	0.5	42.4	8.4
Finance, Insurance and Real Estate	7,059	100	2,095	29.7	26.9	2.8	4,507	63.8	1.9	25.2	36.7
Services	33,237	100	14,831	44.6	13.0	31.6	8,266	24.9	5.4	2.5	16.9
Private Household	749	100	13	1.7	0.4	1.3	13	1.7	0.4	0.3	1.1
Other Services Industries	32,488	100	14,818	45.6	13.3	32.3	8,253	25.4	5.5	2.6	17.3
Professional Services	21,584	100	11,690	54.2	11.1	43.1	5,659	26.2	6.7	0.7	18.9
Public Administration	4,579	100	1,676	36.6	22.4	14.2	1,434	31.3	4.6	0.5	26.3

Continued...

Appendix Table A.2 (Continued)

Industry & Race	In All Occupations		In Professional/Managerial				In Technical, Sales, & Administrative Support				
	No. (000s)	All (%)	No. (000s)	All (%)	Executive, Admin. & Managerial (%)	Professional Specialty (%)	No. (000s)	All (%)	Technical & Related Support (%)	Sales (%)	Admin. Support (%)
Blacks											
Agriculture	140	100	4	0.7	0.7	*	2	1.4	*	*	1.4
Mining	38	100	4	10.5	5.3	5.3	7	18.4	7.9	*	10.5
Construction	498	100	36	7.2	6.0	1.2	23	4.6	0.8	0.6	3.2
Manufacturing	2,141	100	142	6.6	3.7	2.9	270	12.6	2.2	1.2	9.2
Durable Goods	1,079	100	86	8.0	4.1	3.9	132	12.2	2.4	0.6	9.3
Nondurable Goods	1,062	100	56	5.3	3.4	1.9	1,383	13.0	2.1	1.9	9.0
Transportation and Public Utilities	1,141	100	89	7.8	5.3	2.5	419	36.7	2.0	2.3	32.4
Wholesale/Retail	1,997	100	134	6.7	5.7	1.0	885	44.3	0.5	34.7	9.2
Wholesale Trade	280	100	21	7.5	5.7	1.8	100	35.7	1.4	17.5	16.8
Retail Trade	1,716	100	113	6.6	5.7	0.9	784	45.7	0.3	37.5	7.9
Finance, Insurance, and Real Estate	706	100	143	20.3	18.0	2.3	463	65.6	1.6	11.2	52.8
Services	4,459	100	1,122	25.2	6.6	18.5	999	22.4	5.0	1.8	15.6
Private Household	241	100	4	1.7	0.4	1.1	1	0.4	0.4	*	*
Other Services Industries	4,218	100	1,119	26.5	7.0	19.5	997	23.6	5.2	1.9	16.5
Professional Services	n.a.	100	937	n.a.	n.a.	n.a.	733	n.a.	n.a.	n.a.	n.a.
Public Administration	846	100	242	28.6	16.8	11.8	309	36.5	3.4	0.5	32.6

Source: *Employment and Earnings,* January issue, 1991.
Notes: * indicates less than 0.05 percent.; *n.a.* indicates not available.

Employed Civilians in Professional/Managerial and Technical, Sales, and Administrative Support Occupations, by Industry and Race, 1994

Industry & Race	In All Occupations		In Professional/Managerial				In Technical, Sales, & Administrative Support				
	No. (000s)	All (%)	No. (000s)	All (%)	Executive, Admin. & Managerial (%)	Professional Specialty (%)	No. (000s)	All (%)	Technical & Related Support (%)	Sales (%)	Admin. Support (%)
Whites											
Agriculture	3,162	100	179	5.7	2.9	2.7	185	5.9	1.1	0.4	4.3
Mining	626	100	176	28.1	16.9	11.2	92	14.7	3.4	1.6	9.7
Construction	6,810	100	1,123	16.5	14.7	1.8	514	7.5	0.8	0.9	5.9
Manufacturing	17,230	100	4,075	23.7	14.1	9.6	3,063	17.8	3.0	4.0	10.7
Durable Goods	10,253	100	2,530	24.7	14.3	10.4	1,671	16.3	3.5	2.9	10.0
Nondurable Goods	6,977	100	1,546	22.2	13.7	8.4	1,392	20.0	2.4	5.7	11.8
Transportation and Public Utilities	7,168	100	1,372	19.1	13.2	6.0	2,349	32.8	4.0	3.0	25.8
Wholesale/Retail	22,370	100	2,422	10.8	8.8	2.0	11,658	52.1	0.6	42.2	9.3
Wholesale Trade	4,226	100	573	13.6	11.8	1.8	2,480	58.7	0.8	41.4	16.5
Retail Trade	18,144	100	1,849	10.2	8.2	2.0	9,178	50.6	0.6	42.4	7.6
Finance, Insurance and Real Estate	7,100	100	2,192	30.9	27.5	3.4	4,460	62.8	2.0	26.7	34.2
Services	36,095	100	16,732	46.4	14.0	32.4	8,598	23.8	5.3	2.5	16.1
Private Household	761	100	9	1.2	0.5	0.7	9	1.2	*	*	1.2
Other Services Industries	35,333	100	16,723	47.3	14.3	33.1	8,588	24.3	5.4	2.5	16.4
Professional Services	24,396	100	13,577	55.7	13.0	42.7	6,088	25.0	6.8	0.7	17.5
Public Administration	4,629	100	1,773	38.3	23.1	15.3	1,313	28.4	4.1	0.5	23.8

Continued...

Appendix Table A.3 (Continued)

Industry & Race	In All Occupations		In Professional/Managerial				In Technical, Sales, & Administrative Support				
	No. (000s)	All (%)	No. (000s)	All (%)	Executive, Admin. & Managerial (%)	Professional Specialty (%)	No. (000s)	All (%)	Technical & Related Support (%)	Sales (%)	Admin. Support (%)
Blacks											
Agriculture	136	100	3	2.2	1.5	0.7	7	5.1	1.5	*	3.7
Mining	30	100	3	10.0	6.7	3.3	3	10.0	3.3	*	6.7
Construction	482	100	40	8.3	7.5	0.8	21	4.4	0.4	*	3.9
Manufacturing	2,032	100	152	7.5	4.5	3.0	251	12.4	2.4	1.6	8.3
Durable Goods	1,003	100	78	7.8	4.9	2.9	112	11.2	2.7	1.0	7.5
Nondurable Goods	1,029	100	73	7.1	4.2	2.9	139	13.5	2.1	2.2	9.1
Transportation and Public Utilities	1,193	100	119	10.0	6.7	3.3	439	36.8	2.1	2.4	32.3
Wholesale/Retail	2,174	100	150	6.9	5.9	1.0	968	44.5	0.3	36.9	7.3
Wholesale Trade	305	100	20	6.6	3.9	2.6	108	35.4	0.3	20.0	15.1
Retail Trade	1,869	100	129	6.9	6.2	0.7	859	46.0	0.3	39.6	6.0
Finance, Insurance, and Real Estate	737	100	179	24.3	21.3	3.0	463	62.8	1.4	11.9	49.5
Services	5,095	100	1,466	28.8	8.1	20.6	1,170	23.0	5.0	2.0	16.0
Private Household	171	100	2	1.2	*	1.2	1	0.6	*	*	0.6
Other Services Industries	4,924	100	1,464	29.7	8.4	21.3	1,168	23.7	5.2	2.1	16.5
Professional Services	3,498	100	1,250	35.7	8.4	27.3	870	24.9	6.4	0.7	17.8
Public Administration	956	100	293	30.6	20.0	10.7	309	32.2	2.6	*	29.7

Source: *Employment and Earnings*, January issue, 1995.

Notes: * indicates less than 0.05 percent.; *n.a.* indicates not available.

Employed Civilians in Professional/Managerial and Technical, Sales, and Administrative Support Occupations, by Industry and Race, 1995

Industry & Race	In All Occupations		In Professional/Managerial				In Technical, Sales, & Administrative Support				
	No. (000s)	All (%)	No. (000s)	All (%)	Executive, Admin. & Managerial (%)	Professional Specialty (%)	No. (000s)	All (%)	Technical & Related Support (%)	Sales (%)	Admin. Support (%)
Whites											
Agriculture	3,194	100	188	5.9	3.1	2.8	197	6.2	1.3	0.4	4.4
Mining	591	100	153	25.9	16.4	9.5	72	12.2	3.4	0.7	8.1
Construction	6,945	100	1,187	17.1	15.3	1.8	504	7.3	0.5	0.9	5.8
Manufacturing	17,401	100	4,245	24.4	15.1	9.3	3,086	17.7	3.1	4.1	10.6
Durable Goods	10,434	100	2,640	25.3	15.2	10.1	1,633	15.7	3.4	2.8	9.4
Nondurable Goods	6,967	100	1,605	23.0	15.0	8.1	1,451	20.8	2.6	5.9	12.3
Transportation and Public Utilities	7,130	100	1,447	20.3	14.0	6.3	2,335	32.7	3.9	3.1	25.7
Wholesale/Retail	22,678	100	2,524	11.1	9.0	2.1	11,809	52.1	0.8	42.3	9.0
Wholesale Trade	4,500	100	609	13.5	11.4	2.2	2,620	58.2	1.0	41.4	15.9
Retail Trade	18,178	100	1,915	10.5	8.4	2.1	9,189	50.6	0.7	42.5	7.3
Finance, Insurance and Real Estate	6,945	100	2,247	32.4	28.9	3.4	4,272	61.5	1.9	26.3	33.3
Services	36,877	100	17,426	47.3	14.5	32.7	8,633	23.4	5.3	2.5	15.6
Private Household	739	100	10	1.4	0.5	0.8	10	1.4	0.3	*	1.1
Other Services Industries	36,138	100	17,415	48.2	14.8	33.4	8,624	23.9	5.4	2.6	15.9
Professional Services	24,933	100	13,995	56.1	13.1	43.0	6,137	24.6	6.7	0.7	17.2
Public Administration	4,729	100	1,905	40.3	23.5	16.8	1,276	27.0	4.0	0.4	22.5

Continued...

Appendix Table A.4 (Continued)

Industry & Race	In All Occupations		In Professional/Managerial				In Technical, Sales, & Administrative Support				
	No. (000s)	All (%)	No. (000s)	All (%)	Executive, Admin. & Managerial (%)	Professional Specialty (%)	No. (000s)	All (%)	Technical & Related Support (%)	Sales (%)	Admin. Support (%)
Blacks											
Agriculture	101	100	5	5.0	3.0	2.0	3	3.0	1.0	1.0	1.0
Mining	24	100	3	12.5	8.3	4.2	4	16.7	*	*	16.7
Construction	509	100	47	9.2	6.7	2.6	22	4.3	0.8	0.4	3.1
Manufacturing	2,131	100	166	7.8	4.6	3.2	270	12.7	2.2	1.5	9.0
Durable Goods	1,026	100	87	8.5	5.0	3.5	118	11.5	2.3	0.7	8.5
Nondurable Goods	1,105	100	79	7.1	4.2	3.0	152	13.8	2.1	2.2	9.5
Transportation and Public Utilities	1,261	100	129	10.2	7.0	3.3	448	35.5	1.5	2.3	31.7
Wholesale/Retail	2,236	100	168	7.5	6.4	1.2	1,077	48.2	0.5	39.8	7.8
Wholesale Trade	312	100	24	7.7	6.1	1.6	117	37.5	1.3	18.9	17.3
Retail Trade	1,924	100	144	7.5	6.4	1.1	961	49.9	0.4	43.3	6.3
Finance, Insurance, and Real Estate	746	100	192	25.7	23.1	2.7	444	59.5	1.1	14.7	43.7
Services	5,265	100	1,603	30.4	9.4	21.1	1,215	23.1	4.8	2.2	16.1
Private Household	178	100	3	1.7	1.1	0.6	2	1.1	*	*	1.1
Other Services Industries	5,088	100	1,600	31.4	9.7	21.8	1,212	23.8	5.0	2.3	16.6
Professional Services	3,600	100	1,347	37.4	9.5	27.9	877	24.4	6.2	0.6	17.5
Public Administration	1,005	100	339	33.7	20.0	13.7	325	32.3	3.3	0.2	28.9

Source: *Employment and Earnings*, January issue, 1996.
Notes: * indicates less than 0.05 percent.; *n.a.* indicates not available.

Appendix Table A.5

Employed Civilians by Industry, Race, and Occupation, 1985

	Total Number Employed (000s)	Total Percent Employed	Percent Distribution of Occupations					
			Managerial & Professional	Technical, Sales, & Admin. Support	Service	Precision Production, Craft & Repair	Operators, Fabricators & Laborers	Farming, Forestry & Fishing
Whites								
Agriculture	2,936	100	3.9	4.4	0.3	1.2	2.0	88.2
Mining	895	100	25.1	18.2	0.9	32.4	23.1	0.1
Construction	6,409	100	14.4	8.4	0.4	57.9	18.6	0.2
Manufacturing	18,216	100	20.2	20.0	1.7	19.7	38.1	0.4
Durable Goods	11,120	100	21.6	18.9	1.7	23.0	34.3	0.5
Nondurable Goods	7,096	100	18.0	21.6	1.8	14.5	44.0	0.1
Transportation and Public Utilities	6,414	100	17.4	33.5	2.8	18.1	28.0	0.2
Wholesale/Retail	19,965	100	10.3	52.9	17.9	6.7	12.0	0.2
Wholesale Trade	4,017	100	12.6	60.4	0.8	6.9	18.9	0.3
Retail Trade	15,948	100	9.7	51.0	22.2	6.7	10.3	0.1
Finance, Insurance, and Real Estate	6,262	100	26.7	66.9	3.5	1.6	0.6	0.7
Services	28,483	100	43.1	24.1	21.5	5.8	4.3	1.2
Private Household	73	100	1.0	1.6	85.3	0.8	3.2	8.0
Other Services Industries	27,610	100	44.4	24.8	19.5	6.0	4.3	0.9
Professional Services	18,480	100	53.4	25.9	16.2	1.8	2.2	0.4
Public Administration	4,155	100	36.1	31.7	23.6	5.2	2.3	1.2

Continued...

Appendix Table A.5 (Continued)

	Total Number Employed (000s)	Total Percent Employed	Managerial & Professional	Technical, Sales, & Admin. Support	Service	Precision Production, Craft & Repair	Operators, Fabricators & Laborers	Farming, Forestry & Fishing
Blacks								
Agriculture	189	100	1.1	1.1	1.1	1.6	2.6	92.6
Mining	32	100	9.4	28.1	3.1	28.1	31.3	0.0
Construction	473	100	5.1	4.2	1.5	51.6	37.2	0.2
Manufacturing	2,085	100	5.6	12.2	3.9	15.3	62.2	0.8
Durable Goods	1,086	100	6.4	12.1	3.7	18.2	58.2	1.4
Nondurable Goods	1,000	100	4.8	12.3	4.3	12.1	66.4	0.2
Transportation and Public Utilities	947	100	7.9	36.6	5.1	13.1	37.1	0.2
Wholesale/Retail	1,658	100	6.2	41.4	26.8	4.8	20.6	0.1
Wholesale Trade	236	100	6.4	35.2	3.0	6.8	48.3	0.4
Retail Trade	1,422	100	6.2	42.6	30.8	4.4	16.0	0.1
Finance, Insurance, and Real Estate	548	100	15.0	69.9	10.4	2.2	1.5	1.1
Services	3,879	100	24.1	20.7	44.3	3.3	6.2	1.3
Private Household	350	100	0.6	1.1	90.3	0.3	1.4	6.3
Other Services Industries	3,529	100	26.4	22.6	39.8	3.6	6.7	0.8
Professional Services	*	100	n.a.	n.a.	n.a.	n.a.	n.a.	n.a.
Public Administration	90	100	25.2	40.4	23.0	4.2	5.1	2.0

Source: *Employment and Earnings*, January issue, 1986.
Notes: * indicates less than 0.05 percent.; *n.a.* indicates not available.

Appendix Table A.6

Employed Civilians by Industry, Race, and Occupation, 1990

	Total Number Employed (000s)	Total Percent Employed	Percent Distribution of Occupations					
			Managerial & Professional	Technical, Sales, & Admin. Support	Service	Precision Production, Craft & Repair	Operators, Fabricators & Laborers	Farming, Forestry & Fishing
Whites								
Agriculture	2,974	100	5.7	5.1	0.5	1.2	2.3	85.1
Mining	682	100	24.8	15.5	1.0	33.3	25.2	0.3
Construction	7,047	100	14.3	7.5	0.4	57.6	18.5	0.3
Manufacturing	18,338	100	22.0	19.0	1.6	19.0	37.8	0.5
Durable Goods	11,060	100	23.1	18.2	1.5	21.9	34.6	0.7
Nondurable Goods	7,278	100	20.3	20.6	1.9	14.5	42.6	0.1
Transportation and Public Utilities	6,772	100	18.5	33.9	3.2	16.2	28.1	0.2
Wholesale/Retail	21,400	100	10.8	53.0	17.5	6.4	12.2	0.2
Wholesale Trade	4,233	100	13.5	59.6	0.7	6.9	19.1	0.2
Retail Trade	17,166	100	10.1	51.3	21.7	6.2	10.6	0.1
Finance, Insurance, and Real Estate	7,059	100	29.7	63.8	3.2	1.8	0.7	0.8
Services	33,237	100	44.6	24.9	20.3	5.0	4.2	1.0
Private Household	749	100	1.7	1.7	84.0	1.9	2.9	7.7
Other Services Industries	32,488	100	45.6	25.4	18.8	5.0	4.3	0.9
Professional Services	21,584	100	54.2	26.2	15.4	1.6	2.3	0.3
Public Administration	4,579	100	36.6	31.3	24.7	4.3	2.2	0.9

Continued...

Appendix Table A.6 (Continued)

	Total Number Employed (000s)	Total Percent Employed	Percent Distribution of Occupations					
			Managerial & Professional	Technical, Sales, & Admin. Support	Service	Precision Production, Craft & Repair	Operators, Fabricators & Laborers	Farming, Forestry & Fishing
Blacks								
Agriculture	140	100	0.7	1.4	1.4	1.4	7.1	86.4
Mining	38	100	10.5	18.4	5.3	36.8	28.9	0.0
Construction	498	100	7.2	4.6	0.8	53.0	33.5	0.6
Manufacturing	2,141	100	6.6	12.6	3.0	15.6	61.4	0.7
Durable Goods	1,079	100	8.0	12.2	2.4	18.4	57.8	1.1
Nondurable Goods	1,062	100	5.3	13.0	3.6	12.9	65.2	0.2
Transportation and Public Utilities	1,141	100	7.8	36.7	5.4	12.1	37.8	0.2
Wholesale/Retail	1,997	100	6.7	44.3	24.2	4.4	20.3	0.1
Wholesale Trade	280	100	7.5	35.7	2.5	7.1	46.8	0.4
Retail Trade	1,716	100	6.6	45.7	27.8	4.0	15.9	0.1
Finance, Insurance, and Real Estate	706	100	20.3	65.6	8.1	3.5	1.6	1.1
Services	4,459	100	25.2	22.4	41.1	3.8	6.5	1.1
Private Household	241	100	1.7	0.4	90.9	0.8	2.1	4.6
Other Services Industries	4,218	100	26.5	23.6	38.3	3.9	6.7	0.9
Professional Services	*	100	n.a.	n.a.	n.a.	n.a.	n.a.	n.a.
Public Administration	846	100	28.6	36.5	26.1	3.7	4.3	0.8

Source: *Employment and Earnings*, January issue, 1991.
Notes: * indicates less than 0.05 percent; *n.a.* indicates not available.

Appendix Table A.7

Employed Civilians by Industry, Race, and Occupation, 1994

	Total Number Employed (000s)	Total Percent Employed	Percent Distribution of Occupations						
			Managerial & Professional	Technical, Sales, & Admin. Support	Service	Precision Production, Craft & Repair	Operators, Fabricators & Laborers	Farming, Forestry & Fishing	
Whites									
Agriculture	3,162	100	5.7	5.9	0.5	1.2	1.9	84.9	
Mining	626	100	28.1	14.7	1.4	33.4	22.0	0.2	
Construction	6,810	100	16.5	7.5	0.3	57.3	18.0	0.3	
Manufacturing	17,230	100	23.7	17.8	1.4	19.2	37.6	0.4	
Durable Goods	10,253	100	24.7	16.3	1.2	22.4	34.7	0.7	
Nondurable Goods	6,977	100	22.2	22.2	1.6	14.5	41.8	0.1	
Transportation and Public Utilities	7,168	100	19.2	32.8	2.5	15.2	30.2	0.2	
Wholesale/Retail	22,370	100	10.8	52.1	18.5	5.9	12.3	0.3	
Wholesale Trade	4,226	100	13.6	58.7	0.6	6.4	19.6	0.1	
Retail Trade	18,144	100	10.2	50.6	22.7	5.7	10.6	0.1	
Finance, Insurance, and Real Estate	7,100	100	30.9	62.8	3.0	2.0	0.6	0.7	
Services	36,095	100	46.4	23.8	19.7	5.0	4.1	1.0	
Private Household	761	100	1.2	1.2	89.9	0.8	2.0	5.0	
Other Services Industries	35,333	100	47.3	24.3	18.1	5.1	4.1	0.9	
Professional Services	24,396	100	55.7	25.0	15.4	1.6	2.0	0.4	
Public Administration	4,629	100	38.3	28.4	27.1	3.8	1.9	0.5	

Continued...

Appendix Table A. 7 (Continued)

	Total Number Employed (000s)	Total Percent Employed	Percent Distribution of Occupations					
			Managerial & Professional	Technical, Sales, & Admin. Support	Service	Precision Production, Craft & Repair	Operators, Fabricators & Laborers	Farming, Forestry & Fishing
Blacks								
Agriculture	136	100	2.2	5.1	0.0	0.7	3.7	86.8
Mining	30	100	10.0	10.0	0.0	33.3	23.3	0.0
Construction	482	100	8.3	4.4	1.7	54.1	30.9	0.2
Manufacturing	2,032	100	7.5	12.4	2.1	16.3	61.2	0.5
Durable Goods	1,003	100	7.8	11.2	2.6	20.1	57.4	0.9
Nondurable Goods	1,029	100	7.1	13.5	1.7	12.6	64.8	0.0
Transportation and Public Utilities	1,193	100	10.0	36.8	3.9	12.3	37.0	0.1
Wholesale/Retail	2,174	100	6.9	44.5	24.4	3.5	20.4	0.3
Wholesale Trade	305	100	6.6	35.4	2.3	4.6	48.2	2.0
Retail Trade	1,869	100	6.9	46.0	28.0	3.3	15.8	0.0
Finance, Insurance, and Real Estate	737	100	24.3	62.8	7.5	2.7	0.4	1.4
Services	5,095	100	28.8	23.0	37.7	3.2	6.6	0.7
Private Household	171	100	1.2	0.6	94.2	0.6	0.0	0.0
Other Services Industries	4,924	100	29.7	23.7	35.8	3.3	6.8	0.7
Professional Services	3,498	100	35.7	24.9	33.7	1.5	3.8	0.4
Public Administration	956	100	30.6	32.3	29.6	2.8	4.0	0.2

Source: *Employment and Earnings,* January issue, 1995.

Employed Civilians by Industry, Race, and Occupation, 1995

	Total Number Employed (000s)	Total Percent Employed	Managerial & Professional	Technical, Sales, & Admin. Support	Service	Precision Production, Craft & Repair	Operators, Fabricators & Laborers	Farming, Forestry & Fishing
								Percent Distribution of Occupations
Whites								
Agriculture	3,194	100	5.8	6.2	0.4	1.0	2.2	84.3
Mining	591	100	25.9	12.2	0.7	36.7	24.4	0.3
Construction	6,945	100	17.1	7.3	0.4	57.1	17.9	0.2
Manufacturing	17,401	100	24.4	17.7	1.3	18.9	37.1	0.6
Durable Goods	10,434	100	25.3	15.7	1.2	22.3	34.7	0.8
Nondurable Goods	6,967	100	23.0	20.8	1.4	13.9	40.7	0.1
Transportation and Public Utilities	7,130	100	20.3	32.7	2.6	14.9	29.4	0.1
Wholesale/Retail	22,678	100	11.1	52.1	18.1	5.7	12.7	0.3
Wholesale Trade	4,500	100	13.5	58.2	0.7	6.2	20.3	1.1
Retail Trade	18,178	100	10.5	50.6	22.4	5.5	10.8	0.2
Finance, Insurance, and Real Estate	6,945	100	32.4	61.5	2.9	2.0	0.5	0.8
Services	36,877	100	47.3	23.4	19.5	4.8	4.0	1.0
Private Household	739	100	1.4	1.4	91.5	0.7	1.5	3.7
Other Services Industries	36,138	100	48.2	23.9	18.0	4.9	4.1	0.9
Professional Services	24,933	100	56.1	24.6	15.5	1.6	1.8	0.3
Public Administration	4,729	100	40.3	27.0	26.5	4.1	1.8	0.4

Continued...

	Total Number Employed (000s)	Total Percent Employed	Percent Distribution of Occupations					
			Managerial & Professional	Technical, Sales, & Admin. Support	Service	Precision Production, Craft & Repair	Operators, Fabricators & Laborers	Farming, Forestry & Fishing
Blacks								
Agriculture	101	100	5.0	3.0	1.0	0.0	5.0	85.1
Mining	24	100	12.5	16.7	4.2	29.2	37.5	0.0
Construction	509	100	9.2	4.3	0.6	53.4	32.2	0.4
Manufacturing	2,131	100	7.8	12.7	2.7	17.0	59.3	5.2
Durable Goods	1,026	100	8.5	11.5	2.3	20.0	56.7	1.1
Nondurable Goods	1,105	100	7.1	13.8	3.1	14.2	61.7	0.0
Transportation and Public Utilities	1,261	100	10.2	35.5	4.0	10.0	40.2	0.1
Wholesale/Retail	2,236	100	7.5	46.8	21.9	3.8	18.2	0.4
Wholesale Trade	312	100	7.7	37.5	1.3	6.7	45.2	2.2
Retail Trade	1,924	100	7.5	49.9	25.3	3.3	13.9	0.1
Finance, Insurance, and Real Estate	746	100	25.7	59.5	6.8	5.2	1.5	1.2
Services	5,265	100	30.4	23.1	37.0	2.9	6.0	0.6
Private Household	178	100	1.7	1.1	92.1	0.6	2.8	1.1
Other Services Industries	5,088	100	31.4	23.8	35.0	3.0	6.1	0.6
Professional Services	3,600	100	37.4	24.4	33.6	1.4	2.8	0.4
Public Administration	1,005	100	33.7	32.3	28.1	2.9	2.7	0.4

Source: *Employment and Earnings*, January issue, 1996.

Timothy Bates

Dr. Bates is distinguished professor of labor and urban affairs at Wayne State University. He previously served as chair of the urban policy analysis graduate program at the New School for Social Research and as chair of the department of economics at the University of Vermont. Dr. Bates earned his bachelor's degree in economic history from the University of Illinois and masters and doctoral degrees in economics from the University of Wisconsin. He has written more than 50 articles about minority business development for academic journals. In 1993, his book, *Banking on Black Enterprise*, was published by the Joint Center for Political and Economic Studies. His latest book, *Race, Self-Employment, and Upward Mobility: An Illusive American Dream*, was published by Johns Hopkins University Press in 1997. Professor Bates is a consultant to various government agencies, including the Civil Rights division of the U.S. Department of Justice and the U.S. General Accounting Office.

Randall W. Eberts

Dr. Eberts is executive director of the W.E. Upjohn Institute for Employment Research. Dr. Eberts has M.A. and Ph.D. degrees in economics from Northwestern University. During 1991 to 1992, he served as senior staff economist on the President's Council of Economic Advisers. His primary areas of responsibility included monitoring and analyzing issues related to unemployment insurance, job training, income distribution, education, and public infrastructure investment. Dr. Eberts was also a professor of economics at the University of Oregon between 1977 and 1987 and a visiting professor at Texas A&M University in 1981. He has published extensively in academic journals. He also has written and edited several books and served on numerous advisory boards and committees, most recently a committee of the National Academy of Sciences on infrastructure and economic development.

Harry J. Holzer

Dr. Holzer is professor of economics at Michigan State University. He obtained his Ph.D. in economics from Harvard University in 1983. Since then, he has worked extensively on the employment problems of inner-city minorities. His books include *The Black Youth Employment Crisis* (with Richard Freeman) and *What Employers Want: Job Prospects of Less-Educated Workers*. He also is the author or coauthor of numerous journal articles and discussion and working papers.

Wilhelmina A. Leigh

A senior research associate at the Joint Center for Political and Economic Studies in Washington, D.C., Dr. Leigh is an economist who specializes in policy research in the area of health. Prior to joining the Joint Center in 1991, she was a principal analyst at the U.S. Congressional Budget Office where she focused on housing policy. Before that she worked for the Bureau of Labor Statistics (U.S. Department of Labor), the U.S. Department of Housing and Urban Development, the Urban Institute, and the National Urban League Research Department. Dr. Leigh also has taught at Harvard University, Howard University, the University of Virginia, and Georgetown University. Recent publications include *Women of Color Health Data Book: Adolescents to Seniors*, published in 1997 by the Office of Research on Women's Health at the National Institutes of Health; a chapter in the 1996 issue of the National Urban League's *The State of Black America* entitled "U.S. Housing Policy in 1996: The Outlook for Black Americans"; and *Employment Trends 1980-1992: A Black-White Comparison*, a 1996 Joint Center report. Dr. Leigh received her M.A. and Ph.D. in economics from the Johns Hopkins University and her A.B., also in economics, from Cornell University.

Edward B. Montgomery

While on leave from his positions as professor of economics at the University of Maryland and as a research associate at the National Bureau of Economic Research, Dr. Montgomery served as the chief economist at the U.S. Department of Labor during 1997 and 1998. He has been a member of the faculties of Michigan State University (1986-1990) and Carnegie Mellon University (1981-1986), a senior research associate at the Joint Center for Political and Economic Studies, and a visiting scholar at the Board of Governors of the Federal Reserve System (1983). He received his undergraduate degree with honors from Pennsylvania State University (1976) and his masters (1980) and Ph.D. (1982) in economics from Harvard University. Professor Montgomery has published more than 30 papers and articles on state and local job creation strategies, earnings inequality, pensions and savings behavior, affirmative action, workplace smoking policies, the impact of welfare and Medicaid on employment, and similar issues. His work has appeared in numerous edited volumes and professional journals. He has served on the Advisory Council on Employee Welfare and Pension Benefit Plans at the U.S. Department of Labor and on the Advisory Panel in Economics for the National Science Foundation.

William M. Rodgers III

Dr. Rodgers is an associate professor and holds the Francis L. and Edwin L. Cummings Professorship of Economics at the College of William and Mary. He is also an adjunct-associate of the Humphrey Institute, University of Minnesota. He received his B.A. from Dartmouth College, an M.A. from the University of California at Santa Barbara, and M.A. and Ph.D. degrees from Harvard University. His primary research is in labor economics, although he has also written in the areas of public finance and development. He has testified before the Joint Economic Committee of the U.S. Congress on raising the federal minimum wage and served as consultant to the Chief Economist of the Secretary of Labor.

Margaret C. Simms

Dr. Simms is vice president for research at the Joint Center for Political and Economic Studies in Washington, D.C. Prior to joining the staff of the Joint Center in 1986, she was a program director at the Urban Institute. Dr. Simms holds a B.A. in economics from Carleton College and M.A. and Ph.D. degrees in economics from Stanford University. Dr. Simms has edited many books, including *Economic Perspectives on Affirmative Action, Young Black Males in Jeopardy, The Economics of Race and Crime* (co-edited with Samuel L. Myers, Jr.) and *Slipping Through the Cracks: The Status of Black Women* (co-edited with Julianne Malveaux). She is the author or coauthor of numerous articles on minority business issues and on employment and training. She has served on the *Black Enterprise* Board of Economists and currently is a member of the Policy Council for the Association for Public Policy Analysis and Management.

Joint Center for Political and Economic Studies

Eddie N. Williams, President
Robert J. Warren, Executive Vice President
Denise L. Dugas, Vice President, Communications and Marketing
Brenda Watkins Noel, Vice President, Finance and Administration
Margaret C. Simms, Vice President, Research
Kathleen P. Vander Horst, Vice President, Program Development

Job Creation Prospects and Strategies

Volume editors: Wilhelmina A. Leigh and Margaret C. Simms
Editing and proofreading: Mary K. Garber, Marc DeFrancis
Wordprocessing: Noreen R. Battle
Cover design: Carol Francis, Laurel Prucha Moran
Text design: Laurel Prucha Moran